A Violent World

A Violent World
Modern Threats to Economic Stability

Jean-Hervé Lorenzi
*Professor of Economics, Paris-Dauphine University and President,
Le Cercle des Economistes, France*

Mickaël Berrebi
Actuary, France

Translated by Josephine Bacon
Foreword by Anthony Giddens

© Jean-Hervé Lorenzi and Mickaël Berrebi 2016
Foreword © Anthony Giddens 2016

All rights reserved. No reproduction, copy or transmission of this publication may be made without written permission.

No portion of this publication may be reproduced, copied or transmitted save with written permission or in accordance with the provisions of the Copyright, Designs and Patents Act 1988, or under the terms of any licence permitting limited copying issued by the Copyright Licensing Agency, Saffron House, 6–10 Kirby Street, London EC1N 8TS.

Any person who does any unauthorized act in relation to this publication may be liable to criminal prosecution and civil claims for damages.

The authors have asserted their rights to be identified as the authors of this work in accordance with the Copyright, Designs and Patents Act 1988.

Originally published in French 2014 as *Un Monde de Violences: L'économie mondiale 2015–2030*, by Groupe Eyrolles, ISBN: 978–2–212–56001–5 (www.editions-eyrolles.com)

This edition first published 2016 by
PALGRAVE MACMILLAN

Palgrave Macmillan in the UK is an imprint of Macmillan Publishers Limited, registered in England, company number 785998, of Houndmills, Basingstoke, Hampshire RG21 6XS.

Palgrave Macmillan in the US is a division of St Martin's Press LLC,
175 Fifth Avenue, New York, NY 10010.

Palgrave Macmillan is the global academic imprint of the above companies and has companies and representatives throughout the world.

Palgrave® and Macmillan® are registered trademarks in the United States, the United Kingdom, Europe and other countries.

ISBN: 978–1–137–58992–7

This book is printed on paper suitable for recycling and made from fully managed and sustained forest sources. Logging, pulping and manufacturing processes are expected to conform to the environmental regulations of the country of origin.

A catalogue record for this book is available from the British Library.

Library of Congress Cataloging-in-Publication Data

Names: Lorenzi, Jean-Hervé, author. | Berrebi, Mickaël, author.

Title: A violent world : modern threats to economic stability / Jean-Hervé Lorenzi, Executive Board Member, Compagnie Financière Edmond de Rothschild, France, Mickaël Berrebi, Actuary, France.

Other titles: Monde de violences. English

Description: New York : Palgrave Macmillan, 2016. | Includes index.

Identifiers: LCCN 2015035441 | ISBN 9781137589927 (hardback)

Subjects: LCSH: Economic forecasting. | Economic history – 1990– | International economic relations. | International finance. | Economic history – 21st century – Forecasting. | BISAC: BUSINESS & ECONOMICS / Economic Conditions. | BUSINESS & ECONOMICS / Economic History. | BUSINESS & ECONOMICS / Economics / General. | BUSINESS & ECONOMICS / Economics / Theory.

Classification: LCC HB3730 .L6713 2016 | DDC 330.9001/12—dc23

LC record available at http://lccn.loc.gov/2015035441

This book could never have seen the light of day without the intelligent, friendly and talented assistance of Isabelle Albaret

Contents

List of Figures	ix
List of Tables	xi
Foreword Anthony Giddens	xii
Introduction	**1**
1 The Major Breakdown in Technical Progress	**6**
Innovation, a disruptive phenomenon	7
The major part played by technical progress in promoting growth	12
Slowdown: the great debate	16
Increasingly rare resources	21
The war of intelligence	26
2 The Curse of Ageing	**30**
The weight of demographics in history	32
The three impacts of ageing	36
A blessing in disguise?	40
Towards intergenerational conflict	44
3 The Irresistible Explosion of Inequalities	**50**
Inequalities and growth: a return to the old controversy	51
The end of the egalitarian myth	58
The patrimonial society against the middle classes	66
Inequality lies at the heart of a new conflict	71
4 The Impact of Deindustrialization	**74**
1995–2005: deindustrialization, offshoring, outsourcing	76
The London temptation	83
The American hope	87
Terrible uncertainty over globalization	93
5 The Illusion of Definancialization	**102**
The explosion of liquidity	103
The dismemberment of the financial system	107
The utopia of regulation	112

	The impossible debt equation	115
	Finance versus the real economy	119
6	**Savings, the Ultimate Rare Resource**	**125**
	The enigma of the balance between savings and investment	126
	Three decades of an over-abundance of savings	129
	The world is changing, savings are decreasing	133
	The world is changing, investment is increasing	136
	Towards a major imbalance	138
7	**Avoiding the Major Crisis of the Twenty-First Century**	**143**
	Refocusing the world on youth	146
	Socializing rare resources	149
	Taming pensions	151
	A new Bretton Woods?	155
	Risk-sharing	156
Notes		160
Index		175

List of Figures

4.1	Industry's share of added value on a world scale (developed countries and emerging nations)	78
4.2	Industry's share of added value on a world scale (Germany, France, the United Kingdom, Japan, the United States, China)	78
4.3	Share of exports of goods on a world scale	79
4.4	Outflows of capital and stock in foreign direct investments (FDIs) in billions of U.S. dollars at current prices and current rates of exchange	80
4.5	Share of jobs in industry as a proportion of all jobs	82
4.6	Manufacturing jobs (in thousands) and wages costs in industry and corporations (2009 = 100)	88
4.7	Manufacturing jobs (in thousands) and cost of gas in the United States and in the euro zone (2009 = 100)	89
4.8	Trend in U.S. dollar-based exchange rates	100
5.1	Monetary base of the central banks as a percentage of GDP	104
5.2	Notional amounts outstanding in OTC derivatives in billions of U.S. dollars	105
5.3	Total bank credit in the United States, the euro zone and in Japan, in billions of dollars	106
5.4	Development of shadow banking's financial assets in comparison with the financial institutions in thousands of billions of dollars	109
5.5	Projection for 2015–2030 of private debt from non-financial entities and overall debt as a percentage of GDP	117
6.1	Current account balances as a percentage of GDP	130
6.2	Rate of savings as a percentage of GDP	130
6.3	Investment levels as a percentage of GDP	131
6.4	Interest rates and ten-year swap rates as percentages	132
6.5	Savings rate forecast as a percentage of GDP for China and Japan	135
6.6	Provisions of world savings and investment rates as a percentage of GDP	137

6.7	Projections of the rates of savings as a percentage of GDP	139
6.8	Projections of the rates of investment as a percentage of GDP	140
6.9	Forecasts of the world rate of savings and investment as a percentage of GDP	141

List of Tables

1.1	Percentage growth of GDP per hour worked (average annual growth rate)	13
1.2	Rate of GDP as percentages (1500–2012) and potential growth rate of GDP as percentages (2012–2060) (annual average growth rate)	17
1.3	Total factor productivity growth rate of factors as percentages	19
1.4	Technology ranking on the world scale	27
2.1	Unemployment by age group, 2000 and 2013	46
4.1	Number of technological inventions recorded	85
5.1	Profitability of physical capital as percentages (after-tax profits, before interest and dividends/net capital in value)	120
5.2	Annual performance of a few hedge fund strategies as percentages	121
5.3	Annual performance of certain stock exchange indices as percentages	121
5.4	Estimates of the profitability of retail banking equity in 2010	122
5.5	Profitability of equity from market trading for the world's 13 largest merchant banks in 2010	122
6.1	'Savings–investment' differential	141

Foreword

This is an extraordinary book, which deserves to reach a wide audience across the world. It is clear that the opening period of the twenty-first century will be in some core respects very different from the closing decades of the twentieth. I do not agree with everything the authors have to say. For example, they speak of a 'slow down in technical progress', while I think we are in a period of accelerating technological innovation, driven by the digital revolution, whose outcomes at the moment are quite unknown. Yet I know of no other work that attempts such an ambitious, and enlightening, analysis of the dislocated period of history that we have now entered. The authors identify a series of master trends that are shaping the contemporary world – we cannot be sure where any of them will lead, let alone be able to say at this point how they will connect with each other. Nor do we know whether, as collective humanity, we will be able to control and shape the forces we have unleashed to positive social and economic ends.

One such force is the vast expansion in financial capital, creating levels of global liquidity way beyond anything ever observed before. I would relate this precisely to the digital revolution, because for the first time ever almost all money has become electronic – the role of cash is today relatively marginal. The authors are right to say that this process of the creation of liquid capital has become an unstoppable flood. A second is the acceleration of economic inequality at the very top. Overlapping with each of these is the large-scale transfer of industrial production from the richer countries to the emerging economies – the process of the deindustrialization of the West.

These are operating against the backdrop of further deep structural trends, affecting many if not yet all societies in the world. Such trends include the ageing population in the developed countries – a trend that reflects advances in diet and medicine, and obviously embodies many positives, but creates a host of problems of its own. The strain this situation will produce in welfare systems is already evident: it overlaps with a final source of deep worry – where will investment come from, when all of the industrial countries, and many others besides, have run up huge levels of debt? To all of these one can add a further factor: the fact that, if left unchecked, climate change, even in the short term, will exacerbate all of these problems.

As the authors emphasize, some of the core ideas that were prominent twenty years or so ago today seem naive or simply erroneous. For instance, it was widely thought that accelerating global interdependence would bring transnational collaboration on the large scale. The European Union appeared to many to be a model for other parts of the globe. One author, Mark Leonard, even proclaimed that the EU 'would run the twenty-first century'. Today, the Union is fighting its way through no less than five or six concurrent crises and the press – at least for the moment – is full of articles suggesting that it may even collapse.

Two decades ago, many authors were predicting the demise of the nation-state in the face of accelerating global interdependence – Keniche Ohmae, for example, spoke of the emergence of a 'borderless world'. Today, national identity looms as large as ever, as do conflicts originating in sectional divisions and forms of identity politics. The most significant powers in the world once again seem to be nations and groups of nations. It is a sobering situation indeed, since the capability of even clusters of nations to create effective global governance is limited, given the level of interdependence in the world economy. It is matched by the emergence of new forms of terrorism, possibly capable of much greater impact than was true of previous eras. Thus Islamic State mixes barbarism with cutting-edge digital technology in a way that has no analogue previously.

As the authors quite rightly point out, we should beware of overgeneralizing from these trends. We cannot say with any certainty at the moment how far they will prove enduring, or lead to serious world conflicts, even large-scale breakdown, in the social and economic order. Marx said many years ago that 'human beings only set themselves such problems as they can resolve', and he might turn out to be right. To me the correct way to interpret the world today is as a huge mixture of opportunity and risk, in which it is not possible to use stochastic methods to identify how that balance will play out. This is because, at least in some core respects – well identified in the book – we are living in a world 'off the edge of history'. That is to say, we have opportunities, but we also face risks that simply did not exist for preceding civilizations. Take, for example, global interdependence itself, now dramatically accelerating as we move further into the digital age – no one has ever lived in such a world in previous periods of history and therefore we can only learn from the past to a limited degree in interpreting its likely consequences.

Most of this book is about diagnosis. Lorenzi and Berrebi only offer a short discussion of the policy implications of the trends they dissect so acutely. They see no hope in the possibility of reversing deindustrialization in the developed countries. (I don't wholly agree. We just don't know at the current time what the implications of current advances – such as 3D printing and other technological developments – might be.) Nor can we hold back the tide of financialization. However, the authors say we can and must seek to reshape it, and in so doing turn away from unfettered consumption towards investment both in people and in infrastructure.

There has to be an active rebalancing between the generations. Older people have long been thought of as those most in need. Today the balance has to shift back towards the young. The most difficult task will be to encourage population migration at just the time when nations are starting again to consolidate their borders. The tensions involved are very evident when we look at the vast influx of refugees into Europe today, or the movements of population from Latin America into the United States. And then there is the issue of debt. Perhaps, the authors conclude by saying, we should seek to live with it rather than imposing new regimes of austerity. 'Perpetual debt' has in fact a long historical lineage, albeit in much smaller contexts than is the case today. Innovative thinking in this area, however, will be absolutely crucial. My own belief is that the idea that we can run the world as an unfettered marketplace has reached its end point. A retrieval of the public domain – not all necessarily the same thing as the state – will be a key task. Since the policy prescriptions with which this magisterial book ends are so brief perhaps the authors will consider developing them further in a companion volume to this one?

Anthony Giddens

Introduction

Economists are overfond of the word 'crisis'. They tirelessly explore history in an attempt to find explanations, analyses and opinions that might throw light on our vision of the current situation.

Is the world really in crisis? Nothing is less certain; although the year 2009 could rightly be considered as having been a disastrous one, 2010 and 2011 saw a soon-aborted attempt to create a world government. Since 2012 each country has gone its own way. This has been brilliant for some, average for others, but a subject for despair in a third group of nations.

This book is based on a paradox. Unlike other periods of global macroeconomic disruption, the future is not defined by eventually overcoming the current crisis. The crash of 1929 gave birth to Fordist mass production, simply as a consequence of the major imbalance between world supply and demand. The organization of the labour market and the social changes that occurred post-World War II made it possible to overcome difficulties of this kind. The period in which we live today will probably end in a few years' time once the major Western countries are able to settle their private and public debts.

Notwithstanding all this, the twenty-first century will not be able to discover a new balance through such simple restructuring. In reality, six new constraints will emerge, together with the policies used to control them at major world economic level. Conflict is bound to take over by default. In the best case scenario, this conflict will take the form of radical change, but it may also adopt a more bellicose manifestation. Regardless of the form adopted, these six limitations will structure the world of the future. Three of them already exist and will almost certainly affect the course of events as they have played out between 2007 and today. The world has experienced accelerated financialization, an explosion of inequality and a massive, unprecedented transfer of business activity from the Organization for Economic Co-operation and Development (OECD) countries to the emerging nations. These three limitations may govern worldwide economic policy and national policy and they will probably be applied to consolidated geographical areas.

Three other constraints, newer, will take some time to emerge. They are those that could, to some extent, be extremely difficult to overcome, but they can be controlled and exploited, and their massive effects could be mitigated. All this is foreseeable, but the only certainty is that it will be impossible to avoid them. What are they? The first, an inevitable constraint, is the fact of an ageing population and the additional financial burden it places on social welfare, its aversion to structural risk and the major changes it introduces to patterns of consumption. The second is more ambiguous. It is currently the subject of a debate that is far from over. Beyond misleading appearances, hasn't there been a slowdown in technical progress over the last twenty years? This is an important point since technical progress has been the main factor for growth for two centuries and such a slowdown will mark a progressive form of decline. It will not be case for everyone nor will it be forever; this phenomenon will eventually come to an end. The countries that win the forthcoming economic war will be those that will have been able to catch the new wave of technological innovation. Yet no one knows how to encourage the emergence of such advances, reduce their time frames and ensure their wide distribution. In a word, all that counts is to be a country that, like Britain in the nineteenth century or Germany and France in the late nineteenth century, is capable of being the origin, source and beneficiary of such future technological revolutions.

Finally, there is a third constraint, linked to the first two. The future of the world has always been conditional upon the ability to balance world investment with available savings. Yet the long period of surplus savings is behind us. We are embarking on what could reveal itself to be a true tragedy, a period in which savings will become the rarest of resources *par excellence*.

The 1990s allowed Francis Fukuyama[1] to announce the end of history. The 2000s showed how delusional it was to imagine the world as being pacified, free of conflict, free of the immeasurable dark forces, before their terrible consequences could re-emerge. No one today can predict the future course of history except by being content to imagine a scenario tinged with narrow determinism. There is no doubt, however, that violence, whether explicit or implicit, has emerged unheralded from the deepest constraints that are currently tightening their grip on the world.

The searing brutality of the most recent economic, social and even environmental crises now seems to be setting the pace that is currently paralysing political action. To tell the truth, the third globalization has sketched the outlines of what is anything but a 'global village'; the truth is that this world lacks instructions for use, it rushes around extinguishing one conflagration after another, with no end in sight.

The breakdown in technical progress, the ageing population, the explosion of inequality, the massive transfer of business activity from one end of the world to the other, the limitless financialization of the economy, the impossibility of financing our investments – these are like tectonic plates, whose pressures will cause new disruptions that will be as unexpected in date as they will be in intensity. Are we capable of meeting the challenge of these future impacts, with all the subjective and objective violence that they will inevitably cause?

Humility is required, the humility of being capable of describing the cracks in our economic, social and political system that are liable to destroy it, a system that, despite its deficiencies, still inspires many populations throughout the world. What paths deserve to be retained or forged in order to mitigate the threat of the conflicts which are wars in all but name.

This book is based on the description of the three constraints originating in the recent past that constitute the origins of our current difficulties and three future constraints that are harder to identify. It could easily be believed that the markets will find their own response – as they have always managed to do in the past – to these immense difficulties. Even the greatest pessimists, when asked how the market can be saved, believe that even though it may take some time, everything will nevertheless end happily. What a mistake, how naïve! We are entering a world in which these constraints have a name – that name is conflict. For each expression so typical of the language of economists, the confrontation between countries, between social groups and between generations is now so firmly entrenched that there is no knowing whether compromise is possible. What is exceptional in the present time in which we live is that we sense the massive difficulties ahead, though without much success in conceptualizing the threats, yet we hesitate to name them as threats, we hesitate to mention the unmentionable, of stating the explicit, dangerous, cruel conflict known as war. We are convinced that if nothing is done our inability to overcome the constraints will doubtless lead us into a conflict. While we still find it hard to put into words what the wars of the future will be like, we have been reduced to being inspired by what we are told by the futurists of the CIA[2] or the Ministry of Defence[3] in a country such as France. They are the only ones who dare to do so because it is their job. If today we tend to conceal from ourselves the cruel evidence that there will be conflicts in the future, they will eventually describe them.

This is how, with a certain degree of audacity, our 'experts' have traced the outlines of a world that tends to lack harmony by allowing the escape of the well-known *genie-out-of-the-bottle*.[4] Consequently, the centre of conformity and world domination does not hesitate to imagine a world full of conflict, due to the massive inequalities between countries and especially within those very countries, as the United States progressively withdraws from its role as world leader. It is the world of Kishore Mahbubani,[5] the Singaporean philosopher and diplomat who supports the idea of a de-westernized world and, in reality, of a world that is neither globalized nor multicentric. But, in a context still reeling from the financial crisis of 2008 and the loss of influence of the West, from the Arab revolutions whose outcome remains unknown, from the strategic turning of the US towards Asia or the Pacific regions in which tensions exist between countries, from the unsuitability of the instruments of world governance, in which the picture of risk, especially insidious risk, has increased, who knows? These risks are of a political nature, of course, with the threat of bellicose nationalisms as an outlet for disappointed populations, economic risk through the new dominance of China, risk relating to energy as competition increases for rare resources, and risks relating to information technology, public health and climate. There is another new element, that of the powerlessness of certain states that have become sanctuaries for criminal gangs or terrorists, transit points for various types of trafficking – the list is so long, so impressive, that it causes a more or less widespread feeling of insecurity and anxiety. The dialectic between fiction and fact is rebellious. It is because they are virtual that cyber-attacks are part of this bellicose reality and are therefore destructive.

The first signs of a new human folly emerged more than ten years ago. On either side of the West, there was talk of a 'just war', the 'clash of civilizations', ideological and religious systems that were bound to lead to victory, and thus the annihilation of one side or the other.

It has always been assumed that the world would become wiser following the fall of the Berlin Wall, that a generalized market economy would lead to a pacified and uniform world under the aegis of the great international institutions. This was the result of a very inadequate understanding of Samuel Huntington,[6] but, above all, it created a new hysteria relating to a just war, making it possible to define, and even legitimize, the killings that were to come. It is precisely here that Michael Walzer,[7] and the very controversial Carl Schmitt, show the sombre way, one that is unfortunately so revelatory of our probable future. Our world is not that of diplomatic conflicts but of economy. The economists' initiatives are specific and reveal the uncertainty and limitations that are no doubt in danger of overwhelming us. Our anxieties are based on the difficulty of understanding and perceiving this new trajectory in a world economy which, unless rethought, will lead to the sort of conflicts that human history has always demonstrated.

The worst is never certain, however. Without repeating our own account of the often too naïve view of governance of the world economy, we intend to respond to the challenge of imagining and even offering solutions that are liable, while upsetting the current modes of regulation, to make the threat of such conflict more remote. If one manages to perceive the importance, the innovation and the impact of these six constraints, we consider that a future could be contemplated and, moving beyond the contradictions, compromises could be found and habits changed radically on a world scale, as well as on the scale of each country.

1
The Major Breakdown in Technical Progress

A strange destiny awaited the analysis of technical progress as produced by economists two centuries ago. The difficulty in measuring such progress is patent. In the context of an approach from the total factor productivity perspective, it depends on how a given country's economy grows and the division of its business activities into sectors. Even more important is the fact that technical progress was conceived through the contemplation of a particular history, that of the Industrial Revolution, an expression developed by Adolphe Blanqui.[1] An Industrial Revolution represents the passage of a society from one technical system to another, illustrated first and foremost by the original Industrial Revolution that occurred in the late nineteenth century, in which the steam engine, the iron and steel industry and extensive coal-mining defined just such a new technical system. Certain economists subsequently identified other major changes that they considered to be worthy of the definition of 'Industrial Revolution'.

The term 'revolution' evokes the idea of radical change, of profound alteration to the economic and social structures. Thus, mentioning the great breakdown in technical progress amounts to, once again, asking what could be termed such and what could become a true technological disruption. Does the moment of the explosion of information and communication technology merit such a definition? It might do if one remembers that it started nearly thirty years ago and that today's real challenges are of a different order, namely, scarcity of energy and the inadequacy of its associated technologies. These include biotechnology, the innovations of which have not yet been translated *en masse* into fields such as healthcare and, finally, nanotechnology, which is more in the planning stage than a reality. Dealing with technical progress no longer boils down to imagining brutal disruptions; it is more of a linear, peaceful, continuous positive development. That is no easy matter. Recent decades may have been typified by a deceleration in the growth of such progress. Hence the question, is it possible to envisage the emergence of a new technical system whose contours cannot yet be precisely defined, but that would completely upset patterns of consumption and production methods, i.e. the way in which the production system could be transformed? Put like this, the major question of growth arises again today as it did several times during the nineteenth century. For economists, it is necessary to take an initial detour so as to examine the major role played by technical progress in the pursuit of growth, whose irregular nature needs to be identified since, for those who monitor the regularity of economic developments, it reveals itself to be anything but cyclical.

The discussion is legitimate. When scientific and technological changes are observed, seeming as they do to alternate between swift progress and stagnation, it is impossible to detect a current major development in technical progress. This has been suggested by some American authors, first among them, Robert Gordon, who has explicitly challenged the idea of real progress. As far as he is concerned the statistics are there, stubbornly pointing to a characteristic slowdown.

Doubt is inevitable. One needs to take the exact measure of this recent constraint, the difficulty of developing science and innovation. That is because, in the future, the world will be led by countries capable of resolving the uncertainty as to the nature of the technological frontier and which new areas need to be developed. These are the countries that will be the dominant powers of the twenty-first century.

Innovation, a disruptive phenomenon

Technical progress has always been the most aspirational dream of naïve economists. In their eyes, as development proceeds a sort of peaceful and regular continuity will be established in scientific progress and innovation. The cyclical nature of this major variable in growth thus makes it possible to reassure everyone by proposing the idea that expenditure on R&D will have an effect on technical progress. This applies to the classic, reassuring view, linked to the first Industrial Revolution, of the endogenous growth models of the 1980s and Bill Clinton's government investments, the dominance of this way of thinking not having diminished. In practice this vision has proved rather unreliable. In fact, history illustrates the serious tensions that enable economies at the end of their tether to revive and come back to life.

The name for this phenomenon is 'Industrial Revolution', an exceptional convergence of technological transformations that enable a new technical system to emerge. In fact, the term 'revolution' invokes nothing more than a radical change, a deep overhaul of economic structures, a moment of releasing growth acceleration, directing towards a real economy of new inventions that are ready to find their markets. It is here that the expression can be found of a new technical equilibrium, the establishment of new economic growth and a new social model.

This change is based on the simultaneous emergence of what Clayton M. Christensen[2] has called the 'disruptive technologies', whereby a very important distinction is made between technology itself and the use to which it is put or, what that author terms, its 'strategic use'.

Although scientific research is continuous and although the rate of invention may also be continuous, it is only during certain historically identifiable eras that sudden changes presage a new technical balance, upholder of a new economic and social organization. From scientific research and technical progress to the growth of the production system, the process is complex and involves stages of discovery, experimentation and the adoption of new products and processes. At the core lies technological innovation or, to be more precise and to echo Schumpeter, a cluster of technological innovations. This vision of history is, and remains, polemical. Did these disruptive moments, which would make it possible to divide human economic history into periods, really exist? If, for the sake of example, symbolic dates were mentioned, these could include 1783 for Watt's steam engine, so that economic history could be shortened by several months. Why do such revolutions emerge in one place rather than another? What are the factors that trigger such revolutions? Are they governed by supply or demand?

To take an interest in this issue today is simply to review the events of the last two centuries, in which disruption has resulted in technical progress unprecedented in human history. It can be said without fear of contradiction that the growth of technical progress, and thus progress itself, emerged in these very special periods. The question that arises today is whether any possible slowdown of technical progress that we appear to be witnessing today could be reversed into the creation of a sustained recovery.

There is nothing currently that might give rise to a denial that we are on the verge of a long period of stagnation. No one today can be content with saying that the future lies anywhere but in the old, industrialized countries. No one knows where the eventual turning point will occur and spread. Why not in Europe or, more widely, in the countries of the

OECD? After all, Europe was the cradle of capitalist development and has been so since the fifteenth century, when, it is important to understand, a huge wave of socio-economic innovations and transformations broke over Europe.

As Jacques Brasseul[3] and Robert Heilbroner[4] have stated from a millennial perspective: 'Western Europe has been the theatre of a major event, a genuine cataclysm that no other great civilization has experienced. It is the complete and radical disappearance of a centralized and authoritarian power, the fall of the Roman Empire in the fourth and fifth centuries. The central power vacuum created left room for much greater freedom which the cities managed to successfully adopt. The rise of the cities, natural crossroads and the most important places for trade, i.e. market specialization, explains the emergence of capitalism in the West. Nowhere else, whether in China, India or the Islamic countries, were cities, under the control of a strong centralized power, able to develop these economic freedoms, freedoms that were preserved in Europe, despite the revival of authoritarian regimes, the absolute monarchies that predominated from the fifteenth to the eighteenth centuries.'

Rosenberg and Birdzell[5] took the same approach. According to them, the West's big chance came from its initial misfortune, the disappearance of political unification from the imperial Roman system and from the more recent permanent competition between new, smaller, independent political units.

The authors stress the positive effect that this dispersal has had on innovation: 'This division into numerous nations guarantees a sort of collective insurance for society: among all the technical innovations produced by the numerous craftsmen, peasants and entrepreneurs on the continent, one is sure not to lose an interesting idea'. One revealing example is the gradual replacement of the ancient practices of confiscation and spoliation by the ruling power through regular taxation, thus favouring economic development.

Another factor explains this dynamic, namely the fall of Constantinople, hitherto the capital of the Byzantine Empire, in 1453. The new empire, now in the hands of the Turks, definitively cut off the land route for trading with Europeans to the benefit of a sea route controlled by Arab merchants. The response was not long in coming, as Europe opened up its own commercial trading routes using the navigation techniques that the Portuguese had mastered to perfection.

Another just as decisive event in the history of Europe was the collapse of the feudal system. Is there need for a reminder? The Industrial Revolution and, consequently, the processes of world expansion, were also the result of the collapse of European feudal society between 1300 and 1450. This society, built on the relationship of submission by the serf to his lord, prevented the peasant, once his excess crops had been confiscated, from adopting more productive farming methods or taking commercial initiatives. In order to move from this economic system to one in which the forces of production were more mobile, the feudal structure needed to be challenged by a series of crises, the first of which was demographic.

The early fifteenth century marked a turning point in changes to the European economy. A period of continuous population growth caused the limit of European territorial *ecumene* to be reached, triggering a crisis in the feudal system. The population of Europe increased from 45 million in 1450 to more than 100 million by 1650, aggravating the problems of food production. The technical inadequacy of the feudal system had become obvious.

At the same time, the growth of trade gave cities an increasingly important role such that, after becoming centres of administrative power, they now became centres of industry. Wealth was no longer concentrated exclusively in the hands of the land-owners but was now also in the hands of those who controlled trade. This is when the feudal system virtually ceased to exist.

The period of commercial and financial development in sixteenth-century Europe paved the way for the boost in industry in the eighteenth century. In the course of the sixteenth and seventeenth centuries, a certain number of upsets disrupted the economic life of the western world. This was the time of the great discoveries, of new spaces, of the accumulation of capital, all of them forerunners of the future financial system. It was also the period of the formation of nation-states and the growing awareness of the unity and importance of territorial interests. These changes, which interacted with each other, created a context favourable to the emergence of an industrial society, one that could be dubbed the first industrial revolution.

From then onwards, the western world would experience strong growth of a kind that had previously been unimaginable, mainly as the result of the numerous innovations that were constantly challenging the ways in which the economy was organized and how the cards were dealt to the various economic powers. Niall Ferguson, in his definition of the 'six killer apps', has covered everything about the origin of the West's success:[6] competition, knowledge, private property, the applied sciences (such as medicine), mass consumption and, finally, the work ethic. It is their convergence that explains why the first industrial revolution began in the mid-eighteenth century in the West rather than elsewhere.

The emergence of English power corresponds to what historians consider the country's era of technological domination. However, historians such as Musson[7] have put forward the innovative idea that the countries of continental Europe experienced similar developments: 'We have been led to exaggerate British industrial supremacy and to forget the numerous contributions made by the Continent to its own industrial revolution'. This has had little effect on our consideration of a forthcoming new technological impact but it involves a condition that applies for all time.

Yesterday, as well as today, this is a return to the major role of the distribution of new consumer goods and services which is closely linked to social structures, as shown by Patrick Verley[8] when he recalls the extent to which the distribution of wealth affects demand and, thus, the ability of new technologies to take hold. England was the first country to have a large middle class. If one looks admiringly at the emerging nations and their formidable potential, it is indeed their ability to develop the middle classes that renders us so optimistic about them, even if time remains the determining constraint. Of course, the disruption may be swift, but the changes it implies, the changes it will impose, need more time. According to Paul Bairoch, 'In the long term, disruption can be considered as a phenomenon resulting in very profound changes within a relatively short space of time, in comparison with the duration of the previous phase. Taking account of these reservations, it is accepted that the industrial revolution was one of the two most important disruptions in the whole history of humanity and that is why they are described as fundamental breaches'.[9]

In reality, from the late eighteenth century, the industrial revolution opened up a new era of capitalism in the western economies. On the scale of economic world history, this involved a radical change in the principles by which the economy functioned and established the bases for the globalization that reached its apogee in the early twentieth century. It was also the origin of most of the technical innovations that changed the processes for producing consumer goods.

The question is whether we are now experiencing similar conditions. The answer is yes and no. Yes, through the emergence of the middle classes. No, in that the fundamental difference between the changes that occurred at the beginning of this century is that they are based on the emergence of a huge new working class that is largely Asian in origin.

Nothing more than that. The evidence remains that technical progress lies at the heart of all changes in society, past and future.

The major part played by technical progress in promoting growth

In the 1950s economists did much to advance knowledge by attributing most of the results of growth to technical progress. This was the work of such economists as Abramovitz, Kendrick, Denison and, especially, Solow. It was after this that Romer, initiator of a very creative intellectual movement, suggested re-endogenizing technical progress and considering that it is, in itself, only the product of the resources allocated to scientific and technological development. Nevertheless, the facts have been established that technical progress lies behind two-thirds of the increase in annual wealth. To judge by the previous two centuries, this formidable acceleration in production and in production per inhabitant appears to be one that is closely linked to successive waves of innovation.

Since 1783, the emblematic date of the first Industrial Revolution, two or three moments can be said to signify a change in the conditions of production and consumption, appearing as generators of a new growth model. This was definitely the case in the late eighteenth century, the twentieth century, probably as a result of the 1930s crisis, with the emergence of Fordism (mass production), and possibly as a result of the extraordinary convergence of the 1980s when informatics, telecommunications and the internet transformed consumption practices in the same way they did goods and services. This change, though expressed through our lifestyles, was not as the current times if the productivity gains figures are anything to go by. Perhaps this is merely one stage whose importance is increased by the flood of a billion workers who are paid a pittance and produce low-priced consumer goods.

Is this what is happening today? No, at least not if the figures are anything to go by. In studying the trends in GDP in relation to hours worked in certain developed countries such as France, Germany, the United Kingdom, Japan and the United States, the findings are clear. While there was a net growth in GDP per hour worked in the period 1950–1973, with an annual growth rate reaching nearly 8% for Japan, and growth rates of between 3% and 5% for the remaining countries, there was a massive slowdown in the most recent period, between 2007 and 2012.

Table 1.1 Percentage growth of GDP per hour worked (average annual growth rate)

	1870–1913	1913–1950	1950–1973	1973–1990	1990–2001	2001–2007	2007–2012
France	1.7	1.9	5.0	2.9	1.9	1.5	0.2
Germany	1.6	0.8	5.9	2.4	2.3	1.6	0.3
United Kingdom	1.2	1.7	3.1	1.7	2.4	2.5	–0.6
United States	1.9	2.5	2.8	1.4	1.9	2.1	1.5
Japan	2.0	1.8	7.7	3.0	2.3	1.6	0.9

Sources: OECD StatExtracts, Angus Maddison (The World Economy: A Millennial Perspective), OECD (2002), US Bureau of Economic Analysis, Eurostat, International Labour Organization and the authors.

The link between growth and technical progress is clear. What is less clear, despite Romer's work, are the reasons that cause this mechanism to come into play. And it is here that another factor emerges whose role is misleadingly evident, that of scientific progress.

By the eighteenth century innovation was not only the result of the application of scientific discoveries. Initially it met a new need. The groupings of empiricism are typical of the start of profound change. The first engineers attempted, through trial and error, to apply new methods of production. It was due to new demand that inventions were born. The role of science, at least in the case of the first Industrial Revolution, only emerged subsequently.

Of course, in the eighteenth century, there were regular meetings between scientists and practitioners who were members of the learned societies, the main institutions for the dissemination of knowledge. An example is that symbol of the first Industrial Revolution, the steam engine. It operates on a simple technique, but one that eventually proved to be vital. Steam engines became one of the first applications of science to industry. In fact, the power of steam, while known since Antiquity, had not until that moment been the subject of research destined to give it a practical dimension. This new use of steam became a major technical innovation. The mining industry used it to pump water and thus enable deeper and more efficient mining. In 1705 the Englishman Thomas Newcomen perfected a steam pump, but it was not until Watt's innovations in 1783 that really efficient machines were made. These engines soon became indispensable in branches of metal-working and in the iron and steel industry, and this is why their power and their heat output were constantly being improved. The steam engine is the perfect illustration of a series of innovations that were based on both empirical investigations and scientific research in order to produce the most promising improvements.

Why return to this issue? Simply because today's great enigma could be summarized as: if scientific developments are exceptional, amazing, affecting virtually every known field, they do not support our idea that they would be capable of conversion into innovation, let alone into technological progress and, ultimately, into a new industrial revolution.

Perhaps such scientific progress ought nevertheless to be considered as a benefit that, if properly used, would enable society to improve its living conditions. In France today, does the principle of precaution prevent the growth of technical progress? Yet, if science is to be converted into innovation, what is needed is something that might be called a favourable breeding ground, a suitable form of civilization.

For Fernand Braudel, Arnold Joseph Toynbee, Marcel Mauss and Paul Valéry, the concept of civilization appeared to be a matrix for the economic history of a nation. The finest expression of the life and death of civilizations is to be found in the words of Paul Valéry: 'Elam, Nineveh, Babylon were beautiful but vague names, and the total destruction of these worlds had as little significance for us as their very existence. But France, England, Russia [...] these are also beautiful names. Lusitania is also a beautiful name. And we now see that the abyss of history is great enough for everyone. We feel that a civilization has the same fragility as a life. The circumstances that sent the works of Keats and of Baudelaire to join the works of Menander are no longer inconceivable, they are to be found in the newspapers'.[10] Yet is this funeral elegy not also, paradoxically, a hymn to the greatness of civilizations?

Marcel Mauss describes the capacity of civilizations to expand, develop and create their own dynamic while silently imposing a specific technological form.[11] There are countless historical examples of this phenomenon. The return of China to the world scene is an exceptional illustration when it is realized, as David Landes[12] indeed reminds us, that metallurgy was invented in China, nearly fifteen centuries earlier than in the West, as was printing, at a time when the West, between the fall of the Roman Empire and the tenth century, experienced a real stagnation in technical development.

The revolution that occurred in the Middle Ages, described by Marc Bloch,[13] was the result of a period of social progress, a milder climate and sudden scientific progress. Bloch reminds us that between 1050 and 1250 'the development of the economy resulted in a true revision of social values. There had always been craftsmen and merchants. Individually, the latter at least had been able, here and there, to play an important role. Yet as groups, neither of them accounted for much. From the eleventh century onwards, the artisan class and the merchant class both became much more numerous and much more indispensable to the life of everyone, asserting themselves ever more vigorously'.

Then there is twelfth-century Muslim Spain. Al-Andalus, whose prosperity and refinement, inherited from the Umayyad period, were much admired by western contemporaries and those of the Maghreb and, even more so, by the historians who have fashioned this part of the world into a sort of golden age of civilization, something that is only partially true. It is true that the Al-Mohad Caliph Abu Yusuf Yakoub al-Mansur made his mark in southern Spain in a manner envied by the Catholic kingdom to the north. While first and foremost a warrior, he was also a great builder, in a form of continuity with the Muslim dynasties that preceded him. If he embarked on major fortifications to protect the great cities of Al-Andalus, he also ordered the construction of bridges, mosques, baths and La Giralda in Seville, the Caliphate's new capital. Contemporary prosperity was translated into an urban society of a kind unknown in the rest of Europe, with markets reflecting the most flourishing trade in the Mediterranean basin, greatly favouring locally produced goods such as ceramics, paper and silk. The cities were also centres for brilliant intellectual activity among all disciplines. Thus, it is not by chance that a 'breeding-ground' as fertile as Cordoba, the former Andalusian capital, saw the birth in the twelfth century of the two greatest minds of the time, Moses Maimonides and Averroës. The extent of their knowledge is impressive, as is that rare intelligence that enabled them to master disciplines as different as those of medicine and philosophy. Yet they were very much men of their time, of that Andalusian civilization that boasted an art of living and a refinement that were at the time unknown in the West, combined with an economic and cultural dynamism that was very much open to technical and scientific progress and to the history of ideas.

Angus Maddison[14] also described the position perfectly when writing about Venice, Portugal, China, the Netherlands and Britain. He claims that economic growth depends on three clearly identifiable economic phenomena. These are 'the conquest or colonization of relatively depopulated areas that possess fertile land and new biological resources; international trade and the movement of capital; technological and institutional innovation'. It is this last point that most concerns us, that which inscribes history in the force of institutions. One can thus say that in the sixteenth and seventeenth centuries, western science underwent a sort of revolution dictated by the close collaboration between intellectuals and scientists such as Copernicus, Erasmus, Bacon, Galileo, Hobbes, Descartes, Petty, Leibniz, Huygens, Halley and Newton. They all corresponded regularly with their colleagues abroad and travelled extensively. This sort of informal cooperation then became institutionalized in the new scientific academies, promoting confrontation and discussion, publishing the results of research. These works were not intended to remain stored away in libraries but were associated with the definition of public policy.

The question remains today of knowing where to find favourable environments such as these. Everyone thinks today of the brilliance of California, everyone is also convinced that the Internet breaks down all barriers and permits the generalized diffusion of knowledge. Yet there are, and there will be, places that are more favourable to creativity and the ability to translate science into innovation.

Where are they?

Slowdown: the great debate

For economists, prospects are traditionally based on what is known as 'potential growth'. This is defined as growth that makes it possible to attain the maximum level of production without accelerating inflation and without creating a major imbalance. This is calculated on the basis of growth in the active population and increased overall productivity, i.e. in technical progress. Whether one looks at the work of the IMF, the OECD or the many other economic research organizations, while their forecasts are in all probability inaccurate, they nevertheless express the idea we have of the future, and it is much less optimistic than could be imagined. That is because the forecasts are a continuum of the development of technical progress in recent years. The results are very eloquent, especially for the West – the United States, Europe and France. Yet the forecast growth rates of between only 1% and 2% per annum are, in the end, not so surprising with respect to those of the last two centuries, even if they express disruption, hence the implicit perception that we are entering a period of virtual stagnation.

Table 1.2 Rate of GDP as percentages (1500–2012) and potential growth rate of GDP as percentages (2012–2060) (annual average growth rate)

	1500–1820	1820–1870	1870–1913	1913–1950	1950–1973	1973–1990	1990–2001	2001–2007	2007–2012	2012–2017	2017–2030	2030–2060
France	0.4	1.3	1.6	1.2	5.1	2.8	2.0	1.8	0.5	*1.8*	*2.1*	*1.4*
Germany	0.4	2.0	2.8	0.3	5.7	2.5	2.2	1.4	1.2	*1.6*	*1.2*	*1.0*
United Kingdom	0.8	2.1	1.9	1.2	2.9	4.2	1.4	3.1	0.1	*1.6*	*2.2*	*2.2*
United States	0.9	4.2	3.9	2.8	3.9	2.3	2.8	2.7	1.0	*2.1*	*2.4*	*2.0*
Japan	0.3	0.4	2.4	2.2	9.3	3.1	3.1	1.6	0.2	*0.9*	*1.4*	*1.4*

Sources: OECD, Angus Maddison (The World Economy: A Millennial Perspective), OECD (2002), Eurostat and the authors.

Of course, the feeling that the world is entering an irreversible decline is not a new one. Millenarian thinkers have not evaporated as if by magic. However, the present time is quite simply confronted with what some people would call a major technological breakdown. It appears to lie in the way in which total productivity gains have been developing over the last fifteen years. It is from this finding that the major debate was born that currently brings numerous economists into opposition with each other over the issue of the existence of technical progress. For us, that issue is critical. We believe that, in reality, the world is confronted with absolute uncertainty on the question of growth. Of course, we are astonished by the speed at which certain emerging nations have caught up, but that will not be the major issue during the next twenty years.

To illustrate the debate, one name emerges prominently, that of Robert Gordon[15] who has written 'the phase of rapid technological progress that followed the Industrial Revolution was to be an exception of 250 years in the long stagnation that typifies human history'. He thus implies that current technological innovation does not represent much in comparison with the introduction of electricity, piped water, the internal combustion engine and other inventions of more than one hundred years ago.

Is there a need to seek specific responsibility at the very heart of the way our modern society operates? Gordon identifies six major handicaps, six headwinds, which can be briefly mentioned here. They are: the demographic dividend, exacerbated by the retirement of the 'babyboomers'; the decline in education with, on the one hand, a deterioration in university results and, on the other, the rising cost of education, which either means falling deeper into debt or students abandoning their studies; the increase in inequalities; the consequences of globalization and outsourcing; the energy challenge and environmental protection; and, finally, the burden of government and household debt. Anyone would subscribe without difficulty to this description of today's world. Gordon even goes beyond this simple thought. He is the initiator of a deeper movement which judges that the current technical system is inappropriate for the eternal pursuit of a mechanism such as Moore's Law, i.e. doubling the power of calculation by a semi-conductor every 18 months. He claims that average growth in the United States between 1891 and 2007 was 2.1%, borne on the successive waves of innovation, but it will probably drop to 0.9% in the next decades.[16]

This is how a school of thought is born, on this apprehension of what one might call 'the great stagnation'. Everything began in the mid-1970s which, for the middle classes of the western world, signified a turning point with a buying power that progressed little if at all, unemployment having become a virtually permanent threat and prospects for the future becoming ever darker. In practice, the oil crisis of the 1970s inaugurated a succession of crises with brief lulls for the western economies. As far as Tyler Cowen[17] was concerned, the downturn in innovation and productivity gains since the 1970s was linked to a continuous decrease in productivity in education, administration and health. This decrease, for which advances in industry and technology provided insufficient compensation, dragged down the whole of the economy with it. 'The period between 1880 and 1940 introduced numerous major technological innovations into our lives. This long list includes electricity, electric light, powerful machines, the car, the aeroplane, electrical household appliances, the telephone, mass production, radio, television, etc.', Cowen writes. Apart from the Internet, 'life in the material sense is not much different from how it was in 1953. We drive cars, we use refrigerators and we turn on our electric lights'. Although information technology and the Internet have had an effect on our lifestyle, consumption and production, as far as Cowen is concerned, they have not created jobs in mass production industries such as the automotive industry. So much so that the Internet is an innovation that has barely affected wages and buying power.

To measure this technical progress, let us take the total factor productivity of elements from five countries, France, Germany, the United Kingdom, Japan and the United States. The total factor productivity of these elements in fact corresponds to a relative growth in wealth that cannot be explained by labour or capital. Clearly, this 'residue' of riches is not the optimal means of assessing technical progress, but it indeed consists largely of

Table 1.3 Total factor productivity growth rate of factors as percentages

	1985–1990	1990–1995	1995–2000	2001–2007	2007–2012
France	1.7	1.1	1.3	0.9	−0.3
Germany		1.4	1.1	1.1	0.1
United Kingdom	0.4	1.6	1.4	1.5	−1.1
United States	0.7	0.7	1.5	1.4	0.9
Japan	3.1	0.7	0.7	1.1	0.4

Sources: OECD, The Conference Board and the authors.

this resource. According to our reconstruction, the most recent years have been marked, taking all countries together, by a significant slowing down of total factor productivity in the countries in question.

In this discussion, a strong voice makes itself heard, that of Kenneth Rogoff: 'I recently mentioned the theory of technological stagnation to Thiel and Kasparov at Oxford University, and also to Mark Shuttleworth, pioneer of free software. Kasparov asked me, not without a certain irony, what a product such as the iPhone 5 adds to our capacities and he stressed that most of the science that underlies modern computing dates from the 1970s. Thiel defended the idea that the monetary relaxation measures and hyper-aggressive budgetary stimulation that were designed to counter the recession were not targeting the right malaise and were consequently potentially very dangerous. These are interesting ideas, yet it is virtually indisputable that the slowdown in the world economy is the result of a severe systemic financial crisis and not of a long-term crisis in matters of innovation. [...] So there needs to be a reply to the question, is the main cause of the recent slowdown a crisis in innovation or a financial crisis? Perhaps it is a little of both, but the economic trauma of recent years is above all the consequence of the financial crisis even if, in order to cure it, one has had to deal simultaneously with other obstacles to sustainable growth'.[18]

The difficulty in finding explanations remains palpable, with the downside of how they are represented by the consequences of the massive obstacle of patents, costs linked to oil exploration, the accelerated move into service industries coupled with slight increases in productivity.[19]

Now that the debate has been launched, it is important to ask oneself what sort of a world would there need to be in which innovation could recover its strength. And first and foremost, how can this recovery be promoted? This is the question that Edmund Phelps[20] attempts to answer. He claims that the industrialized countries need to break with corporatism and conservative values. Innovation and productivity can be relaunched without adopting the values of 'modernity'. This Nobel Prize winner, famous for having shown that a return to full employment does not mean a return to inflation, asks himself about the underlying cause of the reduction in productivity, which he dates to the 1960s; namely, the lack of innovation. In the course of five decades, this lack has only been halted once during the years of the Internet bubble. The finding is as applicable to Europe as it is to the United States. A true recovery would thus involve a challenge to the established hierarchies, an inversion of priorities to the benefit of enterprises, start-ups and investors. This is to the detriment of a statist and centralist approach. The forthcoming scene is, for him, as cultural as it is institutional and ought to promote the values of modernity, adventure and discovery, wagering on humans and their creativity. One of the original thoughts in his book *Mass Flourishing* is the description of most current economies as being tributaries of corporatism, a control system that combines capitalism, solidarity and tradition, that emerged in the 1920s and survived World War II. It is defined by a prosperous public sector and constantly increasing regulation, with greater importance being assigned to unions and lobbying pressure groups. France, Italy and Spain, Phelps claims, are the most corporatist states and consequently their results are very poor in terms of productivity and employment. Excessive state intervention, as well as intervention by all those institutions that favour the short term, and the uniformity and conformity of mentalities propagated by social networks, constitute just so many obstacles to innovation. Edmund Phelps defends a new type of capitalism, one of adventure, challenge, exploration, individuality and dynamism, in contrast to the values of prevention, acquired wisdom or precaution.

Let us imagine for an instant that the dynamic of innovation were to resume its course. What would happen? That is the question that futurologists are being asked. For most of them, tomorrow's world does not appear to be that idyllic. For Erik Brynjolfsson and Andrew McAfee, Carl Frey and Michael Osborne, Jeffrey Sachs and Laurence Kotlikoff, there will be many victims of these possible industrial revolutions. For example, Erik Brynjolfsson and Andrew McAfee[21] have produced an inventory of what they call the second machine age, that of driverless cars, super-computers that will defeat humans at knowledge games, robots that will perform complex tasks in the factory, and personal phones that will be more powerful than the largest computers of the previous generation. Hence the need to rethink work, education and the relationship with machines. We would therefore live less in a period of recession than in a technological torment, with a profound recasting of the labour market and a necessarily painful transition phase.

Carl Frey and Michael Osborne[22] have costed the effects. They mention the possibility that 47% of American jobs will be endangered. Jeffrey Sachs and Laurence Kotlikoff[23] stress, even more worryingly, that in the case of an increase in productivity, future generations will be the first victims, since the replacement of workers by robots could redirect income from the workers to the owners of robots, most of whom being retirees. Inter-generational warfare can already be imagined. Of course, this nervousness has always existed, linked to a technical process that requires the substitution of capital for work, with the painful consequences of adaptation that are already known. Optimists such as Alfred Sauvy have been able to say that productivity gains would create new wealth, directly and indirectly, and there would also be increasing demand causing a revival of growth. Compensation between the positive effects and the negative effects would thus occur to the benefit of the former. But when will this be? That is the whole issue and, according to Gordon or Rogoff, it is not yet on an agenda that, today, is essentially preoccupied with stagnation.

Increasingly rare resources

If the weakness of technical progress is confirmed, the first victim would be the natural resources sector, with the consequence that they will become increasing rare. Remember that, according to Jeremy Rifkin,[24] we have engaged in an energy crisis that is likely to deteriorate in future years.

In reality, the financial crisis occurred in economies that were already seriously weakened by the impact of high prices of raw materials in previous years. This price increase, and especially that of oil, has been continuous, starting from the American recovery of 2002 and accompanied by the exceptional world crisis that lasted from 2002 to 2007. Starting in 2005, specialists identified the existence of an impact from raw materials, ranging from oil to metals via rubber and cereals,[25] an impact that rose to a peak in mid-2008. A raw materials price index indicates a similar development, when prices increased by 1.5% between 2002 and 2007, then by another 1.5% until they reached a peak in July 2008.[26]

Cereals, that constitute the first link in the food chain, followed the same course. Wheat holds the price increase record, rising from around 120 dollars per tonne to 400–450 dollars at its peak. The sudden rise was similar for rice, slightly less for maize. The general price index for food products, calculated by the specialists of the FAO[27] on the basis of the prices of 55 different products representing the market, increased by 54% between May 2007 and May 2008. Oil was at its most expensive a few weeks after cereal prices shot up, with an accompanying succession of hunger riots.

From mid-July 2008, a price drop began that subsequently accelerated. This resulted in a return to 2004–2005[28] prices. This reduction ought nevertheless to be viewed in relative terms since, in the long term, price increases remain the rule.[29]

The reduction in the prices of raw materials was clearly caused by the worldwide slowdown and a recession in the developed economies. The crisis thus reveals that strong worldwide growth will henceforth be unsustainable in the long term, since an increase in the price of raw materials is of such a nature as to smash any genuine resumption of growth in the world economy, unless the exploitation of rare resources produces one or two major innovations. That is true today and will be even more so tomorrow. This is due to the tendency to underestimate the demographic dynamic in this first part of the twenty-first century and the geopolitical changes it could cause. In 2015, the world's population was 7.3 billion, with those living in OECD countries accounting for just over a billion. In 2050, the world population will have reached a peak, but the population of the OECD area will hardly have changed. The challenge for this century is to meet the essential needs of the inhabitants of the emerging nations and of the poorest countries.

There will be a requirement to meet needs in terms of food, water and energy while collectively managing a climate change that is sustainable. The scarcities which we shall have to face, and which will probably generate violent tensions, involve food crops as much as water, land, energy and raw materials.

In fact, the scarcity of energy and climate challenges pose the question of the unsustainability of our growth model. But there is something more important and more serious. Energy consumption conceals major disparities between countries whose consumption will more or less converge in the next 30 years.

Inequalities in energy and fuel poverty are reflected in consumption per head. The American citizen consumes the equivalent of an average 8 tonnes of oil annually, the European citizen 4 tonnes, the Chinese citizen 1 tonne and the African 0.5 tonnes.

Faced with the energy consumption of the wealthy nations, fuel poverty affects about 1.2 billion people who are still living without access to electricity and 2.8 billion without access to modern domestic fuel,[30] electricity and petroleum products. How can the 'Johannesburg equation' be resolved in future decades by providing more energy for economic development to the poorest and fewer greenhouse gas emissions, all this in energy systems that are notorious for their inertia and inflexibility? Combined with increasing rarity, this should considerably increase geopolitical tensions.

Oil and gas reserves are concentrated in thirty or so countries, most of which are risk-prone. Competition for access to these reserves can only increase in view of the ever-increasing needs of the emerging nations. Even though important discoveries have been made in the North Sea and off the coasts of Brazil and West Africa, geopolitics counts for more than geology. The main question, in any case, is not the volume of reserves, but putting them into production. The level of investment to be made depends, essentially, on the price level and the geopolitics of the countries that own the deposits. Today, a balance cannot be imagined between existing technological conditions and the market. If one only takes into account the current level of reserves, the question of the rarity of resources of fossil origin only seems to have arisen yesterday. Yet every country, aware of the exhaustible nature of this wealth, has anticipated this depletion that is already causing tensions today. These are not limited to competition between the North, the traditional consumer, and the emerging nations whose appetite for resources is growing. Playing on this competition between the two areas, the exporting countries want to retain absolute control of their resources by thinking of the future.

We are therefore witnessing a restriction in the conditions of access to exploration and production, the toughening of taxation arrangements, the introduction of fixed internal pricing and export conditions with respect to quantity and price that are evidence of an increase in the power of a form of nationalism. This competition is magnified by the volatility of energy prices, fed by economic, climatic, geopolitical and financial factors and the difficulty of conceiving of any major technological advances.

The same uncertainty prevails with respect to the issue of water. The figures are well-known. Nearly 780 million people on earth have no access to clean drinking water, 2.5 billion have no adequate sanitation and 20,000 human beings, half of them children, die every day due to lack of clean water.[31] By 2030, five billion people – 67% of the world's population – will probably have no access to decent sanitation. Yet Goal 10 of the Millennium Development Goals was a reduction by half in the percentage of this population. The original difficulty thus remains the inequality of access to water – an inequality between countries, regions, cities and towns, and even neighbourhoods.

Water is a major key to the distribution of the world population. In 2020, some 60 million people will have abandoned the deserts of sub-Saharan Africa for the Maghreb (Morocco, Tunisia and Algeria) and thence to Europe. Whether producing drought or floods, resulting from deforestation, desertification, pollution or climate change, the vagaries of rainfall are the origin of mass population movements. Between now and 2050, the number of so-called ecological migrants may reach 250 million. The key word here is *conflict*. Instability and disputes in the host countries, the countries of origin or within a region are all the result of the depletion of resources that were not abundant in the first place, overpopulation, lack of drinking water and sanitation conditions in which epidemics thrive.

What is even more serious is that fights to appropriate water are becoming increasingly bitter and are a risk factor in outbreaks of conflict across the globe. The major areas of tension are well known and include the Nile basin, fought over by Ethiopia, Sudan and Egypt; the Tigris and the Euphrates, subjects of tension between Turkey, Syria and Iraq; The Jordan Valley, between Israel and its Arab neighbours; while India is concerned about the water originating in Tibet, and thus in China, from the Brahmaputra and the Indus rivers. As for Russia and China, they are uneasy about having to share the waters of the Amur river.

Poverty and water-related stress often go together. As proof, the number of people living on less than 1.25 U.S. dollars a day more or less corresponds to the number of people who have no access to drinking water. The approximately 2.8 billion human beings who live on less than two dollars a day have no access to decent sanitation. Remember, there is no aqueous stock exchange, there is no speculation on a litre of water in Singapore, in Wall Street or in the City of London. In a world in which everything has become a marketable commodity, the vital importance of water is forgotten, as it has no price and suffers from every type of neglect, including economic.

Yet water is also associated with feeding and land use. It is the insurmountable constraint for any type of food production. Yet the food impasse, the predictable imbalance between supply and need, is not restricted by rarity. It depends on our inability to identify problems in the medium term and devise solutions for them. Not only do the inhabitants of Nigeria and Bangladesh not get enough to eat to satisfy their hunger – their diet is below the threshold of 2,300 calories a day which the FAO defines as malnutrition – but their diet consists almost exclusively of vegetables. On the other hand, most animals consumed in the United States and France are farmed animals, fed on grains and soya beans. Thus, of the quantity of cereals and soya beans produced, the French consume 13,680 calories while a Bangladeshi is content with 1,450 calories derived from plants, nearly ten times less. This leads to unbearable conclusions. The number of humans who can be fed is closely dependent on their diet. Yet this figure varies depending on the relationship between the share of vegetable crops that is consumed directly and the share of these same plants that is used to feed animals that are subsequently eaten.

Thus, if humans choose to eat meat as a priority, the planet will not be able to meet the demand. Only four billion of the population will be able to eat. The possibility of being able to meet the food needs of the entire human race thus depends on sharing food between the feeding of animals and the feeding of humans. The current trend, however, is in sustained support for food of animal origin. That is because the new middle classes of the large emerging nations, China, Brazil and India, have adopted western eating habits. In comparison with the level attained in 1961, China has multiplied its meat production by 32% and Brazil by 12%. The progression tripled in the United States and doubled in Europe.[32] With the development of the world economy, the demand for meat-eating will probably continue to grow and adversely affect the grain market.

More recently, the conversion of grain into ethanol is contributing to a new deal of the cards. The question of subsistence plays a role in production between people, animals and engines, the absolute opposite of the Malthusian vision. It is no longer overall numbers of humans and livelihoods that need to be looked at, but sharing livelihoods between different usages. An economic subsistence theory remains to be constructed that will involve the price of fuel, the elasticity of meat consumption in relation to income, dietary habits and a number of other factors. The Malthusian paradigm had the advantage of evidence and simplicity. Yet for the past fifty years it has not been able to withstand the facts, since plant production has increased faster than the population, thus invalidating the comparison between the arithmetical progression of food production and the geometric progression of the population. Yet, despite the greatest availability of food, hunger has unfortunately continued to affect a significant proportion of humanity.

Food security has apparently become the leading strategic challenge. China is in the first rank of countries that are launching themselves into the frenetic race to purchase arable farmland abroad. In fact, China represents 22% of the world's population, but has only 10% of the world's farmland.[33] Forty or so Chinese agricultural companies are operating in thirty or so countries throughout the world to create reserves of land in the name of self-sufficiency in food. Other neighbouring countries have also chosen to become large landowners. Thus, South Korea acquired land in Argentina to supply itself with meat; Japan is interested in Egypt for its vegetable oil and sugar; India is looking at Malaysia for its palm oil. Leasing agricultural land is an alternative if financial and/or political reasons do not permit certain countries to become landowners abroad. These purchases or leases of arable land are continuing relentlessly, mainly for reasons of food security.

Whether considering energy, water or arable land, it has to be acknowledged that the conditions for the production of these resources are very uncertain. All the major resources appear to be potentially available but produced or used under conditions that are either deteriorating or are making hardly any progress. For each, one can only envisage salvation through 'disruptive technologies'.

The war of intelligence

When will this disruption occur? What process will make it possible to revive the movement of an economic growth? Which is the most favourable ecosystem? Who will be capable of developing this process?

Economists have analysed the, so-called, technological frontier that defines the current period by making it possible to separate two groups of countries, the innovators and the imitators. A few years ago, a basic text,[34] focusing on the member-countries of the OECD for the period 1985–2003, taught us a lot about the impact of the level of training in the population, the rigidity of markets and the development of total factor productivity factors. This series of studies, developed by Philippe Aghion and his colleagues, is instructive in the methods it recommends for moving the technological boundaries. Technological revolutions may be of a more social nature, associated with populations, groups and the ability to share resources. In a few words, what could be termed 'a favourable breeding-ground' for innovation.

Of course, nowadays growth is largely in the hands of the 'imitator' countries, the emerging nations and a few developed countries. California, as far as the field of new information and communications technology is concerned, remains, without a doubt, a sort of haven. This is where everything happens and everyone tries to imitate or gain possession – often by questionable means. Silicon Valley itself offers us improvements that are purported to be incremental, yet all linked in some way or another to the Internet, and yet there is nothing here that might give rise to imagining a radical transformation. What is true for this sector is even truer for the rest. Nothing is either fully satisfying or the harbinger of better times ahead.

In order to try to provide a theory/solution that will be submitted to interrogation by the leading countries in future decades, there needs to be a return to the prospect of the endogenization of technical progress. Unlike the exogenous growth theory, the endogenous growth theory suggests that economic growth is the result of endogenous and not external forces. For example: investments, R&D, education, etc. Such classifications are open to criticism but show that ten countries are apparently devoting considerable resources to developing the intelligence industries.

Richard Florida[35] is one of a number of authors who subscribe to the rather banal idea that it is no longer technological innovation and the presence of certain material resources that are the engines of economic development, but rather the 'talent' or the concentration of a certain category of professionals and creative people. One has the feeling here that history is nothing but an eternal recommencement. Remember what David Landes[36] said: this Industrial Revolution was born in England and spread throughout Europe, and that is not by chance. The culture of

Table 1.4 Technology ranking on the world scale

Pays	Technology 2011	Research 2011	Investment 2010	Investment 2011	Innovation 2011	Innovation 2013
Finland	1	1	3	3	4	6
Japan	2	3	4	4	2	22
United States	3	7	6	6	1	5
Israel	4	–	1	1	5	14
Sweden	5	2	2	2	6	2
Switzerland	6	11	5	5	3	1
Denmark	7	5	9	9	9	9
Republic of Korea	8	16	7	7	–	18
Germany	9	13	8	8	7	15
Singapore	10	4	11	11	11	8

Sources: Martin Prosperity Institute (2011), World Bank (2010), World Intellectual Property Organization (2013) and the authors.

those countries, their institutions and their legal systems predisposed them to welcome a change of this kind, something that has not been the case for either India or China, nor distant Latin America, all of which have been incapable of espousing the European model. Why is this so? It is because the engine for growth remains human behaviour and peoples' 'cultural values'.

Gregory Clark's[37] approach is more useful to us for our research into what can distance us from the spectre of stagnation or, worse, of recession. He considers that industrial revolutions emerge from cultural developments and their supporting institutions. What could a revolution such as this rely on today? Places that support the idea of scientific and social progress, shared progress? On this point, one is struck by a certain paucity in the forecasting abilities of the economic literature. Little is learned from reading it unless it is that concentrating resources into teaching and research could favour scientific and technological progress. A more important question remains; namely, why has technical progress slowed down today, even though everyone knows that science can make available all of the results that, unfortunately, are not being used? And this is where the main uncertainty remains. Perhaps it could be imagined that the ageing that affects wealthy societies does not encourage them to launch into true investment in the future whereas, at the same time, the emerging nations are merely developing technologies supplied by the leading nations. Immobility is favoured through this difficulty in understanding the areas in which investment is needed as a priority.

Technological revolutions are the product of very special circumstances in which innovative technologies reinforce each other to the point where they construct a new technical system. Do we have the elements today of this gridlock that could simultaneously produce radical change in goods and services consumed as well as in their means of production? Many studies are beginning to deal with this very specific connection between innovations.

To illustrate the point, there is the work by McKinsey,[38] the thirty-four points of a recent report,[39] or, again, the seven ambitions for innovation.[40] What is striking is that these initial studies only provide a very partial response to the real upsets with which the world will be confronted – the scarcity of resources. This would mean very quickly forgetting that it is here that the inevitable conflicts will lie, in the appropriation of that which enables life. It is also to forget the lesson taught by Fernand Braudel about the impacts to come, perhaps in the form of armed conflict, between the new centres of prosperity and the impoverished periphery, both old and new. In examining the Pisa classifications of research and development investment worldwide, one is entitled to ask, in the spirit of Dipesh Chakrabarty,[41] the Bengali historian, whether Europe, once a prosperous centre, now caught in the infernal cycle of injunctions by the European authority and financial operators, will be able to absorb the impact of a balancing movement that is not in its favour, without the loss of an ancient hegemony and that this will result in bitterness and tension among its populations.

2
The Curse of Ageing

Japan is supremely well suited to the aphorism: 'land of contrasts'. Japanese society has indeed experienced the fastest demographic ageing, due to its low birth rate and the exceptional longevity of its inhabitants. It is hard not to imagine a link between the very real weakening of an economy in the long term – a phase that has already lasted for twenty years – and the demographic impact so perfectly illustrated by Japan. The most surprising aspect of this intriguing development, which may represent both a positive and a negative, is the fact that the economic structure of this country reflects a dual constraint, one conjectural, the other structural. Firstly, there is an income distribution that would be hard to change and that favours capital over labour while blocking any increase in internal demand. Even worse, as the eminent Japanese demographer Shigesato Takahashi reminds us, 'the decline in the rate of fertility is closely linked to the change in the work force [...]. The number of young women in the job market has increased, especially in the service sector. [...]

Consequently, this phenomenon has produced an increase in people who have remained unmarried, leading to a very low fertility rate in Japanese society'.[1] Is it a curse or a blessing? Ageing has aspects of both, since the longevity of the population is also exceptional in comparison with the rest of the world. It is the result of numerous factors, including the national diet, lifestyle and genetics. It might be imagined that Japanese society, torn between the effects of such obvious longevity and such a fragile economic recovery, would not be able to support itself. Yet solidarities exist. Arata Tendō, in his novel *The Mourner*,[2] imagines a society that has outlawed intergenerational conflict. The 'weeper', in his progress towards the death of those he has loved, or 'the forgotten ones', cultivates this close connection between the generations, between the living and the departed, the darker face of Japanese society. In fact, the Japanese example forces us to confront the huge challenge we shall have to overcome, that of deciding how to accept an ageing society. How are we going to be able to deal with the consequences and avoid a fatal slowing down of the economy? How can we avoid intergenerational conflict? These three issues restore demographics to their major role in human history. Fernand Braudel has demonstrated their importance. The global phenomenon needs to be understood as a sequence that combines migratory flows, epidemics, wars and all those factors which, at one time or another, see the population of a geographical region increase and change its configuration; namely, the distribution between the various age groups and generations. In this millennial development, the nineteenth and twentieth centuries have played a particularly important role. There is an awareness of this new phenomenon, the ageing of the population, defined as a change to the average age of the population. Three processes have occurred successively and have altered the outlines of societies in the same way. The first is none other than the reduction in infant mortality; the second is the falling fertility rate; and the third, the lengthening of the human life span.

The special feature of this trend that began more than two centuries ago is that these three phenomena occurred and continue to occur throughout the world, with the possible exception of Africa, based on a time frame that varies depending on the level of scientific, social and cultural development of the various societies. Whatever the case, ageing has affected, continues to affect and will in future affect the whole world. For a so-called traditional economist, this phenomenon has a negative impact on growth, since ageing is regularly associated with the idea of weakening, slowing down and a lack of dynamism, eventually resulting in a greater burden of cost involving health and welfare benefits paid to the elderly. Yet there is nothing that makes it possible to state that this ageing, which we consider to be a second constraint in our new world macroeconomic trajectory, can be summarized by these additional negative effects.

Could a new, imaginative management of ageing result in an upheaval of the very conditions in which the job market operates? If the organization of work and the length of the working life take account of ageing, it would not be impossible for a large part of activity, and thus of growth, and consequently of jobs, to be linked to the needs of the elderly. There is thus a need to insist on a complete re-reading of this constraint and its implications, by questioning whether the traditional impacts of ageing will continue to exist, as well as the ability to bounce back that ageing population assumes and possible schemes to positively manage this change in the relationship between the generations. Here again, there are unique constraints; here again, there is an assumption that there will be a radical change in the way we analyse the macro-economic balance in order to convert a *de facto* weakness into an opportunity and a new form of growth.

After all, nothing has yet been written about this new human adventure, confronted as we are with an increase in the elderly population on a world scale. How can a single type of vocational training last a lifetime? How can consumption habits be changed in the elderly, imagining new industrial sectors associated with adapted technology, making progress in considering the respective incomes of different generations, considering transferring money between them? These are the challenges that are all our societies face and that an attempt must be made to solve unless we want to be mired in the terrible curse of ageing. It is a curse of which one of the possible ramifications is the birth and subsequent expansion of intergenerational conflict.

The weight of demographics in history[3]

The links between demographics and the economy, and the way in which economists have been tackling the subject for the past two centuries are decisive, even if the results are not definitive and have been the subject of much debate. In fact, a consideration of the role of populations in human history, a delicate subject and a minefield since it is conducive to digression, is nevertheless essential if we are to imagine our future. Everything has been said on this subject, all of the arguments have long been discussed and all the truths and counter-truths have been evoked, since behind these words about populations there lie the profiles of domination, slavery or integration, migration, respect or contempt, the ownership of land and its riches, in a word; war or peace. In reality, there is a certain logic in all this unpacking of basic philosophical reflections or simplistic ideas. What is called for in this adventure of ideas is to separate truth from fiction or identify the uncertainties. For example, today, the demographics that appear to be so serious, so entrenched, are the subject of theories and forecasts that are hotly debated and even result in relentless conflict. Let us very briefly survey this eternal discussion about people, their migrations and where they choose to settle.

Two words have faced off against each other during the course of the past twenty centuries with an almost mechanical regularity – domination, assimilation and once again domination – without any justification other than the power that can be exerted. At the same time, a philosophical debate is taking shape and it has a famous protagonist in Thomas Malthus. It is here, in the economy, that this intellectual discipline was born. The complete overlap between the economy and contemplation of population statistics continues to concern us, even today. If one wonders which of the great economists have left their mark on the development of this discipline, one cannot help evoking Malthus and Marx. Each of them considered and expounded on the role of the population in economic growth, causing their thoughts to become a major angle of attack. Another even more worrying issue is that these positions appeared to have been determined by demographic changes, considered to be a sign of prosperity when the population grows rapidly, and an indication of misfortune in a time of depopulation. Thus, in the Middle Ages, between the eleventh and the fourteenth centuries, the population of Europe increased, and this was accompanied by prosperity. Niccolò Machiavelli said it all in his commentary, stating the three principles, so often repeated subsequently. These are that the human population is limited by the decreasing productivity of the land which constitutes a curb on growth; where there is sufficient for subsistence, humankind rapidly increases; a numerous population constitutes an element of power for the state.

Let's change the scene. In the early eighteenth century, the small size of the population was a source of anxiety. Montesquieu wondered about depopulation and pronounced himself to be in favour of legislation to promote a population increase. As if to illustrate the correlation between action and thought in the eighteenth century, the demographics reversed, the population began to increase once again and the discussion resumed about the risks of overpopulation.

Let's skip a century. Demographics and economics, with their strengths and inadequacies, were now definitively entrenched. Yet a concern for being scientific restricted economists to making predictions that turned out to be wrong and formal statements that were sometimes pointless. This formidable debate between economists showed Braudel to be in the right: 'In the short as well as in the long term, on the scale of local realities, as on the vast scale of world realities, everything is linked to the number and oscillations of the mass of human beings'.[4]

Each specialist will interpret things in his/her own way. The demographers stress changes in fertility, marriages and births in early or later life and the mortality rate. Climatologists more often look to the skies for the great events of climate change, while the economists are more interested in increases in productivity, and, above all, cereal production and the ambivalent relationship between population growth and the increase in the human capacity for production. Finally, the historian of epidemics is interested in a return of the 'plagues', while political and social historians cannot forget wars and social unrest.

The optimists and the pessimists were in opposite camps, with Malthus at the heart of this permanent confrontation. Those who believed in the infinite growth of wealth, driven by permanent scientific progress, opposed those who claimed that there were physical limits to our growth. The religion of science versus that of realism! The discussion was revived every twenty years, but now, in the early twenty-first century, it has acquired an unparalleled acuity. It is a case of ecology versus productivism. The end of our world versus infinite development. This is an old debate that relentlessly pits the ancients against the moderns without our knowing exactly who is who.

Malthus was writing in the late eighteenth century, at exactly the time when the old constraints had begun to disappear. Starting from the tragic lessons of the past, a past that is still very recent, there is good reason to be frightened of the runaway growth of the British, European and even the world population, a movement that is only just beginning. Land is limited in area and in fertility, yields are decreasing. If agricultural production can only progress arithmetically, like the right-hand side of a given gradient, the population, by contrast, is growing at a constant rate, i.e. exponentially, as long as it does not encounter the food restrictions that will force it to return tragically, due to famine, to the growth gradient of quantities of wheat. Consider that there was a time in France, a country in which fertile soil abounds, when, for every hundred people, eighty were engaged in farming to feed the population. How could Malthus have imagined that in the early twenty-first century two people would be enough for this purpose, and even then working on a great deal less land? His ideas were imposed on everyone, even those who criticized this 'enemy of humanity', for his bad, black genius. In fact, he was relying on recent events, geography and history, and his theory was both relevant and a nice logical construction. He was wrong, of course. In 1400, there were 350 million inhabitants in the world; in 1600, 550 million. By the late eighteenth century, there might already have been a billion, certainly there were 2.5 billion in 1950 and, in 2014, there were more than seven billion. Despite malnutrition, famine and diseases that feed on the poverty of less developed countries, the food situation for these seven billion human beings has improved in comparison with the way it was for the billion individuals who were alive in 1800. But hasn't the time come for Malthus to get his revenge?

The phenomenon of ageing can actually upset the hand that has been dealt. It would therefore be the number of people, but their age, which is significant. The 'demographic transition' represents the transition from traditional demographics in which the birth and death rates are very high to a so-called modern demographic, in which these rates are low, yet barely differentiated. The ageing of the population, born of this movement, follows several stages in time.

Firstly, the mortality rate among the youngest has fallen drastically thanks to the development and spread of medicine, the improvement in public health and better nutrition.[5] The birth rate will also progressively decrease in the future, due to various factors such as contraception, education, working women and birth control policies, in order to reach a level close to that of the death rate. This last trend, which is fairly recent in developed countries, has led to a significant increase in life expectancy.

The significant changes that began in the eighteenth century sped up in the twentieth century. The proportion of people who lived until over the age of 60 increased from 8% of the total population in 1950 to 11% in 2009. This phenomenon would continue and would accelerate in future decades. By 2050, 22% of the world population will be aged over 60. It is nevertheless difficult to predict accurately the future state of demographics. In fact, behind the ageing of the population lie two uncertainties, one concerning the extension of life span and the other the development in fertility rates. Ageing can accelerate while the fertility rate continues to decline. Life expectancy can also increase solely thanks to the progressive extension of the life span in the most elderly. The age pyramid will retain the same base but will grow higher. Not every country will experience the same type of ageing, even if it seems to be difficult to predict the pattern that will be typical of each of them in the coming decades. That is because the asynchronous nature of the development in each country is evident.[6] According to the United Nations,[7] the over-sixties will represent about 30% of the population of the developed regions in 2050, as against a current 20% of the population, but it will be only 20% in the developing parts of the world. These areas will thus attain the current level of ageing in the developed regions 40 years later.

The reality of the world will thus change, for better or worse, and will be determined by four characteristics. To return to the official sources, the ageing of the population will occur in almost every country in the world.

'The global proportion of people aged 60 or over increased by 9.2% in 1990 to 11.7% in 2013, and will continue to grow in proportion to the world population, reaching 21.1% in 2050'.[8] The intergenerational relationship will be crucial. 'Overall, the number of people aged 60 or over ought to more than double, from 841 million people in 2013 to more than two billion in 2050. The number of the elderly should exceed the number of children for the first time in 2047'.[9] Work will become a heavy constraint. 'Many elderly people still need to work, especially in the developing countries. In 2010, the number of people aged 65 or over in the working population was about 31% in the less developed regions and 8% in more developed regions'. Finally, in certain parts of the world, poverty will be the essential problem. The 'prevalence of poverty among the elderly throughout most of Africa is either slightly less than or slightly more than the average in the total population', according to the same source.

The three impacts of ageing

The discussion among economists has sprung back to life. The concern is now that the problem is not being dealing with globally. Andrew Mason and Ronald Lee[10] have stressed that, until recently, changes to the age structure favoured most countries, since populations were more and more heavily concentrated in the working age group. In certain Asian countries and most of those in Africa, this trend continues. But elsewhere, in the West, East Asia and in Latin America, the number of people in the working age population is in decline or soon will be, unlike the ageing population that is growing exponentially.

Problems that we in the West are already facing today will thus arise, namely failing health and state-funded welfare systems, little economic growth,[11] and even a decline in growth, effort orientated towards the oldest to the detriment of the youngest, the possible collapse of the money markets and a debt burden to be borne by future generations.

This development concerns the whole world. The most typical traits, contrary to what is usually thought, might be found in Asia. Donghyun Park, Sang Hyop Lee and Andrew Mason[12] are very clear on this point. The ageing of the population is the greatest economic and social obstacle for the future of Asia and it needs to be dealt with. The demographic transition of the whole region towards an older population is in the process of radically transforming the demographic landscape. This raises major socio-economic challenges. First of all, Asia needs to find resources that will be capable of sustaining rapid economic growth in the context of an unfavourable demographic, i.e. an increasingly small working-age population. Secondly, again according to the above authors, Asia needs to meet the demand for affordable housing and sustainable financial resources for an ever-increasing ageing population.

Asia is not an homogenous entity, however. Ronald Lee and Andrew Mason[13] have produced a more detailed description. Japan, as the richest country in Asia, was the first to experience the phenomenon of ageing in its population. Unlike other countries in the region, Japan introduced special provisions for the elderly that are relatively similar to what has been done in Europe, consisting of generous pensions and a suitable health and care system. Japan will now have to bear the cost in the long term, which represents a heavy burden on the budget deficit. In the rest of Asia, on the other hand, transfers of public money to the ageing population are very small and, if they remain so, ageing ought not to threaten public expenditure. Yet without such transfers of expenditure could families bear the cost of an ageing population? In east Asia and in Thailand, net family support for the aged is important. In India and south-east Asia, on the other hand, net family payment transfers are not directed at the ageing population. The economic consequences of population ageing in the countries of Asia thus depend on which model has been adopted, whether or not they are based on that of Japan.

It is obvious that the whole world is involved, but initially this will concern the countries that are already affected by the demographic shift. In their case, there is a triple impact based on the cost of ageing, the increase in risk aversion and the lack of innovation. The first impact depends upon expenditure on health and retirement. It might be claimed that an extension of the life span ought to translate into greater investment in human capital. In fact, the extension represents a longer period of viability in expenditure on education.[14] This implies, for each age group, releasing the resources devoted to education, a solution that ultimately reveals itself as being fairly simple if the rest of public expenditure were not being called upon to increase as well. That is because ageing has serious consequences in terms of expenditure on health and welfare, as predicted in projections each of which is more catastrophic than the next. And yet nothing has been decided so far, even if the trend towards increasing costs is hardly disputable. There is a lively debate as to whether ageing is really behind the increase in healthcare expenditure. According to Brigitte Dormont,[15] its projected virtual doubling between 2005 and 2050 is only partially due to this fact, other factors being involved, such as the increase in GDP, technological progress and development of insurance coverage. But the uncertainty in financing the dependence of the elderly is another source of tension in public finances. France may have more than two million dependents in 2040, according to the Charpin Report,[16] even though other theories may be posited.[17]

Refinancing the retirement system lies at the heart of the analysis of the economic consequences of ageing. In fact, again for France, the proportion between the number of contributors to a pension scheme and the number of retirees will fall drastically. In 2050, about 1.2 people will be paying into the scheme for every 1 retiree[18] as against the current situation of 1.8 contributors per 1 pensioner in France. In the United Kingdom, this ratio will change from 3.2 to 2.8 by 2030.[19] Our ageing society, like all the societies affected by this phenomenon, will become a very difficult burden to be supported by assets.[20] All of the projections indicate insurmountable deficits if the number of pensioners is maintained. If the acceleration in the rate of reform ought to encourage us to be more prudent in our diagnosis, the impact of ageing on the cost of social protection will nevertheless be far from negligible.

Even more significantly, Lionel Ragot[21] estimates the contrast between the average annual growth rate of the total French population between now and the end of the century at 0.22%, and that of the working age population at 0.06%. These percentages are eloquent with respect to ageing known as 'top down' and concern the dependency ratio that will increase from 26% in 2010 to 48.9% in 2100. This phenomenon will be experienced much earlier by the country that has become the pioneer of ageing – Japan. Its average annual growth rate is already negative and by 2025, the number of people aged 75 years and over will represent 30% of the population.[22]

For many, risk aversion represents the second handicap of an ageing society. There is no consensus on the effects on the savings market, however. As far as we are concerned, we extensively support the position adopted by André Masson who notes the following two characteristics:[23] risk aversion grows with age and individual savings decrease among the oldest. The theory of the life cycle shows, in fact, that periods of inactivity are marked by a divestment of savings rendered possible due to savings accumulated during working life. Nevertheless, the effect of ageing on savings habits is not all that simple. Contrary to economic intuition from the outset, the aggregate rate of savings cannot fall merely due to the extension of the life span and the reserves to be created to constitute financial insurance. Similarly, if, in theory, stocks and shares are a less attractive investment, due to this lessened tolerance of risk, the improvement with age of knowledge of finance, the time available for managing a portfolio, and the lifeline of security provided by a retirement pension are many factors that could reverse the trend. Yet what is involved here is simply many phenomena of the second order in the general attitude of pensioners in the face of risk, since, far more than risk itself, it is the perception of risk that affects the behaviour of the economic agent. If a crisis proves to last longer or be tougher than forecast, if the future of healthcare systems and retirement seem to be increasingly uncertain, the demand for stocks and shares will necessarily decrease among anxiety-prone pensioners, resulting in a flight to safer investments. This poses a real threat to the economy to the extent that innovation is based on risk-taking.

It is here that the third difficulty intervenes, one that is encountered by ageing societies, namely, a low rate of innovation.[24] What is the relationship between the age of assets and creativity, the capacity for innovation and the circulation of such innovations? Individually, the capacity for innovation reduces after a certain age and takes the form of a bell curve throughout the life cycle. According to Jones,[25] the age that represents the creative optimum reduced by several years during the course of the last century, recording a 30% reduction in innovation potential during the life cycle. Could this figure be the sign of an active population that is older, but not really compensated for by the fact that the peak of creativity is becoming correspondingly shorter in the life cycle? Of course, the ability of a society to innovate has never been the sum of its individual capacities. While the proportion of adults of working age is reducing in our ageing societies with, in particular, an increase in the ratio of welfare dependency, what is the effect of such a change on our collective capacity to innovate?

Two schools of thought have been in conflict on this subject for a number of years. On the one hand, Robert Solow,[26] in his brilliant growth model, mentions the 'dilution' of productive resources in a growing number of workers, operating against growth per head of the population. Becker and Lewis, in their note dated 1973,[27] write of the 'dilution' of human capital which curbs innovation in the working age population. Yet for centuries – remember William Petty in the seventeenth century – other intellectuals have hailed the positive role played by the population, a synonym for ingenuity and creativity.[28] There is a genuine controversy that continues to rage with respect to the impact of the rarity of employment on innovation and technical progress. This theoretical discussion is of great interest in assessing the effects of an active population that will become rarer in the future in ageing societies. Will it stimulate[29] technical progress and innovation or is it a hindrance? That is a very difficult question to resolve. The relative scarcity of employment could cause the population to innovate in order to overcome new constraints. Conversely, a larger working age population multiplies the probability of the simultaneous existence of numerous innovators. Econometric research on this issue has not produced any greater certainties since, for Cutler,[30] the reduction in the working age population is a stimulus, while for Sevilla[31] the 'demographic dividend' has had a positive impact on technical progress. And above all, productivity gains will be associated with active 40 to 49-year-olds,[32] who are the most valuable cohort for economic dynamism and technical progress. Yet here again, doubts have been raised.

A final question: is the spread of innovation influenced by demographic growth and the age of the population? For Paul Beaudry and David Green,[33] countries showing strong demographic growth spread new technology faster between 1975 and 1997, thanks to new entrants into the labour market, who were more likely to have been trained in information technology. The ageing of the population seems here to presage anxieties. How able will the ageing countries with a low birth rate be to spread new technologies quickly, even if such anxieties are partially alleviated by an increase in the level of education? How can companies at the forefront of innovation and productivity gains renew themselves? Over and above the complexity of social behaviour linked to ageing, the work of numerous researchers, such as Christian Pfeifer and Joachim Wagner,[34] has produced conclusions. When a representative sample of German manufacturing companies is analysed with respect to the relationship between the composition of their employees and their productivity with respect to innovation, it can be seen that companies whose staff are older spend much less on research and development than the rest. Does population ageing endanger the process of creative destruction?

While the destiny of ageing societies seems to be predetermined here to some extent, there is nothing is final about it.

A blessing in disguise?

Productivity appears to be contradicting this pessimistic vision. In an ageing economy in which social security contributions account for ever-increasing expenditure, productivity gains are essential for maintaining the buying power of assets. Yet, traditionally, the ageing of the population is considered to be the enemy of productivity. A reduction in individual productivity is quoted in support of this claim,[35] coupled with a decrease in the active population, the drop in savings among economic operators and the increasing weight of expenditure – on health, retirement and welfare – often depicted as being 'unproductive' and to the detriment of future investment in such areas as education.

Initial growth models have reinforced this opinion.[36] They denounce the decreasing yield in production factors, an exogenous technological change, and they forecast an important drop in the rate of savings and in employment. This list is the principal channel through which ageing affects our economies according to the OECD estimates,[37] an impact assessed at between 0.2 and 0.5% for France and Germany, and at 0.8% for Japan. This pessimism does not entirely translate into the facts. In Japan, the economy that has gone furthest down the line in the ageing process and that is presumed to illustrate a form of stagnation, productivity gains between 2001 and 2007 were up by 1.6% a year, representing the same performance as in other developed countries. Sweden, another example in which more older people are in work, beats all records an experienced impressive productivity gains for the years 2001–2007, with an annual growth rate of 2.0%, higher than that of the United States![38]

In fact, the evidence is our worst enemy, since the results of numerous studies have been inconclusive. On an individual scale, the development of productivity with age can be summarized as follows. Growth increases up to the age of about 50, then there is a decrease, the extent of which depends heavily on the occupation in which the person is engaged. Yet today, productivity in the older person is constantly increasing in comparison to previous generations, as the result of better health and a higher level of education.[39] This does not compensate for the reduction but renders it less drastic.

Then there is the second aspect to ageing, namely, the creation of new opportunities. To assess the ability of older people to create growth, the markets, both the market for goods and services and the labour market, need to be taken into account. People aged 65 have a standard of living equivalent to that of the rest of the population, with the exception of the extremes, the poorest 10% and the richest 10%.[40] The level of consumption is in effect levelled out over the whole life cycle of individuals.[41] Thus, the ageing of the population does not result in a tangible change to the level of demand. The structure of consumption nevertheless varies tangibly depending on the age groups, a typical generational effect. For example, people born before World War II are affected by the culture of scarcity and are inclined to concentrate their consumption on basic needs. Conversely, generations born after World War II are major consumers of leisure and cultural goods.[42]

Finally, behaviour changes as life progresses. Ageing is likely to involve greater consumption in terms of housing, domestic services, leisure and health, expenditure on clothing, food and gadgets. In future, the elderly will have to devote an important share of their income to technologies for the aged, technical systems that are designed to assist them in coping with daily life. This development ought to create jobs that cannot be outsourced abroad, since they are linked to residential consumption, i.e. to goods and services consumed at the place in which they are produced. We nevertheless ought not to celebrate too soon, since this contribution will remain modest, creating between 100,000 and 400,000 jobs in France between now and 2030, especially in the health sector and services for the aged.[43] Here again, this is not a natural change in the demand for goods and services and it will not be the engine that will motivate the creation of a large number of jobs.

With respect to employment, ageing is not without effect on the flow of those leaving the job market. In theory, the number of departures due to retirement increased 1.5 times in the decade from 1995 to 2005 and the years 2005–2012. Between now and 2020, according to current projections, one third of the people who were in work in 2005 will be retiring. Definitive departures from the job market will therefore be almost as numerous as the number of people entering it by 2020.[44] But who knows what the attitude will be of retirees in the future, who will discover that their pension, or at least the pension for which they saved, is in danger of reducing over time? This question could also suggest that the ratio of dependence between pensioners and those active in the job market could be less of a concern than has been forecast.

Finally, the issue of health is no doubt less simple than it appears. Does the traditional assertion whereby a price cannot be put on health make it possible to understand the conduct of some of the economic operators in advanced societies? Whether or not these economic operators are disposed to devote such a large part of their income to healthcare expenditure depends on their wealth. Their needs are fully met by material and non-material assets whose marginal utility is rapidly decreasing. So much so that, as the standard of living rises, individuals are channelling their expenditure into anything that operates in favour of a long life span. Health will therefore become a superior asset and an implicit value of life that is constantly increasing. Hence the growing preference for new medical procedures that notably increase the chances of living as long as possible under the right conditions. Health is a powerful engine of consumption in ageing countries. But to what extent?

For Hall and Jones,[45] the value of life grows faster – up to twice as fast – as the income from operators. These researchers estimate that the optimal rate of the share of health in GDP will reach nearly 30% in 2050 in the case of the United States. There is thus little to do to arrest the increase in expenditure on health since this is a deep-rooted movement in our society.

To return to productivity. We expect an individual in good health to be more productive, with fewer absences and better physical and cognitive abilities. Before 2009, economists were unable to demonstrate the link between expenditure on healthcare and productivity. Since then, the link has been shown for 47 countries at every stage of development and for the period between 1940 and 2000. The conclusion, that expenditure on healthcare increases productivity in the economy in the long term, is unchallengeable. The improvement in the state of health of a society therefore has a positive effect on the growth of GDP per inhabitant. That is hardly surprising, but it should be noted that the vision is changing; healthcare expenditure is moving from the status of 'unproductive expenditure' to that of investment. Such expenditure allows for increasing longevity which, in return, nourishes growth; it accelerates the productivity of the labour force and thus an increase in income. In return, the labour force shows its preferences for goods and healthcare services.

In this new approach to healthcare expenditure, what happens to innovation? Can it be directed as a priority to the over-sixties without adversely affecting the shared benefits of advances in medicine? For expensive pharmaceuticals and the benefits of medical instruments that represent the most significant factor in expenditure, the incentive to innovate is all the stronger when private and public insurance exists to cover the costs. Innovation could thus naturally be directed to the elderly who have little to pay in, but whose consumption of expensive medicines and instrumentation is virtually exclusive.

Another effect is that the caring professions, assisting people who are dependent, will suffer from a lack of those willing to take employment in home care due to the progressive disappearance of the traditional pool of uneducated women aged 35 to 50. Thus, only technological innovation, in other words geronto-technology, will be able to provide a satisfactory response to the need for helping the infirm with their domestic chores. Certain aids exist for those with reduced mobility, others for age-related anxiety attacks and memory disorders. New innovations make it possible for carers to keep in touch remotely with the elderly in their care. Furthermore, technology to help the aged, something that is indispensable for allowing the elderly to remain in their own homes, is just as promising economically, since it puts information and communications technology to good use, with the employment of qualified people, productivity gains and the development of a new, promising sector of activity. It is no surprise that the Japanese have positioned themselves in this market with the aim of becoming world leaders in a new robotics industry. In order to offer products and services suitable for people who are getting older, Japanese industry has, since the early 2000s, networked more than 10,000 companies and 250 universities around several key challenges of ageing. Ambition does not end there, however. The elderly and the dependent have only reached the first stage in the development of a personal robotics industry that will subsequently be aimed at all consumers.

In France, these technologies are put to very limited use at present. Yet in April 2013 the French government, conscious of what is at stake, launched a *Silver Economy* network, dedicated to the elderly and bringing together a number of those involved, including companies, associations, institutions, mutual societies, insurances companies, competition hubs, economists and the world of social medicine. The aim is to cause a sector to emerge that will provide employment and growth in future years. Expenditure on the elderly and those who are dependent could be the source of economic benefits for all of the assets if it stimulates innovation. Above all, the creation of such a virtuous circle should facilitate both the spread of technology to help the aged and the social acceptance of the expenditure while remaining at the heart of a social protection system aiming at investment in the future, overtaking the old concept of a system of expenditure that is considered to be non-productive. This new paradigm should cause society to recognize the economic legitimacy of some of this expenditure and consequently to review the welfare system so as to turn it into an economic advantage as far as such a thing is possible. The welfare state, which started with the development of social security, could be replaced by a social investment state, in step with an economy in which the development of human capital and innovation lies at the heart of our concerns. This would involve a permanent initiative to promote self-sufficiency and the abilities of people throughout their lives, living in an economy that is as destabilized by globalization as it is by technological innovation. At present, these changes are in their infancy. There is hesitation, in a reality that is imposing itself, affecting a society in which the burden of the cost for caring for pensioners will merely become heavier year-on-year.

Towards intergenerational conflict

'You shall stand up before the gray head and honour the face of an old man'.[46] This Judeo-Christian vision has been perpetuated down the centuries until the emergence of an individual released from all the shackles that could previously have placed him or her under the authority of a legitimate otherness, such as the figure of the Sage, the possessor of wisdom and knowledge handed down and enriched from generation to generation. Throughout human history, from the most ancient times to certain contemporary societies, this overlap can be found between the generations, this respect due to the elderly. Whether in the words of Moses I. Finley[47] or the initiation rites of passage into adulthood described by George Steiner, the same transmission of knowledge is imposed: 'There is no occupation more privileged. Awakening in another human being powers and aspirations beyond their own; inducing in others the love of what one loves; making one's internal present into their future. It is a threefold adventure like no other'.[48] The dynamic of transmission of a culture is the means of safeguarding it and enabling it to flourish. Between masters and disciples, the relationship is ambivalent, but presupposes the acquisition of the principle of authority. If a master can destroy a pupil because he refuses to transmit certain knowledge to him – as in the case of Paganini who kept for himself the secret of his triple fermata – if the pupil can destroy the master by taking his place – as Nietzsche would replace Schopenhauer – Steiner considers the 'transmission through the soul' to be the finest exercise of the relationship between master and any pupil he considered to be more gifted than himself. But is it eternal? Steiner deplored the fact that 'pupils no longer stand up when a master enters'[49] because this is an age of what is known as irreverence. This is, to some extent, the result of what happened in 1968. It is not without anger that he invokes Adorno's fatal heart attack. Here was a man who had escaped Nazi persecution, who was subjected to criticisms by the extreme left with students exposing their naked breasts on the dais: 'At the time, the professors were prepared for anything, except ridicule; it is ridicule that kills'.[50] The late twentieth century in the West delivered a vicious blow to the principle of authority, even if it did not take the form of an open breach between the generations.

It is daring even to use the term 'intergenerational conflict'. Yet it is common currency today. It was initiated by Ronald Lee and Andrew Mason [51] who have begun working on a study of ageing and its critics. Yet since then a real fashion has emerged for analysing, interpreting and reading the clashes and misfortunes of our societies through the tensions that exist between young and old. To a certain extent, all of the approaches of the fractures in the labour market between 'insiders' and the rest validate this theory. As is known, the former group consists mostly of women and men aged between 30 and 54. There is a great temptation to say that through the classic view, especially the Marxist perspective, the social classes or social groups have gradually been replaced by a seemingly more relevant classification, one that separates the sexes and, even more decisively, the age groups. Researchers have begun a rigorous and systematic study of the level of activity in the under-25s and the over-55s, the two ends of the chain. The results are worrying, regardless of the country under consideration. The young are major victims of unemployment. To put it crudely, it is a world catastrophe, starting with the United States where the unemployment rate among 15–24-year-olds increased from 9.3% in 2000 to 17.8% in 2013. The same finding holds good for countries including France, the United Kingdom, Greece, Ireland, Portugal, Spain and even Sweden. Germany and Japan seem to be the exceptions.

Here again, the data must be carefully analysed before it is exposed to public opinion that would be appalled yet powerless to deal with it. If the trend in youth unemployment is disastrous, the figures are nevertheless not all black and white. It should not be forgotten that young people continue their education for much longer and this may constitute part of the explanation. Studies and levels of working life are thus negatively correlated. Unfortunately, the answer is not as simple as that. The increase in the amount of time devoted to studies is not the explanation for this fairly recent phenomenon. If that were the case, how could it be explained that between the ages of 25 and 30 there is no significant improvement in the employment statistics? Are we witnessing the sacrifice of a generation, something that was often experienced in times of war but never in this version of competition for jobs? There are many

Table 2.1 Unemployment by age group, 2000 and 2013

Age	15 to 24		25 to 54		55 to 64	
Year	2000	2013	2000	2013	2000	2013
France	20.6	24.1	9.3	8.9	7.3	7.3
Germany	8.5	7.4	7.1	4.7	12.7	5.5
Japan	7.7	6.3	4.1	4.1	5.6	3.3
United Kingdom	12.3	19.4	4.7	5.2	4.4	4.5
United States	9.3	17.8	3.1	6.5	2.5	5.3
OECD countries	12.1	16.3	5.4	7.2	4.9	5.7

Sources: Eurostat, Statistics Bureau of Japan, International Organization of Labour, OECD and the authors.

who currently share that far too simplistic view. To avoid this stumbling block, work needs to be done on all the various components of the life of a generation, their standard of living, access to jobs, knowledge – in a word, about everything that might enable a young woman or a young man to integrate normally into society. It is to the credit of Lee and Mason that they have demonstrated the complexity of what might be termed 'the war of the generations'. As indicated by Bruno Palier, there is a tradition in France of only rarely changing the redistribution structure. Yet today, it is young adults and families with children who are the most heavily exposed to the risk of poverty. Again according to Palier, the elderly are benefiting to an increasing extent from the redistribution structure of our welfare societies.[52] There is consequently a genuine debate about the concept that is so attractive, so modern, of the war between the generations.

Unlike Bruno Palier, Jeroen Spijker and John MacInnes[53] believe that this is a bubble that will collapse by itself and has no foundation in reality for one simple reason, namely that the measurements used to assess population ageing are misleading. 'The *standard* indicator for the ageing of the population is the ratio of dependence of the elderly which consists in dividing the number of people who are of retirement age by the number of people who are of working age. This indicator makes no distinction, however, between the fact of being of working age and the fact of actually having a job, classifying everyone who is old enough to retire as being "dependents"'. They claim that a more relevant measurement of the effect of an ageing population would be the ratio of dependency of people who are *genuinely* old, a ratio that divides the number of people whose life expectancy is 15 years or less by that of people who are in work, regardless of their age: 'This measure takes account of the actual effect of mortality trends, while permitting the limit of true old age to move as progress in healthcare prolongs an individual's active life'. In fact, age represents two things. The number of years of life, something that is easy to measure for individuals as well as for populations; and the number of years they have left to live, an unknown for individuals, but predictable data for populations. With the mortality rate dropping, hope for the remainder of life is increasing in all the age groups in the population. This distinction makes it possible to understand why numerous examples of behaviour and attitudes to health are no longer linked to life expectancy but rather to age. During recent decades, the dependence ratio of the elderly has thus increased in the advanced economies, while the dependence ratio of people who are *really* old has declined. This proportion now appears to have stabilized, but is likely to increase progressively during the next two decades. For Germany as well as for Italy, where the growth in employment and birth rate are lower than anywhere else in the developed world, this ratio has remained at virtually the same level for 20 years.

This long plea for countering the intuition of a sacrificed generation has one merit. Whether true or false, figures now need to be discussed in order to avoid any misunderstanding. The very innovative work performed by Hyppolite d'Albis[54] shows that the 'baby-boomers', often denounced as the winning generation, have made it possible, by introducing changes in families which have continued through subsequent generations, for the welfare system in France to continue to exist. In fact, by investigating the changes to these transfers of wealth between generations over a relatively long period, from 1979 to 2005, in order to monitor the baby-boomers during their working lives and assess their contribution to those who are younger and those who are older than themselves, one conclusion can be drawn. It is that while they have been well-paid, they have been responsible for the redistribution of wealth through various forms of transfer. The statements by Laurence Kotlikoff and Scott Burns[55] hardly lend themselves to controversy, however. Future generations will be caught in the trap of a financial burden. If one considers the future financial commitments linked to social security, i.e. to the future benefits to be paid, the United States is quite simply facing bankruptcy. Due to living on the back of future generations, it would appear that these future generations are *de facto* condemned to experiencing a serious reduction in what they inherit and their buying power. So what can be deduced from these divergent conclusions, these very contradictory points of view? Only that an analysis of the actual situation is complex. Access to jobs is hard but made easier by private transfers of wealth that make it possible to retain a relatively constant standard of living. Nevertheless, for the 55% of young Spaniards who are out of work[56] it is a reality, even if the way in which the statistic is calculated is open to debate.

Are there any signs that give credibility to this idea of an intergenerational war? Perhaps, if one considers the student revolt in Chile in 2011 or the 2014 demonstrations in Venezuela. Such things could not, for the moment, happen in societies such as that of developed countries – or could they? The seeds are there. According to one study,[57] 61% of young French people assert that they are ready to vent their frustrations on a society that does not welcome them and they would join a revolutionary movement of the May 1968 events in France type, not so much in rebellion against authority but so as to demand full and complete social integration. The response rate is the same, regardless of social status and occupation. Of the young people in permanent employment, and thus perceived as being 'out of the woods', 54% say they are ready for 'generational' mobilization. According to the sociologists, the fact that this generation is the best educated that France has ever had makes it particularly aware and critical of its situation. What is true for France is true, at the very least, for the countries of the OECD. For the moment, this generation is everywhere showing itself to be resigned, hunkering down and waiting until the tunnel of traineeships and short-term contracts finally leads to the door of job security. Yet if nothing happens, 'it just needs a spark', warn the sociologists.[58] 'A "group" could form if graduates were joined by young people suffering from social deprivation'.[59]

In reality, the discussion around intergenerational conflict is still very confused, uncertain in its conclusions, but essential if there is to be an understanding of the future of our society. Everything is confused, the availability of savings, the ability to innovate, the ability for young people to enter the labour market, public and private inter-generational transfers of assets. In other words, if one could identify the first symptoms of this early twenty-first century, one would have to stress the difficulties, suffering and, the likely unrest among young people who are being mistreated throughout the world. This means that our view of the future world economy is imprinted with the risks of seeing growth profoundly altered. That is either because when young people are cast aside, they will not be allowed to prosper or because the conflicts between young and old could of themselves put an end to growth, at least as long as the necessary rebalancing does not occur.

3
The Irresistible Explosion of Inequalities

Political economy has always been correctly perceived as an intellectually autonomous discipline, independent in its objectives, solely aiming to represent, understand and possibly predict macro- and micro-economic changes in our societies. This has been the primary aim of well-known and lesser-known economists for three centuries. They have striven to answer the question of income distribution, one that occupies a central place in their approach and their analysis. It is necessary to represent this particularly complex subject as being some sort of pseudo-science and repeatedly attest to the either inevitable or unacceptable nature of the current systems of wealth distribution. In practice, some economists legitimize the rewards of capital while others denounce the exploitation and extortion of added value. When approached in this binary fashion, the theory of the redistribution of wealth questions society in moral and political terms before even mentioning its role in the vigour of economic growth. As far as we are concerned, it is thus a matter of rediscovering, through the economists' train of thought, the basis for a solid analysis of the relationship between the level of inequality and that of growth. This is a regression that will definitely show that everything that appears to be set in stone as the natural order or the clearly expressed collective will, is actually extremely subjective and prey to the greatest uncertainty. Subjective, because the inequalities emerge and disappear depending on the periods in question; uncertain, because no one knows what the 'right' degree of inequality is, one that will favour innovation, investment, growth and jobs.

For about the past 30 years, levels of inequalities, assets and income have witnessed an explosion despite the fact that it has not been possible to determine the exact reasons for this phenomenon. No one can seriously explain why there is an increasingly dizzying, widening gap between the lowest and the highest earners. The world is confronted – and this is a major restriction on social balance in our countries – with a level of inequality that is as ridiculous in scope as it is new in human history. It emerged a few decades ago and is radically challenging the social order experienced by western societies for half a century, one that has been given the name of 'Fordism', defined as the triumph of the middle classes. Everyone was delighted to observe an extensive social group in the emerging nations whose earnings were stable and satisfactory, just as everyone congratulated themselves, half a century ago, on the emergence of a comparable social class in the developed countries. Yet this situation, a comfortable one when all is said and done, has mushroomed. Two new phenomena that are specific to the unique times in which we live, have developed simultaneously without our being aware of whether or not they are related. On the one hand, the gap between income and inheritance that is typical for a member of the middle classes has not ceased to widen with respect to a small fringe of captains of industry whose very high incomes have made it possible for them to create personal wealth of a magnitude that would have been unimaginable only a few decades ago. Yet at the same time, the forgotten victims of globalization, the unskilled workers in the developing countries or those who are not yet integrated in the emerging countries, remain on the breadline, defined as experiencing extreme difficulty in surviving. No one knows where one of the rebel movements will emerge, movements that are frequent in human history.

Will they come from the socially excluded or from elsewhere, from the dispossessed middle classes? One thought emerges; namely, the urgency of replacing the myth of egalitarianism, so well expressed by Ford, Roosevelt, Kennedy and the post-war leaders of Europe; other principles are needed that are just as structuring, whereby a social, comprehensible link can be rebuilt and reshaped, one that is accepted worldwide.

Inequalities and growth: a return to the old controversy

As happens so often, we need to revert to David Ricardo:[1] 'The determination of the laws that govern distribution is the principal problem of the political economy'. Ricardo viewed the situation from a macroeconomic perspective that was very remote from a consideration of the phenomenon of inegalitarianism. Yet it is less a matter of considering the impact of wealth distribution on the dynamism of a society (as would have been the case throughout the second half of the twentieth century); it is now a matter of stressing the benefits for all in the existing order. Nevertheless, understanding the extent to which the very idea of inequality has traversed the centuries is very valuable for an understanding of the importance of the breakdown created by the emergence of an omnipresent post-War social democracy, and the subsequent challenge it has faced.

After Ricardo, there were few attempts to explain the inegalitarian income structure; usually all that was done was to observe that it existed. The importance of the individual would be increasingly taken into account and inequality, whether to a greater or lesser extent, would be defined as being the norm.

There is a long list of authors for whom inequality is a natural given or something that is good in itself, something that Richard H. Tawney[2] calls 'the religion of inequality'. It is nevertheless possible to find two basics in it, namely, belief in the natural nature of ownership and the fact that inequality is the fault of individuals. Naturally, these two pillars of the order of every society often appear to be linked, except perhaps in the case of John Stuart Mill who believed that private property was just one solution among many. He went as far as envisaging a restriction on the right of inheritance in order to get closer to the principle of 'equality of the starting point'.[3] Inequality is therefore based, in relation to earnings, on the need to produce, 'the equality of attraction' of various jobs on the one hand but above all 'the degree of confidence one needs to place in an individual', thus repeating the idea of abilities and talents that are unevenly distributed in individuals.

As for natural inequality, it has a progenitor in John Locke, one of the first to have given it legitimacy through the right of ownership. According to him 'property belonging to everyone is not in the interest of anyone'. 'As much as any one can make use of to any advantage of life before it spoils, so much he may by his labour fix a property in.'[4] Hitherto, this theory may appear to be of egalitarian inspiration, as long as the abilities of most of mankind are similar and the problem of the scarcity of land is resolved. But without this second condition, John Locke's proposal would appear to respect the right of ownership as a natural right. Although labour was originally a way of legitimizing private property, once property had been acquired it did not require continuous reaffirmation of the corresponding rights through repeated labour.

A study of the writings of the Physiocrats – a famous group of eighteenth-century Enlightenment French economists and dominated by François Quesnay – goes a stage further. Their concept of 'the natural order' and of 'natural inequality' is all the more impressive when it refers to the political system. Political authority has no function other than to perpetuate the natural order and, in particular, the right of ownership, a right that takes precedence over any political law. That is why, for these same physiocrats, democracy negates the social order based on property, and thus on inequality. Granting every citizen the right to vote could challenge the established, natural order. Fortunately, human thought, on this subject as on many others, is merely flux and reflux.

The rigour of the physiocratic system needed revision and this was the task that Adam Smith set himself. Each man has the will to improve his fate, at least in a setting that is always natural and fundamentally inegalitarian. It is from this tendency, he claimed, that harmony is born. If the physiocrats considered that the natural order was a system to be achieved, as far as Smith was concerned it achieved itself by the constant role of the psychological factor 'this principle of conservation capable of preventing and correcting, in many respects, the bad effects of a partial and even up to a certain point, an oppressive economy'.[5] Yet, faithful to his naturalistic philosophy, he defends an economy of liberty and individualism. According to him, liberty is imposed as the consequence of a spontaneous order, one that is natural and beneficent and a consequence of the idea that the individual is supremely suited to unravelling and pursuing his personal interest. Inequality can only be established because the ownership from which it derives proceeds from the very nature of human history.

Adam Smith's idea did not stop there. He had a specific vision of his time and the 'secondary' inequalities that arose from the natural inequality resulting from owning private property. These inequalities were either due to the very nature of occupations, or from restrictions on competition. That is because what Smith condemns are the exclusive privileges of the corporations that constitute the origin of the greatest inequalities. It is in this that his contribution lies. Consider a decrease in some of the inequalities of society as possible and desirable. In the same spirit, according to him, a liberal society must do everything it can to improve the lot of its poorest members. This is what separates Smith from his successors, Malthus, Ricardo and Stuart Mill. In his view, the fixing of real wages at minimum subsistence level is not an immutable law, especially if the wealth of a nation grows. But that is not where the consensus lies. The concept of inequality in people's abilities is one that has a long history. The essential argument was advanced by Plato, that of a natural elite characterized by its physical, intellectual and moral qualities, and by Aristotle, who used this argument to justify slavery. 'When men differ between each other, as greatly as the soul differs from the body and man from beast, those are by nature slaves for whom it is preferable to submit to the authority of a master'.[6] The differences in ability between human beings are at the very origin of inequality. Should accents of modernity be added to the theory, by anchoring it in the happy description of a liberal society, especially when, in the first half of the twentieth century, it is confronted by a socialist utopia?

In this way, Friedrich August von Hayek attempts to demonstrate the impossibility for a collectivist society to take into account the differences between individuals in a socialist society. He reaches the conclusion that 'men are capable of weighing each other as on scales, and to attribute, according to their ability and assessment, more to some and less to others, so that such men should either descend from supermen or be sustained by a supernatural terror'.[7]

Hitherto, the foundation of inequalities has been discussed, rather than their relationship to growth. In order to tackle this question, it is necessary to take a detour, and discuss the desirable regulation of society. John Kenneth Galbraith writes 'with Ricardo and Malthus, the concept of general deprivation and great inequality becomes a fundamental given. Smith's optimism is replaced in them by a profound pessimism, resulting from the idea they have of the relationship between man and nature and the relationship of men with each other'.[8] Malthus, he believes, lies at the origin of the justification for inequality as the regulator of society. The inequality produced by a free market regime is beneficial since this makes it possible to improve the lot of certain individuals. It involves a restriction on demographic growth, contrary to an egalitarian regime that would reduce everyone to penury. Only individual consciences and responsibility can curb the population increase and the poverty of which it is the cause. Inequality is the means by which to prevent the harmful effects of development, unless the collective intervenes to disrupt the regulatory system through measures of assistance to the poor. '[...] If the lazy and neglectful are placed, with respect to their level of existence and the security of their family, on the same footing as active and hard-working men, is it believable that each individual will tirelessly strive to perform the activity that constitutes the essential wellspring of the prosperity of nations?'.[9]

This defence of inequality contains the frightening accents of what a Herbert Spencer would make of them. He is the man who advocated 'survival of the fittest', i.e., those best prepared for life. Yet, for Malthus, the disappearance of those who cannot earn a living, due to their lack of finance or their family, would make it possible to maintain population growth in a reasonable relationship with the growth of production.

Based on this sort of arithmetic, the idea developed not only of the necessity but also of the fundamental rightness of inequality. Finally the path of growth had been traced. If Malthus assumed that consumption by persons in productive work would not be sufficient to produce a process of growth, on the other hand, the work of the classes who could spend the most – the class of unproductive consumers – would be the only one capable of doing so. While it is desirable that the working class be well paid, it is even more important to favour luxury and the inequality of wealth.

Growth and inequality, this is the ratio that Malthus was the first to analyse, and in respect of which he proposed ways which he claimed could maintain growth at a satisfactory level. Many other studies would be devoted to the same theme, often in total opposition to it. Kuznets is one example. If Malthus' response constitutes the first step towards a normative theory of growth, in which economic efficiency takes priority over any criteria of justice, the analyses performed by subsequent generations would reverse the order of priorities. Efficiency was no longer a means in the service of a greater justice, greater or less inequality became a measure of the value of the economic system. It remains to be known what best meets the specifications, liberalism or socialism? The market or the plan? The answer is obvious for Frédéric Bastiat. 'The development of capital in no way harms the interests of the working class. As capital increases, the absolute share of capitalists in products increases and their relative share reduces. On the other hand, workers see their share increasing in both directions [...] That is the great, admirable, consoling, necessary and inflexible law of capital'.[10] Paul Leroy-Beaulieu is even more optimistic: 'The real danger for the future of civilized societies is not that there are too many inequalities in the conditions, but that there are not enough of them and that, in a few decades, the same uniformity of resources and of life will produce apathy and torpor'.[11]

The plan also has its defenders, of whom the most brilliant was Nikolai Bukharin,[12] a Russian thinker tragically murdered during the Stalinist purges. Yet, over and above these controversies, the stage has been set.

The two essential questions for creating a theory for measuring economic inequality have been asked. They are, in what context should it be placed and what technical backing should be given to it? Henceforth, inequality has become an objectivizable phenomenon and a stakeholder in the theory of distribution. For economists this means a concern for unusual inequality, that which the collective cannot accept. What remains to be determined is what society considers to be disproportionate and unacceptable. The theories of inequality will provide a reply that makes it possible to judge whether or not a society is progressive, the beneficence or otherwise of any initiative of the political economy and of the domain which can be termed an effective counter-productive inequality.

Economists will now go to work on this theme that lies at the heart of our collective existence. The facts have made us pick up speed. We were feeling the first fruits of a virtually automatic return to this taste for a more brutal, more violent society, one that is in practice more inegalitarian. The extravagances of finance are far from being innocent in this development. The first reply was brilliant, coming from the exceptional trio of French economists, Thomas Piketty, Camille Landais and Emmanuel Saez.

Make no mistake, we are at the beginning of history. In a certain way, this explosion of uninhibited wealth is fascinating. When analysing the explosion in the fees paid to performers or the extravagant pay awarded to the heads of large companies, François Bourguignon[13] stresses the dominant role played by the public or by an institution, linked to an extent to the exponential development of communication technologies and the new globalization of discourse. In the scale of earnings produced by Forbes Magazine in 2013, Madonna came top, having been paid 125 million dollars between June 2012 and June 2013. The golfer Tiger Woods earned 781 million dollars annually, making him the highest paid sportsman in the world in 2013. The same always applies, according to François Bourguignon, to the heads of companies. Their high earnings, often amounting to several million euros per annum, can be partially explained by 'the effects of the renting out of information by these leaders, or the effects of contagion or imitation between companies'. In 2011, Steve Jobs' successor saw his pay increase to 378 million dollars. In the same year, in the United States, Oracle owner Larry Ellison was paid 77.6 million dollars and Ronald B. Johnson, head of J.C. Penney, 53.3 million dollars.[14] As for Lloyd Blankfein, CEO of Goldman Sachs, in 2013, he earned 23 million dollars.[15] Globalization is at work here too. The size of the enterprises depends on the conquest of new markets and having branches outside their country of origin. So much so that it is not surprising, as remarked by Bourguignon, that the income of stars and company owners is soaring in the emerging nations.

It has already been said that our companies are not going to correct their excesses immediately. There is a cycle of inequality that must lead inevitably, one of these days, to unbearable tensions and to a more or less violent rebalancing. As if echoing the theory of great stagnation, a foreseeable return to the scales of reasonable remuneration would seem to be the creative source of new growth. Society has always expressed the need to question itself about the inequalities between people. The nineteenth century was one of inequality between the social classes, the twentieth was one of inequalities between nations, the twenty-first should see a return to the irrational economic hierarchies that are actually challenging economic efficiency. There have been plenty of warnings. John Rawls and Amartya Sen, for instance, have placed at the heart of the debate about the future of our companies the ideal of what is acceptable and reasonable: 'Justice is the first virtue of social institutions in the same way as truth is in thought systems'.[16] Neither of them will brook any compromise. John Rawls suggests reconstructing a social contract, in the same way as Jean-Jacques Rousseau, the only person who was up to the task of establishing the rules of social justice in which the highest level of freedom was combined with an effective equality of opportunity. It is less a matter of reaching complete equality between individuals than of establishing the conditions in which socio-economic inequalities are acceptable for a society to be described as being equitable. Socio-economic inequalities are only acceptable to the extent that equality of opportunity is respected and where inequalities are compensated by benefits for the most underprivileged members of society. The subject is a tough one to deal with and the exceptional interest shown in the work of Rawls and Sen proves that attempts are being made to extricate society from its current predicament. For his part, Sen proposes a wider and more detailed view of the subject, at least as far as economists are concerned. He supports his considerations by creating a category that goes beyond mere equality of opportunity and the fundamental rights defended by Rawls, namely that of *capabilities*. Thus, by carefully avoiding getting stuck in the dangerous rut of egalitarianism, he asks a question about inequality that cannot be summarized merely as the inequality between individuals, but that needs to be extended to equality of freedom, equality of everyone's opportunity to achieve well-being. That is because *capability* is nothing less than 'the set of functioning vectors that indicate that an individual is free to lead a particular lifestyle'. This is a genuine equality in which the parameters must be found via consensus in society. Despite certain criticisms concerning the very nature of these *capabilities*, they make it possible to create a hierarchy and, consequently, convert it into action. This is an instrument that is no doubt capable of reversing the devastating effects of the world explosion in inequalities in terms of income, education, health, etc., and can only operate to the extent that there is no going back on the principle of unconditional freedom. Tyranny, the absence of economic opportunity, non-existent public services, intolerance and poverty are considered to be so many obstacles to freedom and are manifestations of the deprivation of freedom. If this approach to justice as representing a capacity to act is as innovative as it is economically useful for judging inequality, it also lays a moral foundation by presupposing the requirement for a favourable political, economic and social context. Today's world, with its hysterical behaviour and its myopia, is a long way from that.[17]

The end of the egalitarian myth

No one has popularized the myth of egalitarianism better than Kuznets. In his opposition to fatalistic visions of a society in which social groups are in perpetual confrontation, he presents a fundamentally positive image, in which society is continually making progress, a progress based on a pacified society. The 'Kuznets curve' shows, on the basis of empirical data extracted from the late nineteenth century to the end of World War II, that there is a close link between growth and the reduction in inequality. There are three successive phases for increased GDP per head. Inequality is created initially but stabilizes and eventually diminishes.

This curve actually describes the development of western societies until the mid-1970s and throws light on the increasing, and eventually decisive, role of the middle classes in the history of these societies. The financialization of the economy and accelerated globalization have reversed the developments of previous decades with the resumption of a particularly spectacular inegalitarian dynamic.

Thus, in the United States, the wealthiest centile[18] of the population saw its income decrease significantly between the end of the 1929 Depression to the start of the 1980s, only to experience a sudden reversal, starting during the presidency of Ronald Reagan, so that by 2012 it accounted for nearly 20% of total revenue.[19]

The methods and forms of calculation have varied considerably during the exceptional period between the end of the Depression that started in 1929 and the 1980s, the years in which the welfare state triumphed. Throughout the western world, we have witnessed, in varying degrees depending on the country and the period, a simultaneous increase in compulsory contributions and a redistribution of income. The creation of the resulting financial flows has enabled the middle classes to develop so that they have become the engine, the yardstick, of society. We have never abandoned this concept of progress. World progress has been identified in recent years as that of the emergence of a huge middle class in the emerging nations.

In 2009,[20] the middle classes represented about 1.8 billion people, of whom 664 million lived in Europe, 525 million in Asia and 338 million in North America. Even in Africa, the middle classes are shown to have increased and they have contributed to a significant rise in consumption. The world advances at the rate at which these new consumers increase. The rise is not going to slow down. Again, according to the OECD, the world's middle classes will increase from 1.8 billion people in 2009 to 3.2 billion in 2020, and 4.9 billion in 2030. The progression will be particularly strong in Asia which, by 2030, will represent 66% of the world's middle class as opposed to 28% in 2009, and 59% of consumption by the same classes in 2030, as opposed to 23% in 2009.

Of course, these projections could be disputed, since they presume a linear progression without any downturns in the world economy. That is not the issue, however. The uncertainty of the future social balance derives from the fact that the new middle classes remain vulnerable. The weight of the informal or grey economy in terms of employment, the lack of university graduates and lower consumption do not match what is traditionally accepted as the definition of a 'middle class', liable to stabilize strong internal consumption and perennial growth. In Bolivia, Brazil, Chile and Mexico, 44 million middle class workers are employed, according to this report,[21] in the grey economy, representing more than 60% of those that make up this class!

This is an exorbitant figure, since the social welfare contributions system can only be imposed on half of those employed. One finding is clear, namely that these social groups, who were hastily dubbed 'middle class', have little in common with the middle classes of the OECD countries but they have become a real 'engine' for development in their own countries.

Abhijit V. Banerjee and Esther Duflo[22] have studied middle class behaviour in a number of countries; how their income was spent, how they earned a living and how they raised their children, based on a set of household investigations conducted in countries with average or low incomes. The panorama is extensive, as it includes South Africa, Ivory Coast, Guatemala, India, Indonesia, Mexico, Nicaragua, Panama, Pakistan, Papua New Guinea, Peru, Tanzania, and East Timor. According to these researchers, as Ernst Engel[23] observed as long as one hundred years ago, the share of the budget spent on food reduces as the standard of living increases, while spending on leisure activities increases rather than spending money on education.

If there is one country whose virtuous circles of the development of the middle classes have sometimes been mentioned as being too fast, with a balanced and thus sustainable growth, it is China. Here again, a furious debate is ongoing, launched in particular by Zhou Xiaohong.[24] The particular features of the middle classes in the countries and regions of east Asia are, according to him, due to the fact that these classes do not experience daily life in a way that is in any way comparable to that of their American counterparts. There are numerous reasons for this, mainly the lack of arable land. Zhou Xiaohong defines the Chinese middle class by means of three criteria. These are, enjoying a monthly income of at least 5,000 yuan, working as an owner, manager or technician in companies or public institutions and possessing a graduate degree. Yet, for him, contemporary Chinese society offers few real opportunities for personal development in this vast social group. The middle classes are trapped between the extremes of wealth and poverty in a country that is losing its traditional landmarks and is encouraging extremely high expectations which the swiftly changing world will probably not be able to meet. Hence the immense frustration and a feeling of not achieving the same standards as the western middle classes, which this social group cannot possibly emulate in terms of living conditions. In fact, this predominant sentiment reflects great fragility. These men and women are deeply in debt due to the high price of property, living with the spectre of losing their jobs and the fact that they may have to deal with the anguish of lack of job security. Hence this really impertinent question: is the Chinese middle class just a myth? This question leads to the issue of the distribution of fruits of growth: 'It would seem that the benefits of the 10% in annual growth of gross domestic product for the past thirty years have been reaped by an elite minority [...]. Although growth has been beneficial for all Chinese, inequalities in earnings have mushroomed'.[25]

So much so that it could be claimed that in its economic development, China has bypassed the Fordism stage, the structuring of society around a solid middle class, that the countries of the west experienced after the World War II, and moved directly to an exceptional growth model accompanied by very inegalitarian wealth distribution. This phenomenon is surprising in itself, but does this logic of development not contain a more general model that many other countries may experience?

Of course, the diversity of situations and the specific nature of each part of the world could make this question sound very naive, but the impact of accelerated globalization remains likely. 'One of the things one notices in Africa today is the number of owners of mobile phones: 71% of adults in Nigeria, for example, 62% in Botswana and more than half the population of Ghana and Kenya, according to a 2011 Gallup Poll',[26] as reported by Calestous Juma. This is a very revealing finding as a curiosity of our era. The use of these phones has increased faster in Africa since 2003 than anywhere else in the world. Probably it is just a matter of catching up, but also perhaps a sign of the emergence of an embryonic middle class. What does it represent in terms of falling between the very large population of the impoverished, living on less than two dollars a day, and the tiny elite who here, just as elsewhere, are very rich? The statistics are unknown, but one thing is certain, they look nothing like those of the developed or emerging countries. Average annual income is assessed at being somewhere between 1,460 and 7,300 dollars[27] for the whole of sub-Saharan Africa. Moreover, research shows this new trend to be based on the decisive impact of the demographic and economic development of Africa for world growth in the twenty-first century. These are not the mere speculations of an economist. The major chain stores, such as Walmart, that have begun to open shops on the African continent, demonstrate real confidence in the economic momentum that this emerging African middle class can provide. According to certain forecasts,[28] consumption could virtually double in ten years, after long stagnation during previous decades.

This could easily be viewed as the perfect illustration of Kuznets' vision. After a modern form of slavery based on the labour of populations who converged on the cities from the countryside, so well described by Leslie T. Chang,[29] the improvement in the standard of living for hundreds of millions of individuals will translate into the purchase of housing and cars – copying the traditional consumption patterns of the European middle classes in the 1960s. But that is not where the novelty lies. It lies in the fact that simultaneously, a tiny minority of extremely rich people have emerged who are a mixture of politicians, entrepreneurs and family groups, perfectly described by Chrystia Freeland.[30] According to her, the inequalities between richest and poorest in the world have never been as great and are far from having stopped increasing. She observes that in the emerging nations, there is the dizzying ascent of a new elite that has cornered the wealth, within a legal framework that is still in its infancy, and that dedicates itself to merciless competition, a situation well illustrated in the cases of Russia and China. Of course, this was what happened in the past two centuries of industrialization. But the political force of a dominant social democracy very soon rebalanced the system very swiftly prior to today. Are we going to witness the dissemination, a very diversified one perhaps, of this same model? It would be an extraordinary reversal of history.

The worst is never certain. Brazil[31] was also a fine example of the rapid rise of a very wealthy middle class in the past two decades. A minority suffered from grinding poverty, with a Gini index of 0.61, signifying that 1% of the wealthiest accounted for 13% of household incomes. Yet, due to the multiple cases of corruption in which the traditional elites were involved, and in order to avoid conflicts of interest that were not arbitrated by politics, between 2003 and 2011 President Luis Inácio Lula da Silva introduced a host of policies designed to achieve wealth distribution by relying on the virtues of the institutions. This experiment in fighting poverty and bringing about social change was achieved and accepted, thus proving that there is no fatalism in human history.

Despite everything, the world analysis of income inequality is a reminder that the incredible expansion of income is not restricted to a very rapid growth phenomenon in the emerging nations, even though we have produced the daring hypothesis that this development could result in 'world post-Fordism'. Could anyone have failed to believe that the crisis of 2007 might result in the slowing down of this phenomenon? Yet nothing could be less true. The inequalities grew worse, even without taking the economic recession into account.[32] Today, nearly half of the world's wealth is owned by the richest 1%, with 99% of the world's population having to share the other half. The average inequality in income from work and capital[33] in the OECD countries grew by 1.4 points between 2007 and 2010.[34] Added to the increase in inequalities of income noted previously, this development could indicate the maximum level of acceptable inequality for these countries.

One always tends to consider that these phenomena are short-term, something to do with the recession, almost accidental. That is the case with the perception of the increase in inequality. Could this be a logic that is specific to the dynamics of a particular period? In that case, nothing happening in the markets, no recession, could challenge it. It is the apparent reason why the trend has not been halted due to downturns in the economy. The inequality of market income has increased to an even greater extent in the last three years than in the previous three years with respect to the countries of the OECD.

It should be no surprise to learn that this growth was particularly sustained in the countries that experienced the steepest decline in average market income – Ireland, Spain, Estonia, Japan and, especially, Greece.

The role of inequalities, whether structural or otherwise, in world growth has been returned to the heart of the discussion by economists. Thomas Piketty's criticism of Kuznets' theory[35] provides the best illustration of this. Does this mean that we need to concede that Marx was right and consider that the 'Glorious Thirty'[36] was an exception in the history of capitalism? This would be tantamount to inferring that the explosion of inequalities is not a cyclical phenomenon but one that is likely to last for the long term, so that it could dangerously mortgage the cohesion of society and the development of the economy. It would also mean rapidly abandoning our post-World War II history, the successes of social democracy and to admit, rather too readily, that democracy is dead due to its inability to manage the complexity of modern society.

Nevertheless, the influence of Kuznets' theory remains considerable even today. As Thomas Piketty remarked, this was the first in-depth work on inequalities based on statistical data (1913–1948). The two sources are declarations of income resulting from the federal income tax introduced in the United States in 1913 and estimates of the national income of that country established by Kuznets, the results of which were published by him in 1953.[37] He produced a more palatable, more optimistic version, in the following year,[38] the starting point of his famous curve. In fact, Piketty would fan the flames of this theory when he described it as 'magic'. He thus showed that the two world conflicts and the economic and political crises they provoked are the origin of the decrease in inequality.

As Piketty denied that the inevitable nature of Kuznets' 'balanced path of growth' was not without its effect on the interpretation of the explosion in contemporary inequality or the effects of an imbalance in the money markets, in oil and property. As he says again, in view of these profound changes, 'it would be ridiculous [...] to assume via this principle that growth is naturally "balanced" in the long term'. Kuznets' optimism lives on.

What is true for income is perhaps even more so for assets and this also affects Europe. The early 2010 results for France are edifying.[39] This was another time in which the concentration of assets increased. If the 10% most affluent households owned nearly half the total gross assets, the richest 1% individually owned more than 1.9 million of these assets. This figure should be compared with that of the assets owned by the 10% of most underprivileged households, with declared assets of 2,700 euros each, collectively adding up to 0.1% of total assets. In the United Kingdom, the wealthiest 1% own as much as the poorest 55%. The inequalities of ownership are consequently much more marked than those of income. And, in fact, it is in London that the highest concentration of billionaires in the world[40] is to be found.

The finding is even more striking for the United States.[41] Since the 1920s, income inequalities have declined and today, they are at their most marked. The average assets owned by the wealthiest 7% of Americans – 8 million of them own more than 836,000 dollars – increased between 2009 and 2011 by 28%, to almost 3.2 million dollars. The rest of the population, i.e. the vast majority of American households, on the other hand, saw their income fall by exactly 4%. So, in 2011, they were worth on average 134,000 dollars, 24 times less than their wealthy compatriots. In 2011, the richest eight million Americans, who represented only 7% of the total population, owned not 56% of the wealth of the country, as they had in 2009, but 63%. Why was this? The wealthiest mainly own stocks and shares, while the rest of the population mainly owns real property. Stocks and shares have continued to increase in value while the price of real estate collapsed by between 25% and 30% due to the housing crisis.

We have all accepted for a long time that the role of the welfare state, the great regulator of the situation, is to correct such developments. Opinions differ as to the level of wealth transfer, but not about the underlying principles. As François Ewald[42] predicted, the system introduced half a century ago has run out of steam for obvious reasons. It is now too cumbersome to be managed efficiently; it is not suited to dealing with current problems, ranging from mass unemployment to the cost of welfare. It continues to operate, sometimes usefully, sometimes wastefully, with no other prospect in view than increasingly large transfers of wealth, as has been the case in recent years.

While the crisis has its winners – although very few – it mainly has losers. According to the OECD,[43] disposable income per household was less affected than market income thanks to cash payments to the less well-off and the increase in income taxes. During a recession, obviously, the number of people entitled to benefits payments increases. But at the start of the crisis, in 2008 and 2009, a certain number of OECD member countries increased the rate of transfer of wealth so as to make demand more dynamic and counterbalance the fall in household income. These public transfers of funds occurred throughout the countries in the area, with the exception of Turkey, between 2007 and 2010. The countries that were worst affected by the economic downturn were the first to organize public movements such as these to promote the growth of disposable income.

Yet these measures were based on assumptions of the homogeneity of populations that no longer represented the true situation. Both with respect to contributions and to the redistribution of wealth, the challenges and arbitration of public finances revealed new conflicts between the structurally unemployed and the 'insiders', which posed problems for the fabric of social ties that had been created 50 years previously. The problem is often viewed from a quantitative angle. Technical solutions are sought and found through reducing costs and finding new resources. In France, Germany, the United Kingdom, Japan and the United States, public expenditure on social security has increased from between 5 and 15% to more than 25% of GDP. The subject is far from being exhausted because the mere stabilization of the cost of social security does not make it possible to avoid questions of welfare, health and the old age pension. To question this expenditure would be to open Pandora's box, putting initial training as well as vocational training, welfare dependents, etc., under threat.

The welfare state will have great difficulty in transforming itself, inventing new forms of intervention, regulation and management. Hence the interest in a global theoretical consideration and prospects such as those of Gosta Esping-Andersen,[44] one of the first to have condemned the destructive role of the post-industrial economy, a perspective that is hard to avoid, with respect to the compromises operating in the European welfare states. The problem is all the more arduous since current changes such as the ageing population, new inequalities, as well as the mass entry of women into the job market, assume that new interventions will be required. The welfare state thus needs to be rethought and a substitute needs to be found for the 'nanny', 'repairing' or 'compensating' state, such as an 'investment' state that is better capable of solving new social issues posed by post-industrial society.

In reality, the welfare state as we know it is dated. As the child or parent of Fordism, its aim is to support and revive growth through its impact on the economy, job creation, support for consumption, and protecting savings. Beyond this shared logic, there are three great models of the welfare state whose varying levels of generosity reveal the profound differences in their nature. There is the Scandinavian social-democratic model, the liberal model of the English-speaking countries and the conservative and corporatist model adopted by the countries of continental Europe. This typology, established by Esping-Andersen, can help to reveal the strengths and weaknesses of each model; what can be changed, what should be abandoned, and under what conditions. What Esping-Andersen is proposing here is a very stimulating initiative, a new paradigm that is capable of coping with the new risks facing contemporary societies. This 'dynamic perspective' proposes intervening much earlier by immersing individuals, from earliest childhood, into this society of emerging knowledge. The question that arises is no longer in terms of costs but in terms of investment, making it possible to create wealth in the future. The second requirement is to favour jobs for women and to ensure male – female equality. These 'revolutions' could give birth to new resources that, for example, would make it possible to finance retirement while maintaining intergenerational equity and fair wealth distribution within the same generation. As can be seen, contemplation of the subject becomes very prospective. It is no longer a matter of creating a financial rebalancing, but of profound social change. This would presuppose fundamental political choices.

André Masson[45] has dedicated his work to reconsidering these choices. He offers three routes that correspond to three concepts of welfare and, over and above this, three 'ideologies' from which the choice must be made. What is at stake is an exit, via the top, from this welfare state that appears to be condemned. For this economist, whether one prioritizes the markets, in the tradition of a John Locke, the State, following in the footsteps of Jean-Jacques Rousseau, or families, as Thomas Hobbes did, these three rival theories conflict with each other in their solutions to social problems, namely, the free agent, citizen equality and multiple solidarity. The free agent theory implies favouring a withdrawal from the welfare state, criticized for its unproductive largesse and, paradoxically, the production of inequalities that might challenge social cohesion. The second scenario, equality of the citizenry, proposes a reorientation of the transfer of wealth in the context of a welfare state that is unchanged in size, towards 'active expenditure' to the benefit of youth and new risks. The multi-solidarity scenario strives to renew the social contract by basing itself upon an inter-generational pact, creating links and reciprocity between the generations. Imagining a combination of these three scenarios lies in the realm of fantasy and that is not what we are about. It is a matter of tracing three possible paths to meet the mortal failures of the current welfare state and enabling us to choose.

The patrimonial society against the middle classes

Chrystia Freeland's verdict[46] brooks no appeal. During the 1970s, 1% of the wealthiest Americans accounted for 10% of national income. Today, 0.1% alone account for 8% of it. If the wealthiest are growing increasingly rich, the middle and upper middle class is despairing as it sees its income stagnating. This schism between the wealthy 'pro-business, pro-money' Americans and the super-rich is, Freeland claims, 'a much more incendiary threat than the anti-establishment idealism of

"Occupy Wall Street"'. This new plutocracy can only find its legitimacy in what Freeland calls the meritocracy. It has more in common with clannish and thus dangerous dynamics with a definite tendency to use the law to avoid paying taxes, holding on to its hegemonic positions and reproducing itself from generation to generation. For Freeland, this 'feudal' form of capitalism heralds the end of capitalism as it has been – defending fair play in competition and open to new entrants and those with audacity.

Society today has to confront these fundamental challenges concerning the question of the link between democracy and inequalities, as Daron Acemoglu, Suresh Naidu, Pascual Restrepo and James Robinson remind us.[47] Democracy can be captured by certain elites since it overturns the distribution of power *de jure* within society. Yet the inequalities are not in the order of the mere *de jure* distribution of power. They are also part of its *de facto* distribution. The persons who assume power *de jure* tend to keep control of the political process by gaining greater *de facto* power. They are incentivized to control the local application of laws, mobilize little private armies or dominate the party political system. Democracy also needs to deal with those *de jure* institutions – the political parties – or the threats emanating *de facto* from the elite who are tempted to join in the flight of capital and tax evasion. One ultimate contradiction concerns the possibility of a positive link between inequalities and democratic regimes. Autocratic regimes could be more tempted than others to introduce egalitarian policies in order to maintain social peace and thus avoid any social conflict. The contribution of Acemoglu and his co-authors is therefore, based on empirical data, to show how democracy increases inequality in societies in which it is hard to access land ownership, a situation that is interpreted as being the result of a political process of decision-making rather than the action by the major land-owners. The authors also note that democracy increases inequalities through taxation when the middle class is relatively wealthy. These conclusions favour democracy by enabling the middle classes to benefit from a redistribution of income to the detriment of the poor. Acemoglu and his co-authors therefore reject the idea that democracy necessarily leads to a uniform decline in inequality.

There are other links that seem to condemn the middle classes. Tyler Cowen[48] probably offers the most pessimistic view. He claims that the prospects for the middle classes in the rich countries are rather sombre. He even imagines their extinction in the United States, compressed as they are between the wealthy who are growing ever wealthier and more numerous and the poor who are slightly less poor, but also increasing in numbers. Tyler Cowen's central theory rests on the polarization of society between the winners, 10 to 15% of the population, those who understand computing and who are confident of their future as *insiders*, and the losers, who can be replaced by intelligent machines, who feel themselves to be useless and who lack initiative with respect to their income that stagnates or falls. For Cowen, the erosion of the middle classes and the growth of inequality in the ageing countries are not moving in the direction of a riot, but into a sort of 'daze'. This prospect is not fundamentally new. It is in the tradition of the recurring announcement of social disaster linked to technical progress, such as automation and robotics elevated to their highest levels. It is thus the digital divide that is the cause of the social divide, translating into the relegation of a large section of the U.S. population into outer suburbs, isolated from the centres of decision-making. This marginalized population, condemned to living frugally, is unlikely to be able to count on social welfare to enable them to exit from their second-class status. This is not far removed from Hannah Arendt's description in *The Human Condition*[49] of a society that is moving towards total inertia and lack of action.

To try to understand all of the movements that affect our prevailing social model, one key concept should be added, namely that of the property-owning society. Michel Aglietta[50] was the first, in the 1970s, to identify this major transformation, represented by the emergence of property-owning capitalism, in the development of capitalism. This economist, whose theories are inspired as much by history as by anthropology, sheds light on the transition from an economic paradigm from that of Fordist capitalism to capitalism of the property-owning type. What does this mean? For Aglietta this represents a disruption to business that will now place power in the hands of the shareholders rather than in those of the directors. This disruption also affects the world of remuneration, largely now taking the form of capital, and the world of finance, since recourse to the money markets is prioritized over loans.

The question of the division of power, over a period of time, between shareholders and directors is nothing new and can be found in the work of Adolf Berle and Gardiner Means.[51] For 30 years, it was considered that a new law of capitalism had been introduced, that of the seizure of power by the directors. The implications of this were significant, since the latter's remuneration was obviously linked to growth and therefore to investment, and consequently to jobs.

The first challenge to this logic, that appeared to be eternal, was the development of 'private equity' that combined investment funds and directors within a relatively short space of time. Property-owning capital goes far beyond this, however. This is shaped by events through favouring the short term over the long term. A company is now perceived as a financial product. This financial vision of a trading company, the pressure exerted by shareholders to maximize short-term profitability or the remuneration of the directors based on capital, prevents management from making the 'right' decision, restricting investment and thus adversely affecting the long term strategy necessary for the development of a company.

If the question of the origin of power in enterprise is often asked, this is the first time that the absolute preference of shareholders for the short term and the enhancement of the capital they have committed has been established. It should not be forgotten that the nineteenth century was that of virtuous shareholder capital, as described by Max Weber,[52] in which profit was basically destined for reinvestment. It is likely that in this new history the origin of under-investment will be discovered, a phenomenon already seen in western countries from the lack of prospects in our societies.

What drives this property-owning society? One answer was provided by Thomas Piketty in his analysis of the ownership of capital. Yet the concentration of capital that has begun to increase again in recent years is far from achieving the record of the early twentieth century. To take the example of the United Kingdom, for instance, the share of the top decile of ownership of capital decreased from 90% in 1910 to 65% in the 1970s (the share of the top centile decreased from 70% to 25%) then increased again to 70% in the early second decade of the second millennium.

The explanation is simple and relies on the existence of a middle class that owns about one third of national assets. Again according to Piketty, this specifically European phenomenon lies behind the optimism of the Thirty Glorious Years in France (1945–1975) and the difficulty of accepting that since 1980 there has possibly been a slowing of social progress. Piketty concludes that the hyperconcentration of capital in the societies of the *Ancien Régime* or the nineteenth century was linked to reduced growth and to a yield on capital that was greater than the rate of growth.

David Boyle[53] provides a very concrete description of the phenomenon. He paints the picture of an anxious middle class forced to face the very objective difficulties of becoming a property owner, contemplating their children's future as well as their retirement.

The future indeed lies at the origin of these fears, even if the present represents an obstacle course with its stagnating incomes. All of the conditions exist for a form of 'decommissioning', such as the unsuitability of the educational system, polarization of the labour market and the escalation in property prices.

In a more political context, this represents a new game, an unknown logic that defines growth that we will become familiar with in this society based on ownership. To some extent, both Aglietta and Stiglitz have responded to the eternal issue of the complex relationship between inequality and growth. As far as Joseph Stiglitz[54] is concerned, the explosion of inequalities comes at a price, one that is initially economic. The instability is the result of stagnant demand, while indebtedness endangers the financial balance of households. It is the result mainly of the increasingly high earnings of the rich who also save the most and weighs in favour of a policy of deregulation and reduced public expenditure, despite the fact that such expenditure is indispensable for a country's economy. Finally, pensioners are by their very nature an impediment to growth. Yet the cost of the increase in inequalities is also political. It actually encourages abstention from voting and, beyond that, the discrediting of politicians by those who feel themselves to be excluded or on the point of being so. It also indicates the increasingly important place occupied by money in politics and the importance of the wealthy, who represent their special interests as being for the common good.

Is Stiglitz right? No one knows. As far as we are concerned, there is no room for doubt. The middle classes are unlikely to fail to react, they could revolt. The numerous scandals involving concealed wealth and tax havens can only result in an outpouring of anger that has been contained hitherto, and the development of a feeling that there exists a sort of caste system of a minority of untouchables. In Gabriel Zucman's investigation of tax havens,[55] he mentions cities and countries that are synonymous with the sinister reality, in which the tax fraud of a minority of the ultra-rich operates to the detriment of the many. As much as 5,800 billion euros are hidden in Zurich, Hong Kong, the Bahamas, the Cayman Islands and Luxembourg...Switzerland alone manages 1,800 billion euros that are basically undeclared, of which more than half belongs to Europeans. Zucman shows that tax evasion is initially organized by local networks, though this does not stop him taking the road towards financial globalization. Germany (200 billion euros), France (180 billion euros) and Italy (120 billion euros) are Switzerland's three main clients. In general, these 'customers' first go through the British Virgin Islands to conceal their identities and subsequently place their assets in funds in Switzerland or Luxembourg. The 5,800 billion euros sitting in accounts in tax havens are, the author claims, a conservative estimate. He rather opts for an amount in the order of 8,000 billion euros, 80% of which is concealed.

Inequality lies at the heart of a new conflict

Did the inexorable rise of inequalities that began several decades ago play a role in the 2007 crisis? This debate has been revived and some economists claim that it was indeed the direct cause. The IMF economists Michael Kumhof and Romain Rancière[56] have even attempted, with some success, to model these phenomena by comparing them with the equivalent crisis in 1929. A study of the Great Depression could throw light on the little-understood role of inequality.

These two economists stress the similarity between the periods that preceded the crises of 1929 and 2007. There was a serious increase in inequality of earnings and the household debt/income ratio. Hence the legitimate question of whether these phenomena are linked. 'When – as happened in both cases – the wealthy lent a large share of their additional income to the poor and to the middle classes, and when inequalities of income increase for several decades, the debt/income ratio becomes great enough to increase the risk of a serious crisis'. This is indeed what happened during the two periods studied. The debt/income ratio doubled between 1920 and 1932 as it did between 1983 and 2007.

The study performed by these economists also shows that in 1983 the ratio for the 5% of the wealthiest households was 80% but it was 60% for the rest of the population. Twenty-five years later, the turnaround was spectacular. While it was 65% for the wealthiest 5% it was 140% for the remaining 95%.

Other explanations have been given. Some have denounced a lax monetary policy, others an outrageous financial free market. Economists such as Raghuram Rajan[57] claim that the crisis is the result of a long-term process. The growing inequality in income has put pressure on politics, which in turn has dealt the card of easy credit, favourable to demand and job creation even while income is stagnating.

Michael Kumhof and Romain Rancière have modelled the links between inequalities of earnings, indebtedness and crises: 'Our model contains several innovations that reflect the empirical facts described [...]. Firstly, households have been divided into two income groups, the 5% at the top of the income distribution scale (defined as the "owners of capital"), whose total income derives from the yield from the stock of capital and interest on loans; and the remaining 95% (the "workers") who are waged. Secondly, wages are determined through negotiation between the two groups. Finally, all of the households are concerned with their level of consumption but those who own capital are also concerned with the actual amount of physical and financial capital they possess. Consequently, when their income increases at the expense of the workers, they divert it into a threefold increase in consumption, physical investment and financial investment. The latter involves an increase in loans to workers, whose consumption initially represents up to 71% of GDP, enough to maintain production in the economy'.[58]

The increase in savings at the top and the borrowings of the majority mitigate the inequality in consumption in relation to income. This development leads to a reinforcement of intermediation services, producing a doubling in the size of the financial sector, but the increased indebtedness of the middle class generates a financial fragility and the risk of a persistent crisis. 'When it actually occurs – in 30 years' time, it is supposed here – households will be in arrears with 10% of their borrowings and production will decrease suddenly, as witnessed during the American financial crisis of 2007–2008.'[59]

While not totally subscribing to what Romain Rancière and Michael Kumhof write, one cannot but take this cry of alarm extremely seriously. It is also repeated by Robert Reich,[60] for whom the concentration of wealth among the few coincides with the concentration of their power. His attack is brutal. Never in the history of the United States, he claims, has the wealth of the richest 1% financed electoral campaigns so heavily, put pressure on the media and banned the necessary reforms. In 1928, as in 2007, 1% of Americans owned 23% of the income, a record that resulted in the stock market crash, triggering the Great Depression. The 1920s, like the 2000s, are typified by inequalities of income so that the middle classes have no other option, if they are to avoid dropping out of their class, than to fall massively into debt.

Do the economists have solutions to offer? For Michael Kumhof and Romain Rancière an organized disindebtedness could be imagined. Another solution would be to re-assess workers' income to allow them to gradually free themselves from debt. The debt/income ratio would then be impacted immediately by a drop due to an increase in income, and the risk of indebtedness followed by a crisis would be averted.

Against the background of globalization, however, there is a downward trend in wages policy. Diverting income tax on labour to economic levies on land, natural resources and finance is an exercise that would cause many problems, since these represent two different 'orders'. Yet the negotiating power of workers should be taken into account as it might prevent the potentially disastrous consequences of new financial crises that current trends tend to forecast.

Conversely, should one be inspired by the pessimistic view of Paul Collier,[61] when he imagines a world in major difficulty, with a billion individuals who are imprisoned in what he calls 'traps', condemning a large section of the world population to revolt at a given moment? Here again, no one can predict what will happen. Yet there is a high risk of seeing history repeat itself, in a world that has become so irrational and so incomprehensible that not only those who are excluded, but even the middle classes, whether old or new, will no longer accept the rules of the game.

The conflicts will adopt different forms depending on the geographical region in which they occur. Populism and rejection of the other in the developed countries, instrumentalization of religious conflicts in numerous emerging nations, all of this legitimized by ultra-conservative positions in the Robert Kagan mould. Everything is in place for this infernal mechanism of the concentration of financial, economic and ideological power in the hands of the few, throughout the world, that will one day cause diverging interests to descend into hysteria.

4
The Impact of Deindustrialization

Most observers consider that the crisis began in 2007 and has experienced many vicissitudes ever since. Some hope it will resolve itself soon, others suggest analyses leading to different economic policy proposals. The only virtual consensus is in the name, 'financial crisis'. The present authors do not see it that way, however. Of course, finance played a significant role, but it was fundamentally a crisis of the real economy. We believe that the crisis is the result of the massive transfer of business activity, between 1995 and 2005, from the developed countries to those countries which would become known as the emerging nations. This was the unprecedented phenomenon of deindustrialization of the rich countries and submission in the short term to the *diktat* of the western consumer, who was so greatly tempted by the low cost of consumption and investment. This is the period when it was enviously reported that one hour of Chinese labour cost 40 times less[1] than the labour of an American or European having the same qualifications. This miracle needed to be exploited quickly without thinking too much about the consequences, i.e. the price to be paid for supporting the newly unemployed. It would result in an explosion in the costs of social welfare and, above all, the disintegration of the world economy in the face of the brutality of this unprecedented impact. This is what is known as offshoring.

The term 'offshoring' is an ambiguous one. Is any setting up of companies or factories in the emerging nations a sign of offshoring? Is it restricted to transferring business activity to replacing operations that were previously performed in a developed country? This discussion of terminology is of little importance with respect to the unique mechanism that was implemented within a very short space of time, mainly during the period between 1995 and 2005, that led to entire sectors of industry in the developed countries being transferred to the emerging nations. This movement, specific to the late twentieth century, is not restricted to a drastic reduction in the OECD countries' share of industry and the loss of millions of unskilled jobs in these same countries. It has led to deindustrialization, in the sense of a loss of substance in overall industry in this part of the world. The loss is fundamental. It has caused the West to lose the 'leadership' role it enjoyed for the past two centuries, a West that is now convinced that the future will be less favourable to it. The movement in itself appears to be inevitable, although not necessarily in this configuration, one that contains the seeds of an imbalance in the world economy that we have experienced and that we continue to experience.

In fact, deindustrialization is nothing more than a short-term victory of consumption or finance, as was the case in Great Britain in the early twentieth century when it made the choice to sacrifice its industry in favour of creating a financial centre in London. The results are known and have created difficulties, not of production but of creation, for the countries in question. This is the fourth characteristic of the gestating world economy; this fourth restriction may be the hardest to bear. It appears to lie at the heart of the difficulty that the West has had in recovering, especially in the labour market in the United States, and in overcoming the fact that growth, even if solid, has hardly anywhere resulted in a genuine rebalancing of the job market. That is why new hope is incarnated in the word 'reindustrialization' that is now appearing all over the place – and in the United States in particular – in the explicit hope of rediscovering a taste for development and production capacity. The aim of this chapter is to show the extent to which the movements that began in the late twentieth century were underestimated and how they go quite a long way in explaining our current difficulties. They make it possible to understand the slowdown in globalization as we have been experiencing it for the past twenty years, as it translates into reduced direct investment in the emerging nations. Will the United States manage to reconstruct its industry, based on its cheap energy? We hope so, but nothing is certain, even if in this way the country illustrates its legitimate desire to retake control of its economic destiny.

Are these mere illusions? Uncontrolled globalization, conflicts between nations, whether in decline or not, an abortive attempt at world government – to put it briefly, no one knows, or even imagines, what the coordinated management of a world economy subject to less imbalance would look like.

1995–2005: deindustrialization, offshoring, outsourcing

For the economists, the economic crisis was initially a concept before it became an accursed reality. It was a forum for conflict, ambiguity of theories, profound disruption, the impossibility of turning back the clock, the emergence of new systems. Anyone dreaming of a single and sole explanation is seriously mistaken. Others, fewer in number, see it as a special moment, that of the emergence of uncertainty, of new forms of economic regulation, of different social rules.

There is a basic rift between these currents of thought. For some, the situation merely represents more pronounced fluctuations than previously, just some 'turbulence'; for others, it constitutes serious disruption, a subversion of predominant thinking, that condemns the old regulation mechanisms that are now incapable of returning the system to balance. Every strategy, even revolutionary ones, then becomes part of the next crisis as one of the cohort of remedies already tried or assumed to have been so. That is the situation with Keynesianism which, in a single generation, has moved from the status of a genuine breach with the past to that of a mere theory of cycles. Not a single recovery plan has been announced that has not been described as being 'Keynesian'. Yet two fundamental issues arise. Is the economic crisis intrinsically linked to globalization? In other words, is it due to a change in the balance of power between the developed countries and the emerging nations? If the origin of the crisis indeed lies in this confrontation, how will it be possible to re-establish the balance between the parties, both for actual trade as well as for the rates of currency exchange, technology transfers and control of added value chains?

Offshoring actually conceals a complex reality. In the strictest sense of the term, moving businesses, i.e. when a company transfers its factory abroad, represents a tiny part of the issue. Other elements are involved and are interlinked. On the one hand, the northern countries see it as being to their advantage to move services that currently represent the bulk of their GDP. That is the case with Germany, for example, although very little is said about it. On the other hand, the emergence of the countries of the South occurs, of necessity, via the withdrawal of market share from the North, in terms of world trade. The North currently owns the smallest share of the pie, although it has recently become bigger. Europe was withdrawing to a lesser extent, until the crisis, than the United States or Japan. Finally, with respect to offshoring, whether for the United States or Japan, the main fact is that production has been moved to countries in which people are paid low wages, and they comprise a major part of the technology sector. Europe, which has less of a presence in this area, has been less heavily affected. Yet, for a dozen years or so, it has been developing its own offshoring movement within the European Union, from West to East.

Our understanding of the crisis is linked to these movements. This massive transfer of operations can only lead to millions of unskilled workers leaving the job market in the OECD countries and extremely heavy pressure on the level of their pay. This is where formidable tension can be observed on the level of income in the various wage categories. To overcome this problem, two solutions were applied on either side of the Atlantic by respective governments. One consisted of favouring an insane expansion of credit, something that led to the uncontrolled indebtedness of individuals and was the origin of the U.S. housing market crisis. The other tangibly increased welfare payments, making it possible to maintain a slight growth in the purchasing power of these same unskilled workers. Here the effect was not the same because this policy was to result in an uncontrolled increase in public spending deficits. As always happens in the economy, it is the extent of the impacts that creates the event. The reconstructed figures that take account of offshoring businesses between 1995 and today are eloquent and clearly explain the current difficulties.

The first illustration of this phenomenon shows that for the developed countries and the emerging nations, the industrial added values of a country in relation to the industrial added value of the world would suddenly change location. Our calculations are based on the aggregation of a limited number of countries, but have been chosen from among the most important of them. For the countries of the West, they are the United States, Japan, France, Germany, the United Kingdom, Canada and Italy. And for the emerging nations, the combination of six flagship countries, to which we have added Australia, the most interesting link between these two worlds. This produces the following list: China, India, Brazil, South Korea, Mexico, Indonesia and Australia. The movement is of such a scope in comparison with other periods of offshoring, notably the 1970s, that there is no doubt as to the exceptional and unique nature of this phenomenon. The second globalization is here, in a specific form that confers a leading role on the specific location of the production sites.

This movement has affected all of the western countries, including Germany. With respect to the emerging nations, the analysis centred on China but, here again, the whole world is affected by the most massive transfer of activity that has ever taken place.

78 A Violent World

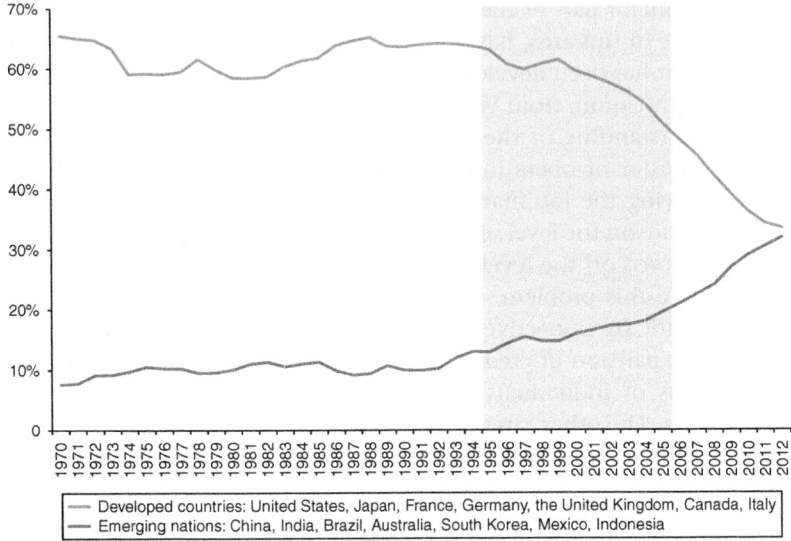

Figure 4.1 Industry's share of added value on a world scale (developed countries and emerging nations)

Sources: World Bank and the authors.

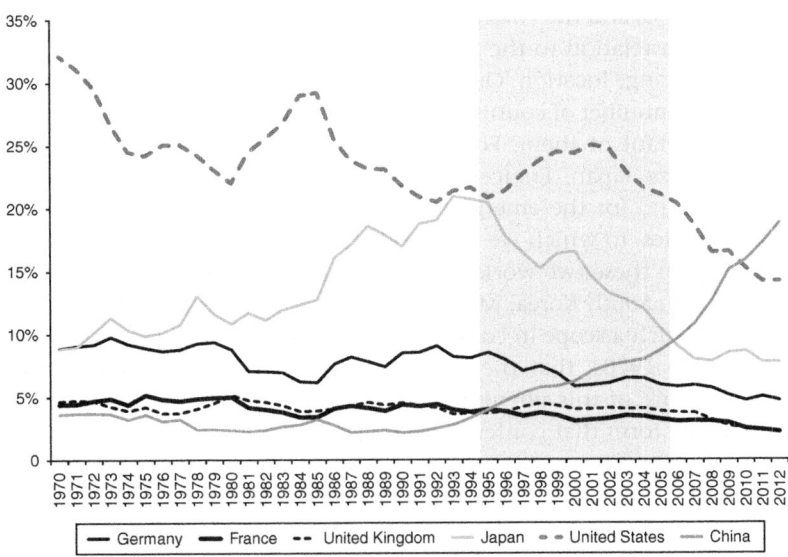

Figure 4.2 Industry's share of added value on a world scale (Germany, France, the United Kingdom, Japan, United States, China)

Sources: World Bank and the authors.

Very naturally, this offshoring movement was accompanied by a reversal of the flow of goods that accelerated sharply from 1995 onwards. Everything was in place for a whole new phase of development of the world economy. China entered the WTO, the World Trade Organization.[2]

Even if this description appears to be simplistic, the division of activities through the chain of our globalization is much more complex than it was in the past. The breach is so clear that it could be considered to be the founder of a new world economic order. For better or worse.

Offshoring also takes place via major transfers of capital. The concept of FDI (Foreign Direct Investment) is a complex one. It is necessary, in fact, to make distinctions that are still not always being taken into account. The first concerns operations of mergers and acquisitions of share capital. This is a particularly interesting category. The second is based on loans between the parent company its subsidiaries, or between subsidiaries in the same group. These are called 'special purpose entities'. The third distinction involves 'green field' investments, the setting up of new subsidiaries abroad, with new means of production and job creation. Finally, there are investments in property and profits reinvested abroad. This is like comparing apples with oranges, but despite these different statistics, the FDIs throw light on a trend. Since the 1980s, the figures have illustrated a movement that is unprecedented in scale.

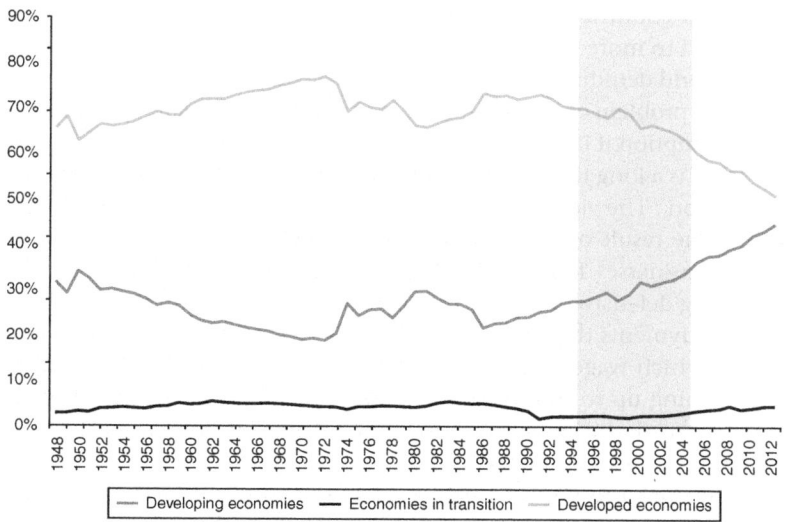

Figure 4.3 Share of exports of goods on a world scale

Sources: United Nations Conference on Trade and Development and the authors.

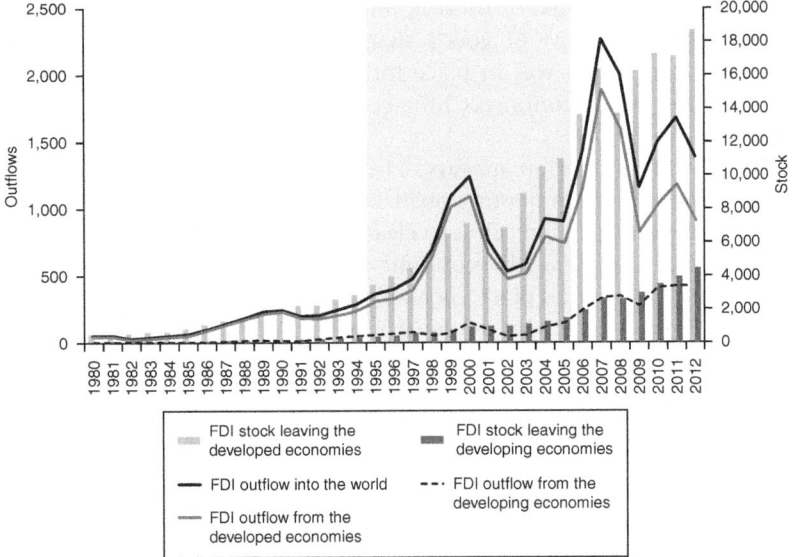

Figure 4.4 Outflows of capital and stock in foreign direct investments (FDIs) in billions of U.S. dollars at current prices and current rates of exchange

Sources: United Nations Conference on Trade and Development and the authors.

Since the 1980s, the outflow of foreign direct investment from developed countries have become enormous in real terms; in 2008, it amounted to more than 1,600 billion dollars.

The world deindustrialization movement could be said to be confined to a mere problem of production efficiency and a change in the structure of consumption if it were not for the very serious consequences in terms of jobs. It is a long time since Paul Krugman was able to write 'there is no connection'. The violent changes in the labour market are evidently not merely the result of technical progress, which is everything but exogenous. Businesses have responded to competition from the South by producing defensive innovations. 'Due to the existence of monopolistic welfare payments that could be destroyed if they were imitated in countries in which wages are low or innovation in the northern countries, [...] opening up to international trade could result in the adoption of innovations that were diverted to specialist jobs in order to protect the existence of such payments'.[3]

To measure the impact on jobs, it is therefore necessary to distinguish between what is due to global changes, such as China's increased power, and what is actually the result of offshoring. Consequently, great caution is required in manipulating the figures so as to be able to judge the impact of international commercial competition on French employment in industry. The average annual volume of jobs in industry that have been destroyed in France is in the order of 71,000 jobs between 1980 and 2007. Furthermore, it would appear that international competition was responsible for 39% of job losses for the 1980–2007 period, and 45% of losses for the 2000–2007 period. All of these figures[4] should be treated with caution but they are an indication of the effect that merely confirms and attempts to quantify the evidence.

In reality, reasoning should depend on the type of job, its 'offshorability', as well as the position of the company concerned. If fortune favours an employee, it is because his/her occupation cannot be offshored and the company is doing well. That is not a problem of job losses, but rather a question of pay. Those who are unlucky enough to have to change jobs will be forced to accept a pay cut. The literature has sought to identify true downgrading which affects workers who are made redundant due to offshoring and, more generally, as a result of international competition.

Other research[5] has shown that offshoring to countries in which costs are low has favoured a drop in wages in the United States for workers who have been downgraded. Obviously, this shows that offshoring to countries having low wages is associated with a reduction in the number of jobs in industry in the United States, but equally – and this is more interesting – that the wages of workers who have remained in the industrial sector are, in general, positively affected by offshoring. Always, according to these studies, most of the negative effects of globalization are the result of the downward pressure on the wages of workers who leave industry for jobs in agriculture or services, a pressure that has had repercussions on U.S. wages in general.

In conclusion, to take the data produced by the International Labour Office, it is no surprise that the same downward movement has been identified in jobs in industry in the developed countries since the 1970s, thus making it possible to relativize the very negative view of French industry. In fact, if, in 1970, the share of jobs in industry represented an average of 28% of jobs for all the countries in question – France, Germany, the United Kingdom, Japan and the United States – today it represents just over 14%, a reduction of nearly half.

The reduction in jobs in industry and a drop in wages are typical features of this movement, even if the description should be viewed with caution, due to the very different situations in which countries find themselves, the sectors of industry, the companies and even the individuals concerned.

How can this profound change be linked to what has already been shown, namely the slowdown in technical progress and the ageing population? Is there a change in the very structure of production and consumption?

In fact, it is a matter of knowing whether the deindustrialization phenomenon, this time on a worldwide scale, will continue in future decades. If it does, it will not be without consequences for jobs, productivity and world trade.

This is not a hypothetical question, since there are numerous indicators to show that this phenomenon is already at work.[6] The whole history of the coming years may well be defined through this movement.

Patrick Artus, who was the first person to mention the problem, considers that several structural factors explain this long-term reduction in the importance of industry throughout the world. Firstly, there is a steep drop in income levels throughout the world, even though GDP per inhabitant increased by 35% between 1995 and 2013. This increase can be explained by a transfer of demand from industry to services, thus causing a higher

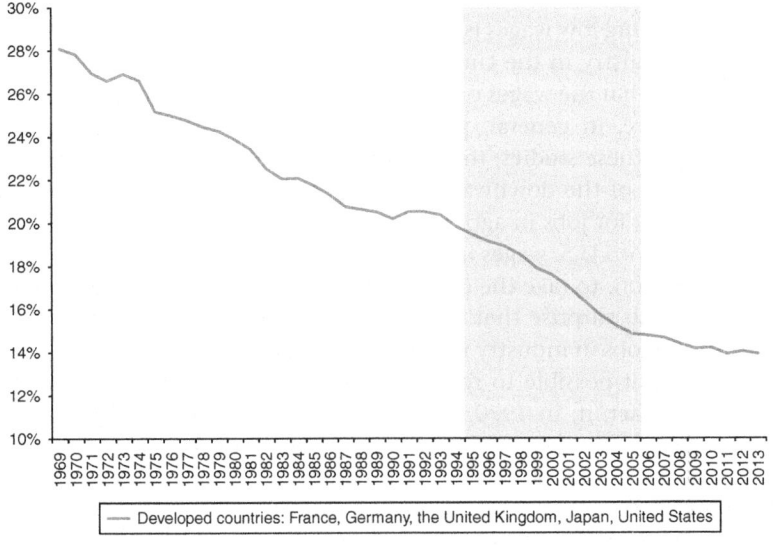

Figure 4.5 Share of jobs in industry as a proportion of all jobs
Sources: International Labour Office, INSEE and the authors.

rise in the cost of services than in the industrial sector. To be convinced of this, all one needs is to realize that the manufacturing sector index only increased by 17% at the very time when the non-manufacturing sector index rose by more than 75%. Subsequently, the theory could be advanced that the worldwide deindustrialization phenomenon could have had two origins. On the one hand, the relative rise in the price of raw materials, which would imply *ipso facto* decreasing industrial demand. On the other hand, the acceleration of new technologies favoured any form of dematerialization. Nor should demographic ageing be forgotten. Structurally, an ageing society consumes a greater amount of services.

The much vaunted and very much desired reindustrialization could certainly be no more than a pale copy of the production systems of the last two centuries.

The London temptation

What makes the industrial history of Great Britain so interesting?[7] The simple reason that it illustrates in an exemplary manner the nature of a normal, inevitable and perhaps positive phenomenon of deindustrialization linked to the opening up of trade. In the course of the nineteenth century, Great Britain gradually disengaged from the industrial sector, giving way to the place of finance and thereby achieving world economic dominance. During the second half of the nineteenth century, other countries caught up with it, and it was overtaken at a later stage by the United States although there was nothing fatal in that movement. Remembering the industrial history of Great Britain would make it possible today to prevent history repeating itself with its accompanying harmful consequences, in an immediate parallel with the rise in power of the emerging nations.

That is because Great Britain, through a badly managed beginning or, more precisely, by pushing it to an extreme, left its technological advance behind. Will this syndrome affect all of the industrialized countries? If we look at the British case again, while the exact date of the first Industrial Revolution in Britain remains a subject of controversy between economists, the period probably began in the eighteenth century, running out of steam in about 1870–1880, during the Great Depression of that era. In the second half of the eighteenth century, the rate of invention accelerated. In addition to innovation in manufacturing processes, new materials arrived, such as the so-called paisley cloth imported from India which was soon be manufactured at home in Great Britain. The textile industry, the coal and iron mines, the mechanical industries, the steam engines, weaving looms and that 'dominant' innovation, the railways that were introduced in the period 1830–1840, constituted a network of mechanical industries. They had very powerful knock-on effects on the rest of the economy.

Finally, Great Britain benefited during that period from a very special position. As the cradle of the Industrial Revolution, it retained this dominant position for nearly half a century, due to the very limited spread of technology linked to the difficulty of communications in the period, the difficulties of travelling and exchanging information and the deterrent of protection by constructing tariff barriers. Yet, mainly between 1790 and 1820, Great Britain maintained its technological progress thanks to protectionism on all sides. In 1820, the phenomenon now known as 'the London temptation' was triggered. Although it had built its power on a defensive strategy, Great Britain proceeded to open up its economy in an uncontrolled fashion, allowing its followers to swiftly gain a competitive advantage.

In 1820, Britain still represented 21% of world industrial production, as against 10% for Germany, 13% for France and 5% for the United States. Thanks to the superiority it enjoyed in three of the industries at the heart of the first wave of industrialization – textile machinery, coke-fired iron and steel foundries and the steam engine – it took full advantage of the liberalization of trade in the initial stage. Subsequently, however, continental companies reacted and sought to bring in English foremen and workers, tempting them with high wages, especially in iron and steel and in construction. In fact, the French and German governments increased their initiatives to offer strong incentives for technology transfers. The German railway network, virtually non-existent in 1850, would catch up with the French network after 1860 and with that of Great Britain after 1880.[8]

From 1840 onwards, Great Britain no longer sought to prevent the export of its technology. The number of meetings between engineers increased. The great universities and technical colleges in France and Europe had already trained a generation of scientists and technicians to a level at least comparable to that of their British counterparts, who would be capable of improving upon and using the standardized technologies. At that time, a certain downturn in British innovation policy could be observed. After 1850, the technological primacy of Britain was soundly beaten by the United States and continental Europe. It is merely enough to count, as did Paul Bairoch, the number of technological innovations developed by the three great centres of economic activity to demonstrate the extraordinary decline of the world's greatest economic and political power, a process that took only a few decades.

Table 4.1 Number of technological inventions recorded

	Great Britain	Continental Europe	United States
1770–1799	32	23	3
1800–1819	20	7	6
1820–1839	22	13	10
1840–1859	12	17	16
1860–1879	11	18	12
1880–1899	13	21	18

Source: Paul Bairoch, Mythes et paradoxes de l'histoire économique [Myths and Paradoxes of Economic History], *La Découverte*, 1995.

The Great Depression, even though it hit the whole of Europe hard, resulted in an end to the hegemony of the British economy. It is true that from the point of view of internal factors, Great Britain did not renew its machinery and technology in the sectors that had driven the Industrial Revolution. Nor did it possess the energy source of the second Industrial Revolution, oil, and it suffered from a serious shortage of metals. Finally, it invested very little in cutting-edge industries, such as chemicals or electricity, whose development it considered to be slow and hazardous. The traditional technical systems of the first Industrial Revolution disappeared after 1870, to be replaced by new leading sectors of the second industrialization, steel and electricity.

Unlike the United States, Germany or France, Great Britain did not seem to realize the danger that opening up to the world could represent if the effects of doing so were not well controlled, as they were liable to cause price reduction and loss of control of technology. This awareness was translated into unsuitable policies for combating the Zollverein Agreements in Germany in 1878, the McKinley Tariff in the United States in 1890 and the Méline Law in France in 1892. That is why Paul Bairoch has written that the United Kingdom 'was a free trade island in the midst of an ocean of protectionism'.[9]

Confronted with such internal and external difficulties, Great Britain fell into a relative decline which was translated into the slowing of its production capacity and its economic growth. Opening up to world trade increased its exposure to technology transfer. International commercial interaction became more frequent and more sustained, foreign producers imitated home-grown technology and the incorporation of their knowledge into their own production processes resulted in a veritable deindustrialization of the British economy in the late nineteenth century. It was a real loss of substance for Britain.

Yet this actually represented a carefully thought-out strategy, because finance took over. The relative decline in British industry was compensated for by a competitive position in the service sector, primarily in financial services.

By the nineteenth century, the City of London had already become a leading commercial centre: 'It is thus against this economic background that monetary and financial relations were woven'.[10] In fact, the development of the City of London as a financial centre is the result of a decision by the Bank of England in 1797 to introduce a forced exchange rate for banknotes. Notes then became currency in their own right, without being representative of convertibility into gold ('the gold standard'). This decision involved a long controversy between its supporters and its detractors. The economically conservative Sir Robert Peel ended it by adopting the 'currency school' position which favoured convertibility, an option that was actually theoretical since it had to be suspended during the economic crises of 1847 and 1857 and eventually could not be put into practice.

More importantly, the City also owed its rise to a total reorganization of the banking structures. After the stock exchange crisis of 1825, the British crown established 'joint-stock banking' based on the issue of stocks or shares and allowing banking capitalization to increase as well as diversification of loans granted. It also created subsidiaries of the Bank of England, the purpose of which was to ensure the necessary liquidity in the markets. This reform gave birth to such institutions as the London and Westminster Joint Bank in 1835, the Union Bank and the London and County Bank in 1839. Access to joint stock banks and London clearing houses in 1854 removed the last trump card still held by private banks, which were gradually eliminated to the benefit of the joint stock banks, who grouped together to extend their provincial networks or gain access to London clearing. The concentration movement that started in the early twentieth century led to the creation of the major deposit banks that represented the strength that lay behind the British financial system. The strategy of prioritizing London as a financial centre, this 'London temptation' was a perfectly consistent one. Its purpose was to reinforce, to its benefit, the pre-eminence and solvency of the Empire.

The financialization of the British economy was initially indispensable for accelerating the development of the Crown's merchant navy which increased its number of vessels by 30% between 1820 and 1860.[11] Furthermore, the British government, aware of the natural wealth of its colonies, realized that financial intermediation was indispensable for channelling wealth from the outer limits to the centre of the Empire, a function that had been taken over by very autonomous local administrations who received permission to develop their own financial engineering and who took the initiative to issue bonds on the London market to finance their projects. In fact, Lance Davis and Robert Gallman[12] have established a positive correlation between the increase in the rate of savings and the acceleration of investments. Since investors were constantly in search of ever-increasing yields, the banks were encouraged to embark on financial innovation in order to attract clients in a competitive climate. In other words, London's financial centre came to have the undisputed monopoly on innovation in financial technology.

The American hope

This is the great enigma at the start of this twenty-first century. After experiencing the implacable reality of the departure of its industries to emerging nations to a greater extent than any other country, the United States may be opening a new chapter in its history. What is surprising is not that one can speak of a revival of the American economy, since it is fundamentally cyclical. What is to be hoped and expected, of course, is a traditional exit from the bottom of the cycle rendered more complicated due to very strict budgetary constraints but facilitated by a particularly accommodating monetary policy. The innovation, however, lies in the fact that this new impetus is supported by a resumption of industrial activity. The way in which the American Empire has cocked a snook at the defunct British Empire is a true irony of history. The movement began in 2010 with an increase in industry's share of GDP and the creation of new jobs in manufacturing.

More specifically, industry's share of added value in U.S. GDP had fallen from 13% in 2005 to 11.9% in 2009.[13] Yet, since 2009, a net rebound is observable in U.S. industrial added value, since it now accounts for more than 12.5% of GDP. As for jobs in manufacturing, the outlook here is also optimistic. While it fell by around 20% between 2004 and 2009, there has been a slight recovery since then.[14]

The origin of this development is clearly based on the relative decrease in wages costs, linked to a weak rate of exchange, wage freezes and productivity gains. In fact, U.S. wages have reduced, in comparison with their commercial partners, by 30% since 2000, if one excludes China. Furthermore, since 2009, U.S. wages costs have decreased by about 5%, while the same costs, taking all sectors together, increased by 2.3% in the same period.

88 A Violent World

Figure 4.6 Manufacturing jobs (in thousands) and wages costs in industry and corporations (2009 = 100)
Sources: Bureau Labour of Statistics, Federal Reserve, OECD and the authors.

The second reason, one that is often quoted, involves the development of shale gas. Since 2008, the prices of natural gas have reduced by 60% in the United States while, at the same time, they increased by more than 15% in the euro zone. If the fact that technology in the energy sector is still very much controlled by the United States is taken into account, it is doubtless easy to understand the extent to which reindustrialization, linked to this advantage in energy costs, has been able to develop in North America.

The automotive industry is obviously the most typical example. The year 2007 was a terrible one for General Motors, Ford and Chrysler. In the case of General Motors, production fell in that year from 5 million to 2 million vehicles. The nadir was reached in 2009, with a 50% drop in production and more than 30% of jobs lost. Yet by the end of 2013, production had returned to 10.5 million vehicles, with nearly 800,000 employees,[15] and in 2014 a ceiling of 16 million was reached, even higher than production had been in 2006.[16]

This genuine recovery is also to be found in the petrochemicals industry.[17] In fact, this sector is one of the big winners in the shale gas 'revolution' with remarkable profits being made in comparison with foreign competition and, for the future, promising production capacities for

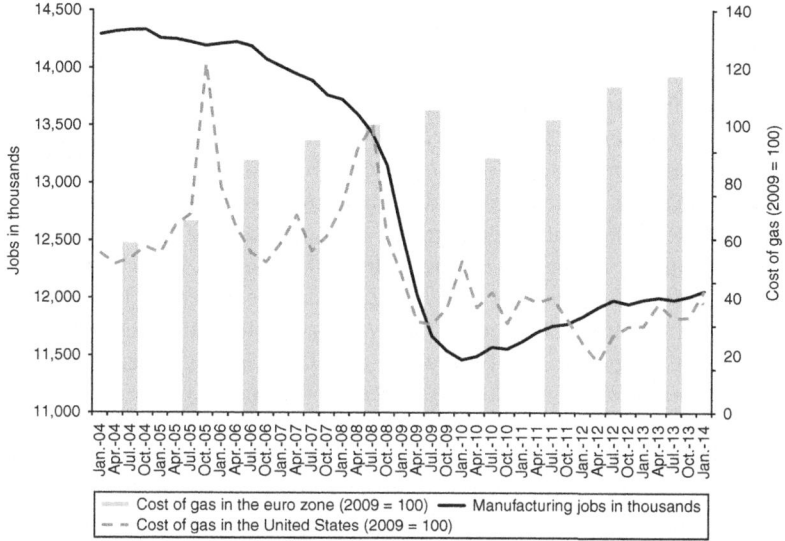

Figure 4.7 Manufacturing jobs (in thousands) and cost of gas in the United States and in the euro zone (2009 = 100)

Sources: Bureau Labour of Statistics, Dow Jones & Company, Federal Reserve and the authors.

ethylene and polyethylene production. Could this be a form of offshoring for this industry? Between 2012 and 2015 increases in existing capacity were planned, the reopening of units or site conversion from naphtha to ethane and propane, and, notably, many new projects of impressive size,[18] almost all of them located in the states bordering the Gulf of Mexico. These are due to come into service in 2016 or 2017.

Even more revealing is the fact that petrochemical companies throughout the world are eager to invest in U.S. petrochemicals. These include SABIC, a Saudi Arabian company and one of the world leaders, Braskem, the Brazilian petrochemicals company, the Indian Reliance Industries and the Thai company Indomara.

The enthusiasm is generalized to such an extent that there is talk of a genuine turnaround.[19] It should be remembered that it is these very petrochemical industries that were heavily offshored during the previous decade to low-cost-energy countries such as those in the Middle East, or those with high demand and low manpower costs such as in south-east Asia and China.

The same story has been produced by the American Chemistry Council[20] in its study of investments linked to the competitive advantage resulting from shale gas. The figures speak for themselves. These projects will increase turnover in the chemical industry by 265 billion dollars for the period 2012–2020 and by 2020 this additional production will translate into the creation of 46,000 jobs in the chemical industries and 537,000 jobs if indirect and induced employment are taken into account. Regardless of judgements as to the reliability of these figures, one can only be impressed by the scale of change that is occurring. The phenomenon is translated into a significant commercial rebalancing in the United States. We are on the way to substantially higher export levels than the growth rate of imports – the latter is very likely to double. Will this adversely affect the exploitation of 'non-conventional' energy sources?

Is it possible to speak of a renewal of U.S. industry, through a measured examination of the various figures and reports[21] published recently that harp on the very attractive theory of a renaissance? It is such a long time since the OECD countries had their wings clipped by the emerging nations, when their supposed technological superiority was threatened, that any growth spurt appears to be decisive and definitive.

It is still too early know whether this industrial recovery is short-term or whether it will translate into a long-term trend. Three factors will determine this reindustrialization. These are the cost of unskilled labour, especially in the countries of the South, the reduction in the energy bill linked to 'non-conventional' sources of gas and the ability of the economic environment to benefit from this cost reduction. One can only speculate as to how these factors will develop. If recent trends continue it could be imagined that from 2015, the cost of labour adjusted to productivity in the United States will be 16% lower than in the United Kingdom, 18% lower than in Japan, 34% lower than in Germany and 35% lower than in France and Italy.[22] Furthermore, the labour market in the U.S. is much more flexible. The U.S. has the third most flexible economy in terms of employment regulation, far ahead of Japan, the United Kingdom, France or Germany.[23] This finding reinforces the feeling that the U.S. has a competitive advantage. The same analysis and the same hypotheses, the same positivity applies to the price of gas. In 2008, a million BTUs, the unit of reference, cost more than 12 U.S. dollars. Four years later, in early 2012, it had fallen below 2 U.S. dollars, before rising again to 4 dollars in 2014.[24] These prices remain three times lower than in Europe, as these sources of energy cannot currently be exported and there is nothing to make one think that that situation will change.

Finally, U.S. reindustrialization is known to be very dependent on an unstable international economic environment. It is nevertheless to be hoped that the macroeconomic changes in the United States will maintain their dynamic. Remember that there is an attempt to reduce unitary wages costs between China and the United States, coupled with the increasing value of the yuan and awareness of the vulnerability of an over-exploited logistics chain. Anything is possible, and even probable, even without excessive optimism. Yet numerous uncertainties persist. There is no guarantee to ensure the future financing of reindustrialization, a process that is very greedy in terms of equity. The process will only happen if the fundamentals of the U.S. economy are robust, if they are based on reliable growth forecasts and on a financial system that is capable of supporting projects requiring large injections of capital, while investing in labour with a high added value.

Similarly, industrial recovery must be accompanied by favourable market conditions. Industry is a sector that is heavily exposed to uncertainties, however. The manufacturing sector is particularly sensitive to change in the economic cycle and more heavily exposed to risk. There are far more cases of insolvency in the manufacturing sector than in the other fields of activity that reached a low point in the economic cycle, while there is a trend in the opposite direction to the top of the economic cycle. A revival can be imagined if these corporate insolvencies are reduced to a minimum. This is a particularly important condition since more than half the products manufactured in the United States are not destined for export.

Above all, would it be possible to imagine that this reindustrialization is based on the U.S.'s trump card, its technological leadership, expressed in the development of new industries? On this subject, Suzanne Berger is pessimistic. She speaks of an innovation process that has become paralyzed, start-ups that can no longer find productive ecosystems in which to develop, as a consequence of previous relocations outside the country. The state needs to intervene in order to contain this 'loss of substance'.[25] Of course, these innovation, research and development programmes are now in competition with those of the emerging nations. Currently, the share of U.S. expenditure on research amounts to 2.79% of GDP.[26] In this, the United States is greatly in advance of China. Investment in the private and federal sectors amounts to 450 billion dollars and is rising by 1.2%, while expenditure on research and development in China lags way behind, at 230 billion dollars, even though, for several years, it has maintained an extraordinary increase in this expenditure.[27] Yet according to current tendencies, China will only outspend the United States on research and development in ten years' time.

The prospect of seeing the emerging nations reducing the innovation gap between themselves and the West by moving closer to the technological frontier would have been unimaginable a few years ago. In comparative terms, their investment in innovation translates into an increase in the scale of their industrial production, in competition with high added-value labour in the developed countries, first and foremost among them the United States. The U.S. multinationals, however, can call on more R&D skills from abroad; in fact, in the case of some of them, currently in the minority, most of their expenditure goes on their foreign subsidiaries.[28]

Another element that relativizes the prospect of uncomplicated reindustrialization is that the United States represents no more than 4% of engineering degrees awarded throughout the world, as against 34% for China and 5% for Japan.[29]

Finally, the average annual 5% growth in the number of patents filed appears low for fuelling robust potential growth. How can this phenomenon be explained in the land of innovation? It is due to heavy legal constraints. It takes twice as long to file a patent today in the United States as it did twenty years ago, and this is not the case in any other country. The substantial advantages that emerged a few years ago do not guarantee that the U.S. industrial turnaround in growth will be long-lasting. Will the formidable energy of the Americans concentrate on this objective? Will all of the efforts of the most powerful nation in the world be directed towards overcoming such major costs?

Whether the role played by industry in the economy and its growth are genuine remains debatable. In recent years, the contribution of the service sector was greater than that of the manufacturing sector. The recovery of industry ought also to be relativized by the reduction in the manufacturing sector's share of total employment since 2000. Industrial employment in the United States has shrunk by 20% since 2000, representing four million people.[30] This phenomenon, which is a natural trend in the advanced nations, is of several origins, including outsourcing services such as transport and security, the consequences of productivity gains which are greater than those achieved in the service sector, the reduction in the relative price of industrial assets as well as a distortion of the consumption structure of households in favour of services.

Consequently, U.S. reindustrialization is a more important reality than one might think, although not as strong as that which is proposed for the future. Its existence is essential, nevertheless, for the redefinition of current globalization.

Terrible uncertainty over globalization

Globalization is the permanent subject of discussion as to its strengths and weaknesses and there is incessant talk about its very existence. The concept and the reality that it implies have lost their robustness, and have been substituted with vagueness and approximation. It is for this reason that the lessons of history need to be learned in order to analyse the current situation. This is what Suzanne Berger[31] did base on a precise definition: '[...] globalization can be understood as a series of changes designed to create a world market for goods and services, labour and capital'. This is indeed the dynamic that operated between 1870 and 1914. The flow of investment from the developed countries to the new worlds and developing countries grew significantly. While the net volume of French investment abroad between 1887 and 1914 represented about 3.5% of GDP, that of Great Britain was as high as 9% in some years, especially when directed at the British colonies.

Even at that time, the question arose of the negative effects that an opening up of the international economy could have on democracy and social progress. The fears were the same as they are today although the situation was far from being identical. Fear of a collapse in wages with competition from China and Japan, fear of a deterioration in working conditions, fear of a reduction in social welfare and finally fear of an environmental disaster.

Suzanne Berger goes even further. She draws two lessons from this analysis of the first globalization, 'the fragility and the reversibility of globalization'. She claims that only governments can respond to the fears created by globalization.

Why is this? It is because the United States is the only country capable of preserving democracy and undertaking the necessary reforms. Then there is Dani Rodrik's 'political trilemma'[32] which links democracy, the nation-states and globalization. A second challenge awaits globalization, that of avoiding exacerbated competition that will end in conflict. That is what happened in 1914. The first worldwide conflict, as the English journalist Norman Angell suspected,[33] would result in the destruction of links of interdependency, globalization and between the property-owning classes of both victors and vanquished. Hence this second lesson, namely that globalization, i.e. the extreme extension of international links, does not result in a peaceful world order but, on the contrary, has the potential to destroy the entire system. Like all advances in human history, it is not a venture that is exempt from dangers, conflicts, an explosion in inequalities of income as well as power struggles. We are now experiencing the same adventure once again. It increases hopes and results but also tensions, rejections and ambition. The road is narrow if the present poorly run wager is to succeed currently. It requires a clear understanding of what is at stake and what is or is not possible.

Dani Rodrik's thoughts on the matter[34] can be seen here to be essential, evoking the structural incompatibility of the three terms – democracy, nation-states and hyperglobalization. We have three choices. The first is ultraliberalism, combining hyper-globalization and nation states. Hyperglobalization is intended to mean commercial and financial integration, in other words the free circulation of capital, which after its initial glory days between 1870 and 1914, was resumed from the mid-1970s, especially between 1995 and 2005. According to Rodrik, democracy is absent from this scenario because the nation-states were content to adjust to the requirements of globalization and its movements of capital. The result of this attitude has been moderate inflation, with strong trading that has translated either into a trading surplus or into a genuine ability to attract capital to finance a deficit in the balance of trade. In this context, the only objective of the nation-state is to adjust to globalization to preserve the competitiveness of its enterprises.

The second scenario combines the current hyperglobalization with anxiety about the power that the markets have acquired and the increasing desire for democracy. This is the expression of a wish for world government which, leaving the current state of functioning of globalization, wishes to retain it within great supranational and public institutions. This is a vision, one that is sometimes utopian, of creating something along the lines of a 'United States of Europe'. It would mean creating a governance of the existing types – the WTO, the IMF, the UN, etc. – but one that would have to develop in order to put the nation-state out of the running while complying with economic cultures and issues. Rodrik considers, however, that world government is an illusion; he is exasperated by the fact that the politics of the smallest common denominator are allowed to supersede important cultural, political and economic differences. If, as he claims, the economic frontiers have disappeared, those of language and law persist. So while goods circulate freely, humans remain largely 'immobile'.

The last possibility of this trilemma consists in preserving nation-states and democracy. This represents a challenge to hyperglobalization.

Contrary to what world government might become, this solution does not seek to abolish the nation-state. Far from it. It actually relies on it in order to achieve global accords thanks to cooperation between nations.

Rodrik's trilemma is unparalleled in its explanation of the European situation and its difficulties. The European Union has chosen globalization and free trade, a choice enshrined in all the European treaties. It further attempts to clothe itself in the mantle of sovereignty in the form of defence, foreign policy, justice, the single currency, etc. Yet budgetary policy remains largely in the hands of the nation-states and is the expression of an ill-conceived architecture resulting in a crisis for a Europe that has abandoned democracy. This is what Rodrik calls the 'golden straitjacket'. National financial regulation, to which the populations of the European Union are very attached, goes against the plan for an integrated economy in which the financial institutions are completely mobile. The states need to admit their powerlessness to regulate finance on pain of seeing their enterprises being established in less demanding countries. This is the sad reality of regulation that sees competition going to the lowest bidder.

We are confronted with three scenarios proposed by Dani Rodrik: nation-state and hyperglobalization, nation-state and democracy, i.e. moderate globalization, hyperglobalization and democracy, i.e. world governance.

One thing is sure in Rodrik's thinking, namely that hyperglobalization, the nation-state and democracy cannot possibly co-exist. Yet the ambient discourse never stresses this impossibility which, if it were to be expressed clearly, would lead to unfortunate choices. Has globalization, over and above its indubitable economic successes, at least had the merit of definitively putting an end to war and conflict?

Suzanne Berger has studied this issue in relation to the first globalization. Does trade pacify international relations[35] dubbed by Montesquieu as that 'sweet trade'?[36] Globalization and the spread of the market economy as we have been experiencing it for the past 25 years, coupled with the democratization of numerous countries after the end of the Cold War, does not allow for a response, except in the case of Europe. Has a quest for individual profit replaced the warlike violence between neighbouring countries since the early 1990s? International trade has had a contradictory effect on the possibility of armed conflict whether one analyses the impact of a bilateral or a multilateral opening. Trade between two countries increases the cost of opportunity of a bilateral war and the destruction of the prior benefits of trading while, in multilateral trading relationships, these same two countries see the cost of opportunity of a bilateral war reducing. That is the reason why globalization encourages bellicose nations to outsource conflicts.

In fact, nothing is certain except a more general idea, dating from the end of World War II that international political cooperation and a sustainable peace depend fundamentally on international economic cooperation. The second globalization, which is nevertheless quite new in its procedures, is based on ageing multilateral economic institutions that are the result of the 1944 Bretton Woods system – the International Monetary Fund (IMF), the World Bank and the General Agreement on Tariffs and Trade (GATT). This arrangement is one that was suitable for the post-war economy, enhancing the extraordinary success of the international economic order and witnessing unprecedented growth and development worldwide. Doubts were again raised, starting in 1971, when the Bretton Woods system failed, heralding a deeper integration model in a system that was profoundly disrupted by the arrival of new economic powers and the relative decline of the United States. This formidable moment occurred without an established concept and without appropriate institutions until the crisis of 2007.

It would appear that we are witnessing an inverse movement; one of withdrawal and slowing. It is limited but it is real, a form of globalization that translates into several protectionist attempts and a slowing of growth in world trade. Is this true and what is the scope of this alleged world change of course? Pankaj Ghemawat[37] has brought us back to reality. Contrary to the current description of semi-achieved globalization, we are currently living in an era of mere 'semi-globalization', since numerous indicators of world integration are surprisingly low. Only 2% of students are enrolled in foreign universities and 3% of the inhabitants of the planet live outside the country in which they were born. Only 7% of the directors of the S&P 500 companies, the companies quoted on the American stock exchange, are foreign. Finally, exports only represent 20% of world GDP. And to conclude on what might appear to be anecdotal, since 11 September 2001, it has taken three times as long to deal with loading a truck that has to cross the border between Canada and the United States. According to Ghemawat, this is a sign of regionalization at work, one that even affects the internet since individual countries are imposing restrictions on its content.

The opening up of markets, as has been shown in the past, remains a very fragile situation. All the more so since it is not always desirable. The World Trade Organization (WTO)[38] confirms that the rising tensions in the labour market and increasing inequality of incomes in many countries have had a negative effect on the public's attitude to globalization and international trade. As long as the majority of citizens believe that both of these are the reason for unemployment and increasing inequalities, governments may find themselves constrained to slow the expansion of free trade and be tempted to introduce forms of protectionism. This is a major challenge for the WTO which has played an important role in recent years in the fight against protectionist pressures: 'Protectionism is like cholesterol: the slow accumulation since 2008 of restrictive measures on trade – currently covering nearly 3% of the world trade in goods and nearly 4% of trade among the G20 – could end by obstructing commercial flows.'[39] It is hard to know whether this represents a true increase in protectionism or mere feverishness resulting from the terrible years of 2008 and 2009.

Of course, barely three years after the start of the crisis, 1,187 discriminatory measures[40] applicable to foreign suppliers have been recorded. If the list of protectionist measures implemented is a long one, the accounting approach should be handled with care. In a world tour of the most protectionist policies, Latin America tops the charts, followed by Russia, India and China. This is a stereoscopic view that does not exempt either the United States or Europe, even if the measures taken are generally less visible or more compatible with the spirit of regulation of the WTO.

So protectionism is doing fine, but is that anything new? One cannot reasonably speak of a breach. The world is actually very open and could find itself undermined in the future by protest votes of people who felt themselves excluded, tempted by the prospect of isolationism through withdrawing behind their own borders. That is a risk for tomorrow, one that is currently present but limited.

Over and above this potential protectionism, one cannot conceal a different and much more significant problem, that of a genuine slowdown in world trade.[41] All the sources have converged. The growth in world trade experienced a fall in 2012 and has remained sluggish ever since. The economic slowdown in Europe has adversely affected world demand for imports and a sharp drop in trade has been the result, as well as numerous uncertainties affecting world growth. These include disruption to the euro zone, procrastination in U.S. monetary policy and the fragility of the Chinese financial system. It could be assumed that this was merely a recessionary phase. Stagnating or falling production and high unemployment in the developed countries reduce imports *ipso facto* and slow the flow of exports from the developed countries as well as from the emerging nations. All that is left is to wait for a recovery. But here again, as elsewhere, the organization of the world economy may be in the process of change.

From the exuberance of the years 1995–2008 and after the impact of the sub-prime mortgage crisis, a net slowdown in the export of goods could be detected. Naturally, the recession played a major role in this development. But is it the only explanation? While the world value of exports at the current prices and exchange rates has doubled, increasing from 8,000 billion dollars to 16,000 billion dollars between 2003 and 2008, [42] the growth in exports decreased substantially from then on and until today. In 2014, the world value of exports amounted to only 18,900 billion dollars.

One can always speak of the world reindustrialization without imagining that it would have no effect on international trade. Is this a genuine disruption or a modest change of trajectory? It is hard to decide. In any case, the real war will take place on the currency exchange markets. The currency war is not new since it is the ultimate weapon of the central bankers. In the past they were always the protagonists who were responsible for this eternal conflict. Depending on the scope of the movements, these wars are of different durations. Above all, they only impose voluntary currency fluctuations which should not appear as anything but the consequence of the natural movements of the markets.

The challenge lies elsewhere, as Nicolas Baverez reminds us: '[...] the currency war is emerging as a major component of the economic war. As a result, it has accompanied all the major crises of capitalism since the nineteenth century (the late nineteenth-century recession, the depression of the 1930s, the late 1970s recession and the globalization crisis since 2007), that caused both the change in production norms and an upsetting of the hierarchies of power'.[43] Currency is a powerful tool, the first instrument of a nation's power in international trade. So it is not surprising that governments want to play with it, especially in times of crisis, whether economic or financial.

The most frequently quoted example, one that is so well known that its origin is sometimes forgotten, is that of the 1930s and currency devaluations. What happened? The Stock Exchange Crash of 24 October 1929 is well-known to have caused the U.S. Federal Reserve to increase its interest rates and this resulted in a series of bank failures and a sudden and heavy depression. On its part, the U.S. government took exemplary protectionist measures in the form of the Smoot-Hawley Tariff Act, which imposed high customs duties on industrial products. It was the devaluation of sterling, however, in 1931, when it came off the gold standard that imported the recession into Europe. Finding themselves incapable of reaching an understanding, all of the leading countries, and first and foremost the United States, devalued their currencies in a sort of race that turned into a competition and raised protectionist barriers at the same rate, leading to the collapse of international trade. This was the lesson, constantly repeated, that should be learned from a generalized conflict and subsequent collapse.

Bretton Woods should be remembered for the desire for stability and durability it represented. The choice implemented between a world currency and a system of fixed parities is always remembered as if this had been at the heart of the discussions. That is not the case, the two proposal being different concerning the dominant role played by one country over the others, something that always comes to an end: 'The Bretton Woods System was the victim of its basic asymmetry, since it was based on the dollar which was not subjected to any discipline'.[44] That is probably true, but it did not prevent the system from lasting for nearly thirty years in a respected framework and a discipline that was accepted by all, until the domination crumbled or was challenged, and, with it, the rules it imposed. All that remains is to attribute a theoretical necessity to the change, expressed in thousands of articles concerning the beauty of flexible exchange rates.

This world disorder restores all their legitimacy to currency exchange rate policies. The undervaluation of certain currencies assumes the overvaluation of others, of which the euro zone and Japan were victims until recently, with the consequences with which we are familiar, namely, loss of competitiveness, mass unemployment, sluggish growth and indebtedness.

This insupportable tension between indebtedness and a strong currency on the one hand and increasing savings and an undervalued currency on the other – the situation in the emerging nations – heralds a new currency war, a war on a planetary scale that will have its winners and losers.

Voices are regularly raised to recall the risks of such a conflict. In March 2009, Ted Truman[45] warned of the temptations of a bellicose policy using the currency weapon. In 2010, it was the turn of Guido Mantega, the Brazilian Minister of Finance, to make an announcement that had an exceptional impact: that the world was 'in the midst of an international monetary war'. The statement was premature and excessive but, as so often happened, the thought preceded the deeds. What followed was an explicit policy of devaluing the currency. This was the case in Japan. Japanese Prime Minister Shinzō Abe's policy was to create a lot of liquidity, via the

Central Bank, so as to cause the yen to fall as a result of his determination, the clarity of his objectives and the transparency of his statements and actions. It marks a break with the past, heralding new times. History prior to the crisis is simple. It is that of U.S. structural trading imbalances in relation to all the emerging nations and China in particular. These imbalances resulted in an influx of U.S. dollars in these countries. Instead of sterilizing this influx, it was reactivated by the Central Bank of China whose aim was to maintain a favourable exchange rate, which caused it to purchase U.S. public or private securities. The consequence was an explosion in world liquidity prior to 2007, a phenomenon that was maintained by virtue of the daring monetary policies adopted by numerous central banks, led by the U.S. Federal Reserve.

The history of exchange rates for the last 15 years translates these movements, with their winners, their losers, high volatility of all currencies (with the exception of the yuan) in relation to the dollar, in the well understood interest of both parties, well beyond their public posturing. The trend in exchange rates complied with what was to be expected, seriously deteriorated as a result of the slump followed by the world

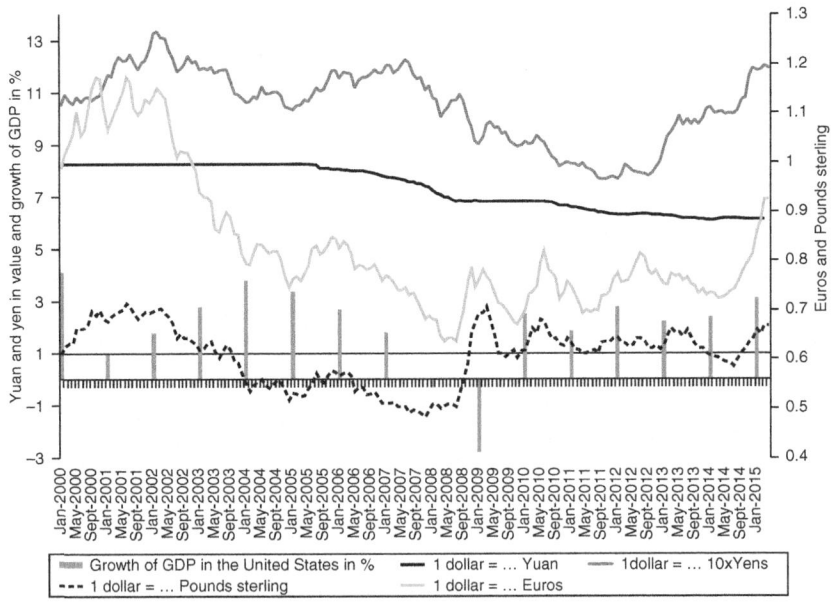

Figure 4.8 Trend in U.S. dollar-based exchange rates
Sources: OECD, IMF, and the authors.

recession, was dominated by the United States and China, and was thus carefully controlled.

Yet the desire to reindustrialize exists. If Europe can emerge from its torpor, if Shinzō Abe pursues his policy we shall be progressing towards a new period, that of currency exchange weapons, that are so easy to implement and so effective in the short term. The daring policy of quantitative easing launched by Mario Draghi is a perfect illustration of this.

The currency wars will reveal themselves to be extremely violent, totally suicidal. Why is this? The dash to devalue currencies implies the creation of liquidity, speculative bubbles and their inevitable explosion. History has taught us something that we tend to forget, namely that monetary peace is a world public asset that should be preserved above all else. Forty years ago, we opened Pandora's box by sanctifying the flexibility of exchange rates. The risks are enormous, the policies could be brutal and the days of reckoning are approaching, according to the convincing warning issued by Jacques Mistral.[46] Underestimating the current dangers, failing to find them a solution on the world scale is leaving the field open to every possible scenario, including those that are the most unmanageable and the most dangerous. That is because this period appears to be dictated by whatever the biggest countries, mainly the United States and Japan, want; to change the situation by rebalancing to their advantage that which has prevailed hitherto.

Of course, reindustrialization is only in its infancy. There is nothing today that would make it possible to claim that the relocation movements could adopt the desired magnitude, though there is nothing to prevent it being imagined. That is not the main thing, but in the policies that will be implemented in order to achieve it, that of exchange rates will be in the lead. The balances established at this start of the twenty-first century will then be profoundly changed by this new will. Industry is only a limited part of the productive structures of developed countries, but it is the yardstick by which the strength and power of nations is measured. The physiocrats are not far away, or, more precisely, they have returned, expressing themselves in this ardent obligation to control the industries of the past, the industries of today and, above all, the industries of the future. Rates of exchange will certainly be playing a major role in this, quite simply because, as we are beginning to realize, the costs of labour will converge in the coming years. This will leave just one weapon in the hands of the politicians, that of the exchange rate. It is in this field that the tensions will be most significant.

5
The Illusion of Definancialization

In this world currently under reconstruction, nothing seems more utopian – or more improbable – than the control or restriction of financial activity. It was the dream of the post-crisis years, the idea that political will could be imposed on all of the movers and shakers of the world of finance. The scenario was soon demolished by the weakness of the U.S. government that was incapable of finding any autonomy in relation to Wall Street. Today, the manifestations of the financial industry are without a doubt more complex and more extensive than they have ever been. For this simple reason, through globalization, finance has the ability to intervene, create and use available liquidity to an unprecedented extent. Yet our whole recent economic history has assigned a key role to the creation of liquid assets at a world, regional and national level as well as via the central banks. In fact, the present authors consider that liquidity is the key to the way in which finance has developed, thus showing the extent to which it would be impossible to imagine a world that was definancialized. Remember that the origin of the evil is to be found in the major imbalance in trades which is itself the product of massive transfers of business from the North to the emerging nations. Even if there is an intention to reduce the trade deficits created by the United States, the reality of deindustrialization of the OECD countries will have two consequences in practice. The first will be the attempt by the emerging nations to maintain and even increase their position in trade. The currency war is even now the concrete translation of this desire, and it will worsen in the future. It is important to stress that this war will yet again result in uncontrolled growth in liquidity on a world scale. The world will have difficulty in extricating itself from this situation. Added to this are the current very expansionist policies of the central banks which are rightly perceived as being extremely fragile.

This combination will result in the uncontrolled growth of financial products, financial transactions and their valuations.

It is against the background of this worrying climate that all governments, without exception, have promoted the very idea of regulation which is, in reality, the mere political expression of a desire to put the world to rights. This is not going to happen, however. While regulation may be desirable, despite an extension of its areas of intervention, and despite its increased technical abilities, it cannot channel the movements of what has now become the world's leading industry. The case rests. If this finding is accepted, i.e. that finance will place a heavy burden on future developments, calculation and action should be directed exclusively at the true vocation of financing the actual economy. It matters little that the financial sector survives on its own logic if it becomes capable of meeting the necessary requirement for investment and the needs of those who are economically active on the markets for goods and services.

Yet surely, we are told, before thinking about growth the problem of our debts needs to be resolved. Debt reduction, a subject often treated in a moralizing, hypocritical manner rather than from the economic aspect, cannot concentrate all our financing efforts; this would be tantamount to definitively condemning the revival of the world economy. This is certainly a problem that is more difficult to deal with, from both the economic and political aspects.

The explosion of liquidity

In the beginning there was liquidity. The development of the financial markets cannot be understood without stressing the growth, unparalleled in human history, of financial assets of all types. Yet the word liquidity is itself complex since it covers a number of different realities. The same word conceals a number of different factors, different realities and different regulations. In short, liquidity covers a number of ambiguities that need to be removed.

Firstly there is macroeconomic liquidity, defined by the set of liquidities created by the central banks and which in practice represent the increase in the monetary base. It is a known, quantified and controllable category. By following its development, one can understand the role of monetary policy operations and grasp the impact of the central banks on economic policy. Then there is bank liquidity, the liquid assets held by the banks. Finally there is a less well-defined space in which astronomical statistics, such as those on global liquidity, not all of them completely verifiable, are concentrated. This area includes all the available assets that can be traded on the markets, including those notorious assets, the derivatives of all types.

These three categories are linked. The growth of macroeconomic liquidity, created by the banks, involves banking liquidity, something that is set by these same central banks. In the same way, global liquidity is largely defined by both the liquidity of the central banks, and thus by banking liquidity, as well as by all of the new assets that the financial system is capable of creating. The explosion in this liquidity since the first decade of the second millennium lies, in reality, behind the financial crisis. In fact, this gigantic set of financial products distributed all over the world needed to be made profitable. Hence the decisions to make unaffordable loans such as the subprimes. Since the origins of everything need to be discovered, macroeconomic liquidity has taken a leading role due to the political choices of the emerging nations, who did not want to sterilize their assets in foreign currencies and preferred to maintain a rate of exchange that was favourable for them.

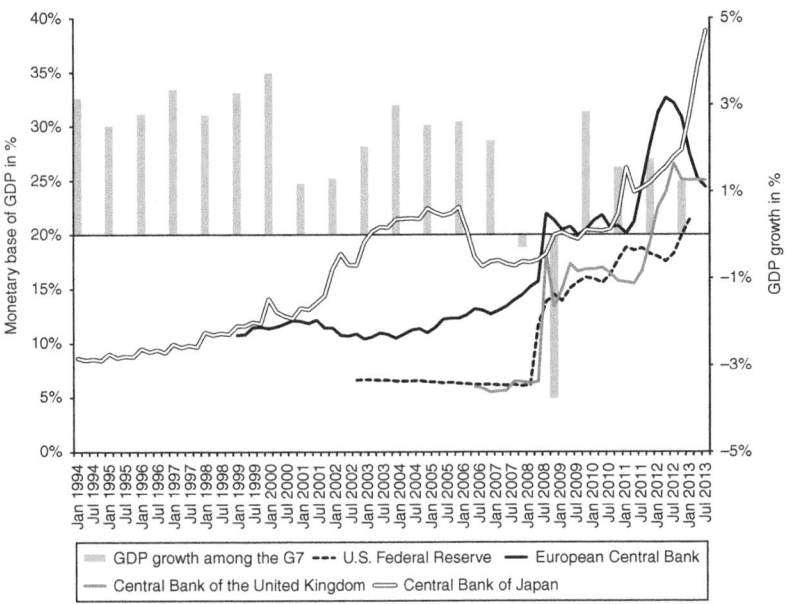

Figure 5.1 Monetary base of the central banks as a percentage of GDP
Sources: Federal Reserve, Bank of Japan, OECD and the authors.

This increase in macroeconomic liquidity on a world scale, linked to policy, never ended, regardless of changes in economic policies in recent years.

The Figure 5.1 shows how macroeconomic liquidity controlled by the central banks has distanced itself from economic reality to the extent that it has grown much faster than wealth produced, i.e. GDP. But what is more worrying is the amount of financial products traded in the markets, whether regulated or unregulated. These figures are quite stupefying. The most recent statistics of the Bank for International Settlements (BIS) on the OTC derivatives market reveal that the total outstanding amounts on which derivatives are based, i.e. the total notional amounts of derivatives outstanding, amounted to 630,000 billion dollars by the end of December 2014.[1] That is the equivalent of ten times world GDP! It has more than tripled in only 15 years.

In particular, these are interest rate contracts that represent the largest sector on the world OTC derivatives market with a notional amount outstanding of 505,000 billion dollars by late December 2014. Another

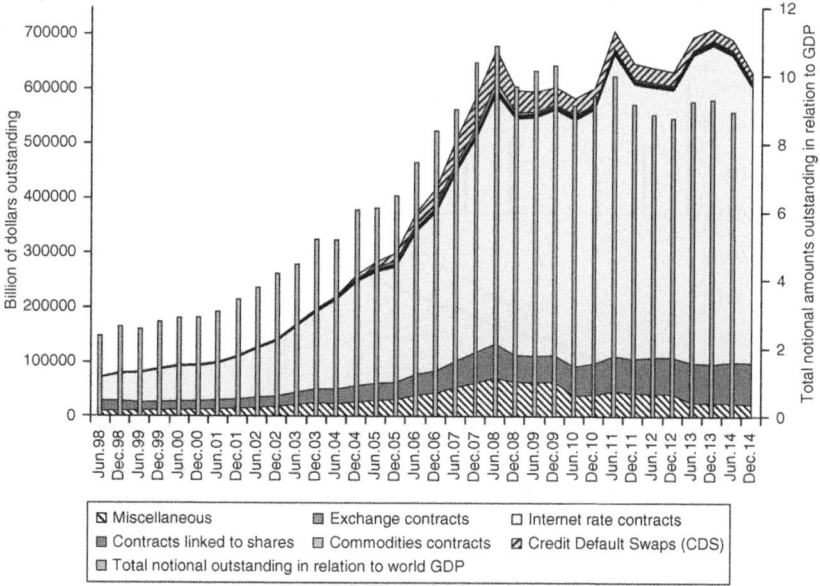

Figure 5.2 Notional amounts outstanding in OTC derivatives in billions of U.S. dollars

Note: Total notional amount outstanding in relation to GDP.

Sources: ISB, IMF and the authors.

106 A Violent World

highlight, again according to the BIS; of the 5,300 billion dollars traded every day just on the exchange market, only 7 to 8% is destined for non-financial operators who are attempting to protect themselves from the risks run by companies.

Of course, in this ocean of money, there has to be a separation between what is done at the discretion of the OTC relationship between financial institutions, that are not truly transparent, and the true purpose of the market transactions. Obviously the former are the most dangerous transactions. Remember the case of Lehman Brothers and the impossibility of calculating the products sold to counterparties throughout the world financial system. One merely has to look at the explosion of OTC products to realize the risks that the world is taking in the market.

Finally, there remains the most reasonable part – or at least the part that ought to be the most reasonable – that of the liquidity of the banking system, defined as global credit global, the most traditional way of financing national economies. It has increased rapidly, more

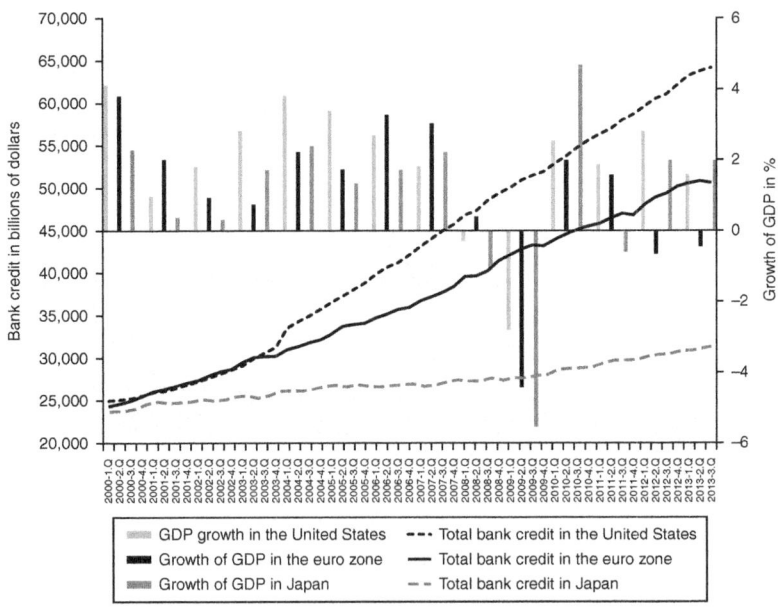

Figure 5.3 Total bank credit in the United States, the euro zone and in Japan, in billions of dollars

Sources: BIS, IMF International Financial Statistics and the authors.

so in the United States than elsewhere, being more or less correlated to growth.

Moreover, the surge in credit in recent years is evidence of the importance and distribution of credit. In the United States, credit to the inhabitants more than doubled between 2000 and 2013, rising from 17,000 billion dollars to more than 41,000 billion in 2013. Again in the United States, credit granted to the government actually tripled. Symmetrically, the Japanese stagnation translates into a meagre 15% increase in credits to inhabitants during the same period. One thus moves from a relatively understandable banking world, consisting of a network of adventurous central banks whose workings are largely transparent, to a new financial world order that is neither perfectly definable, nor transparent, nor controllable. Above all, it is one whose relationship to the real economy is more than distended.

The dismemberment of the financial system

Two key expressions have emerged and are now well-established – 'shadow banking' and 'dark trading'. They are the perfect illustration of this drift that everyone or almost everyone regrets without being able to do anything about it. The circuit introduced by shadow banking is well-known and easy to understand, even if the reality is more complex. A share of household savings passes through unit trusts, then through financial institutions that are generally unregulated and that then create structured products, which are themselves put up for sale. The characteristic of this mechanism is that cannot be subjected to rules of any kind. At the very moment when a massive regulatory arrangement is being introduced for controlling the banks and insurance so as to avoid what has been called systemic bankruptcies, these flows of savings, managed by shadow banking, are only increasing.

It is an irony of history that one hundred years ago the financial system was one of 'shadow' or 'parallel' banking. It worked, in fact, without precise regulation, without true safety nets. It was of an intrinsically unstable and risky nature and caused governments to rethink the system in its entirety and to stabilize it through prudential regulation. The second time shadow banking made its appearance was during the last 30 years, when it radically changed the structure of the financial system and, beyond that, considerably increased the systemic risk. Why did this happen? The answer is because one of the characteristics of this type of parallel banking activity is to increase the financial cycles, in the expansion phase as much as in the retraction phase. This is what happened during the banking and financial crisis of 2008. When in its expansion phase, shadow banking relies in particular on the leverage effects and what are known as asset-liability maturity imbalances. These types of risk do not generally fall within the remit of public regulation, whether by insuring deposits, equity and liquidity requirements or access to cash held in the central banks. These risks therefore weigh heavily on the traditional banking system which itself continues to provide services such as guarantees, lines of credit or the safekeeping of assets to be securitized.

Despite the risks run and the temptations for regulation, shadow banking still has a bright future, perhaps in a different form, within the traditional financial system. That is because the banks and the insurance companies need to confront the increased demand for equity and liquidity and, as always, restrictions produce workaround movements.

If one agrees with Esther Jeffers and Dominique Plihon,[2] the parallel banking system could be defined as a system of financial intermediation that contains entities that are outside the traditional banking sector but that partially fulfil similar functions. If this 'shadow banking' has developed from an OTC market, it consists of a priority around the idea of a new model of financial intermediation. The best known example is securitization based on substituting the traditional model of 'originate to hold', i.e. state the fact of granting credits and keeping them on the bank's balance sheet until the due date with a linked risk control to the borrower, through the 'originate to repackage and sell' model in which debts are not involved. If one had to describe this phenomenon, one could copy Jeffers and Plihon who have made a comparison between these two models of financial intermediation. In the traditional model, household deposits at commercial banks permitted long-term credit. The 'shadow banking' model, on the other hand, using a longer circuit, converts household savings into structured products, backed by bank debt. These products, known as Collateralized Debt Obligations (CDOs), are then transferred to non-banking entities. In this way the bank assigns a portfolio of debts, namely part of its balance sheet assets, to an *ad hoc* company, a special vehicle for investment. The securities are then divided into prioritized tranches based on their yield and the associated risk, then assessd by credit rating agencies and sold to investors to provide a vehicle for refinancing. Ultimately, it is indeed non-banking entities, and thus entities who escape the supervision of the authorities and who do not apply prudential rules who contribute to financing the economy.

What is even more surprising is that the development of shadow banking was in no way slowed down by the 2007 financial crisis. Quite

The Illusion of Definancialization 109

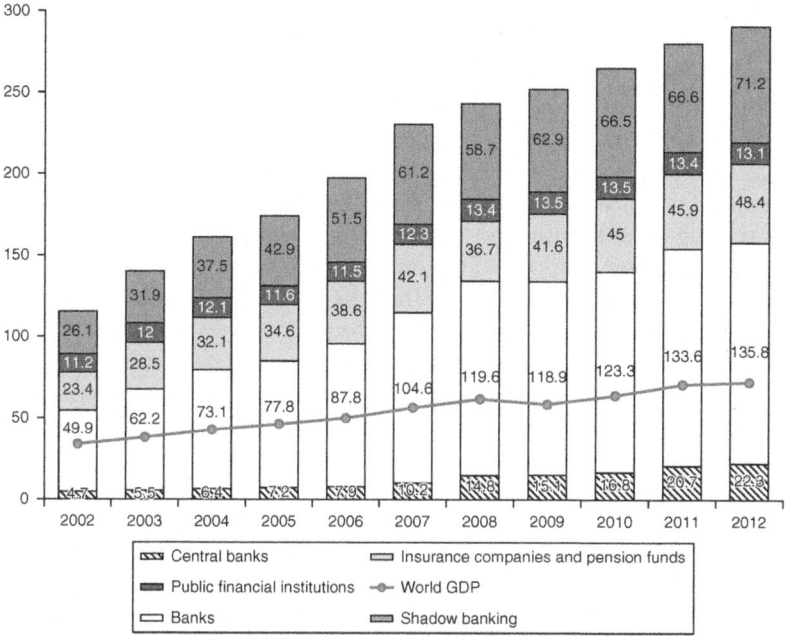

Figure 5.4 Development of shadow banking's financial assets in comparison with the financial institutions in thousands of billions of dollars

Sources: National Flow of Funds Data, BIS, IMF and the authors.

the contrary. It developed again with a 2013 total of 71,000 billion dollars,[3] representing half of the assets managed by the traditional banking sector.

Basically it is the mixture of genres that is worrying. The fruitless attempts at regulation, and especially the discourse surrounding it, have pressured the major banks into creating their own unregulated financial instruments. The risk of another imminent financial crisis that currently threatens the world is linked to this financial world which is so complex at present that regulation is not even capable of defining its frontiers. This problem seems unlikely to be resolved since this method of parallel financing is so widespread. In the United States, the weight of shadow banking is currently much greater than that of the banks, since it represented[4] nearly 165% of GDP in 2012, while the banking sector itself amounted to only 95% of GDP. In other countries – France, Germany and Japan – the weight represented 95%, 70% and 65% of

GDP respectively. As for the United Kingdom, it accounted for as much as 350% of GDP.

With respect to the 'dark pool', this is a system that was launched in the United States in the late 1990s and became legal in Europe in 2007.[5] It authorizes taking a position in the stock markets without such vital data as prices and volumes being immediately revealed. That is why it is known as 'dark trading'. This market is thus distinguished from 'lit trading', the illuminated market which has strict requirements of transparency before and after negotiation. The sums involves are on the increase, representing 'a doubling in two years of the volume of negotiations in the "dark pools" in percentage terms for all transactions'.[6] 'Dark trading' is confined to the OTC market between two parties and has very sophisticated ways of executing orders on the lit markets, which has not failed to attract new operators to it who are attracted by the absence of the restrictions present in the 'traditional' markets.

This means that the extension of finance has not slowed significantly in most recent times. Yet the opposite situation would have been welcome. That is because if one looks again at the history of the most recent financial crisis, its origin can be found in the monetary imbalances in the real economy, yet its initiation and subsequent development were rendered possible thanks to the extraordinary proliferation of financial products that are totally disconnected from the market for goods and services. These products would never have seen the light of day had it not been for the dizzying growth in liquidity that we have witnessed in recent years.

The excessive amount of uncontrolled and largely useless liquidity resulted in a real banking panic, resulting in a freezing of various financial positions, the cessation of transactions between financial institutions taken individually and, eventually, a crisis of liquidity. It was the first time in the history of financial crises, that the growth in risk premiums preceded corporate bankruptcies. It was only subsequently, in the late spring of 2008, that companies experienced the true impact on their funds before their ability to finance was affected in its turn and eventually, by systemic effect, their order books. The result is known, namely that the United States and the rest of the world were plunged into recession.

Of course, this refers to the banking crisis itself. In the absence of sufficiently rapid action, this resulted in a wider – financial – crisis that began in spring 2008. Lessons for today and tomorrow need to be learned from this succession of episodes. As Barry Eichengreen stresses,[7] there is a sort of nostalgia for the days when banks played the simple role of intermediation by lending to households and companies in a perfectly reasonable manner, and they did so against a background of perfectly transparent and adjusted balance sheets. There is a strong temptation for U.S. and European financial authorities to revert to happier times before securitization existed and to establish rigorous regulation that would take us back to the happy days of the 1960s. In reality, the problem is far more complex. Securitization belongs to a global method of financing the world economy of which it is just one element among many, and which has played a positive role, without a doubt, in financing the world economy. In fact, securitization is a product of the deregulation of the financial markets, as well as new forms of banking regulation and an environment in which there has been total dematerialization of the flows of capital on a world scale. As a result, securitizations increased by 150% in the space of ten years. The most extraordinary phenomenon was the acceleration of this movement starting in 2001. There is a reason for this sudden rise, namely, the rapid deterioration in the U.S. trade deficit which needed to be financed in one way or another. The possibility offered to the banks to remove some of the credits from their balance sheets then played a major role in this U.S. indebtedness economy. The trade deficit could never have been financed if the banks had been unable to spread the debts owed to them throughout the world. This financing, which was indeed risky but which resulted in value creation, could never have emerged unless these same banks had not had the option of breaking down and spreading the risk. In reality, these massive transfers of savings from one part of the world to another would never have been possible without this financial innovation that remains one of the positive aspects of globalization. What made it disastrous was the excessive, unrestrained and uncontrolled use thereof.

Can this be remedied? No, let us not fool ourselves, this moment in the world history of finance will not end soon, especially while the respective levels of development in the major areas of the world and the demographic developments in these same areas lead to these streams of finance being judged necessary and even desirable. The question is therefore not to challenge these mechanisms but to establish that they were used thoughtlessly. They were allowed to deviate from their true purpose, i.e. the deconsolidation of a uniform and diversified risk so as to maintain a permanently effective asset-liability management.

This systematic excess found itself an anchoring point in the securitization derivatives. In recent years, securitization, which was based on the dual logic of optimization of equity and management of assets-liabilities in the hands of the finance departments of the banks, has surreptitiously passed into the control of the trading floors with the main aim of launching high-leverage products with a hoped-for very high yield. In order to do so, a specific mechanism was created. Securitization consists of stripping the assets from an institution by assigning them in the form of securities. Financial vehicles are created to which these assets are attached. They issue certificates, view the cash flow generated by the underlying assets and repay the investors.

By describing these operations as they are implemented, it can be seen that the banks, contrary to the basic rules of smooth operation, very often intervene and do so at every level of operations, especially in the creation and financing of specific vehicles. This is what has made the tangled web so difficult to unravel.

The consequence of these excesses, these pointless risks, these design errors was not long in coming. A world without organized liquidity is a frightening one. Yet every financial crisis is founded on a lack of trust. This has affected every form of securitization, well beyond the initial impact in the summer of 2007 and the subprimes crisis. This financial crisis, triggered by property difficulties which, when all is said and done, are fairly traditional problems, is now completely out of control. The cyclical fall in property values that could have been translated into a simple slowing of U.S., British or Spanish growth, has been replaced by financial deregulation with consequences that are far from having disappeared. Successive banking 'stress tests' are performed, in an attempt to re-establish confidence that has been completely undermined. Everything has been tried in the past seven years. Monetary and financial upsets have occurred in succession with no genuine cure in sight. Regulation has been approached as the solution to every evil.

Yet the evidence is staring us in the face. The financial sector is no longer a mere auxiliary of growth. From now on it has its own development logic, and it can only be hoped that this is placed, entirely or partially, in the service of growth.

The utopia of regulation

In 2008, the world took fright, and fear is often a good counsellor. For several months, it was possible to believe in human rationality and wisdom.

Remember what happened on 2 April 2009 in London. The leaders of all the major developed countries and the emerging nations were there to 'confront the greatest challenge the world economy has faced in modern times'.[8] Among the subjects tackled, that of financial regulation was considered to be a priority. The plan was a very ambitious one. A new council, the Financial Stability Council, was set up and the decision was taken to thoroughly reform all the control systems for world finance.

Yet just a few months later, on the initiative of the United States, a new summit met, this time in Pittsburgh. It was now 24 and 25 September 2009 and once again the plan was extremely ambitious. Every subject was tackled and concrete measures taken. Broadly speaking, the world authorities devised a financial regulation programme articulated around the following measures: reinforcement of requirements for equity and bank liquidity buffers, greater solvency for financial institutions, greater transparency and resilience of the market infrastructures for OTC trades and, finally, risk-handling imposed to the parallel banking system,[9] not forgetting the new rules concerning tax havens and a bonus-malus system applied to traders.

So what was the situation five years later? After a series of pointless G20 summits that largely emphasized the ineffectiveness of such meetings, the result achieved was pretty poor. Basically, however, this is of little importance since today's world does not allow any limit to the growth of liquidity. Yet there was no lack of proposals during this period, such as those from Paul Volcker, John Vickers and Erkki Liikanen.

But the results never materialized. While 180 commitments were made at Los Cabos in 17 June 2012 of which were judged to be a priority, it was necessary to get back to reality. The regulation of OTC derivatives was only in its infancy. Most of the structural reforms were never applied. The OECD pulls no punches in the face of this finding since it claims that financial regulation only developed to 20% of what had been planned.[10]

We ought to not be too cruel in respect of the development of the banking system. Basel 3 and Solvency 2 were proposed to limit the risks of the banking and insurance systems. With Basel 3, the equity and liquidity requirements would certainly have reduced risky ventures by the banks. But the problem did not lie there. True regulation exists, without what Paul Volcker, John Vickers and Erkki Liikanen suggested, i.e. introducing a restriction on the ability of the banks to act, either on behalf of their clients or on their own behalf, as hedge funds. Numerous solutions could have been envisaged but all can be summarized as whether one permits or forbids a retail bank to transfer customers' deposits to another part of the bank which happens to be an investment or merchant bank. In fact, it should have been a case of avoiding moral hazards and systematic risk,[11] i.e. the fact that when a bank fails it endangers the very life of the whole financial system. In practice, everyone hesitated when it came to establishing a genuine separation between lending activities and investment bank activities. In the French case, a holding structure should certainly have been maintained to ensure the permanent existence of universal banks. Nevertheless, this separation is no doubt one of the most important measures to be discussed and, using different procedures, to be taken if one wants to accord to it the priority it deserves in relation to the banks, in the general interest.

In Pittsburgh, the aim was to regulate world liquidity, change the behaviour of the banking system and create regulated markets where none existed, as well as limiting speculation by the financial stakeholders. In fact, today that is impossible because only a restriction on the growth of world liquidity would permit it. This is not on the agenda, however, and this would appear to be the case for a long time to come. We shall be experiencing, as we did in the past, an increase in liquidity in all its forms which is very much greater than the world economy. Part of the financial system will remain opaque. One will just have to live with the consequences and attempt to limit them, especially growth. That is because this incomplete regulation possesses instruments, which may be limited but are nonetheless weighty. Basel 3 is not without its effects on economic activity. Some claim, unlike the bankers, that this arrangement will not involve an increase in the cost of credit but it will no doubt increase taxation on the banks, dividends will be taxed though not debt interest. Unfortunately, for these same supporters of reform, this is also likely to deter the banks from transferring an important share of their activities to the financial markets which are considered to be more profitable or to the so-called parallel system that is more flexible in terms of equity. This is how the long-term impact of Basel 3 should be judged, according to the IMF,[12] which is quite modest in terms of an increase in the interest rates on bank loans in the United States, Europe and Japan. If the costs of running banks turns out to be higher after the reform, the lenders will probably adapt to the situation without this adversely affecting the general interest.

Other studies of the issue are much more worrying. That is the case with the very alarmist opinions issued by the Institute of International Finance,[13] a powerful representation of the banking profession on an international scale. The Institute has announced that reform resulted in a true explosion of the cost of credit due to the increase in the cost of equity. This ought to amount to slightly more than 2% in the United States and in the euro zone between 2011 and 2015, 6% in Japan and 10% in the United Kingdom.

If regulation is not going to be trained into a formal garden, it is an absolute requirement that it be adapted to the new rules to ensure that their ability to ensure security does not have the effect of restricting growth.

To summarize, there remain very important loopholes in terms of risk management. So much so that regulation appears to be a sort of derivative with the aim of explicitly acting in a way that implies no overturning of the present balance of power and, especially, the omnipotence of the financial system.

The impossible debt equation

David Graeber[14] poses this question which has no known answer: 'Will man be eternally in debt?' in relation to God, to nature, to other human beings? According to him, the Bible says nothing different – Jubilee, the final redemption or release from debt, or the cancellation of debt every seven years, the law that dates back to Moses. *Merci* in French is a request for mercy, *Obrigado* in Portuguese or *Much obliged* in English say that someone is an 'obligee' of someone – the recognition that he has contracted a debt.

History shows that debt, in other words, culpability, is a weighty argument for the acceptance of asymmetrical relations between debtors and creditors, between the weak and the powerful. In time of war, a life spared is a contractual debt for life to be reimbursed according to the good will of the victor. And it is debt, credits, that are the origin of so many revolts and conflicts between populations.

This enduring truth is a reminder that the moral ground has overtaken that of the economy. Any other vision would make it impossible to find a solution to the debt problem. The first temptation is always the same, that of an external solution, in the present case that of inflation, to decide between the respective interests of the creditor and the debtor. When one really wants to legitimize inflation, one speaks of the euthanasia of the pensioner. This will immediately turn public opinion in favour of the unfortunate debtor. Unhappily and happily, inflation is not and will not be a concern in the short term.

We therefore need to find a reading today that is suited to the sociological reality of the countries in which we live. The first rule for understanding the extent to which the problem as posed has no solution is to deal with debt as a whole, by consolidating its two forms, private and public. Why should this be done? Take a simple example, that of a young student. Whether he is studying at a leading university, public or private, the debt is a public or private one for the collective. Eventually, everyone thus finds themselves to be a debtor and a creditor, through the private regulation of their own constraints or through the taxes they are required to pay. If one were finally to decide to look at debt as a whole, one can only be horrified by the reality of the future and insurmountable difficulties.

Many people believe that the essential difficulty lies in the public debt. In fact, private debt is just as important to the extent that it is impossible, except in generational terms, to separate individuals when it comes to debt repayment. The figures are very eloquent. In 2013, private debt from non-financial entities amounted to between 130 and 170% of GDP in the developed countries.

As for public debt, the figures are known today: nearly 100% of GDP in the euro zone, the United States and the United Kingdom, and nearly 230% of GDP for Japan. If one adds to this the amounts of public debt and those of private debt of non-financial entities, the difficulty becomes insurmountable.

This finding is all the more disturbing when one realizes that the demographic characteristics of the world are not going to improve the situation. Age-related expenditure between 2013 and 2040 will reach an amount that will be decisive for future growth. The estimates vary, but not the orders of magnitude. Age-related expenditure in terms of retirement and health for the period 2013–2040, will represent about 9% of GDP in the United States, 6% in the United Kingdom, 2.5% in France and Germany and 1.5% in Japan.[15]

What growth or inflation would simply make it possible to stabilize this overall debt? In order to do so, let us consider the overall debt of countries such as France, Germany, the United Kingdom, Japan and the United States, weighted according to their respective GDP. Three possible scenarios emerge. The first and most plausible is based on GDP growth amounting to 2–2.5% for the period 2015–2030, accompanied by inflation in the same order of magnitude. In this case, it could be expected that that overall debt will continue to grow at a similar rate to that during the early 2000s. The second scenario, in which growth will reach 4 to 5% a year, again within the context of 2–2.5% inflation, would make it possible to stabilize the level of debt. Finally, the third scenario would be a debt reduction. This would require the Western world, including Japan, to achieve a growth rate of more than 5% annually, and to do so in an environment of high inflation and the introduction of very judicious reforms. That is quite simply unachievable, an impossibility.

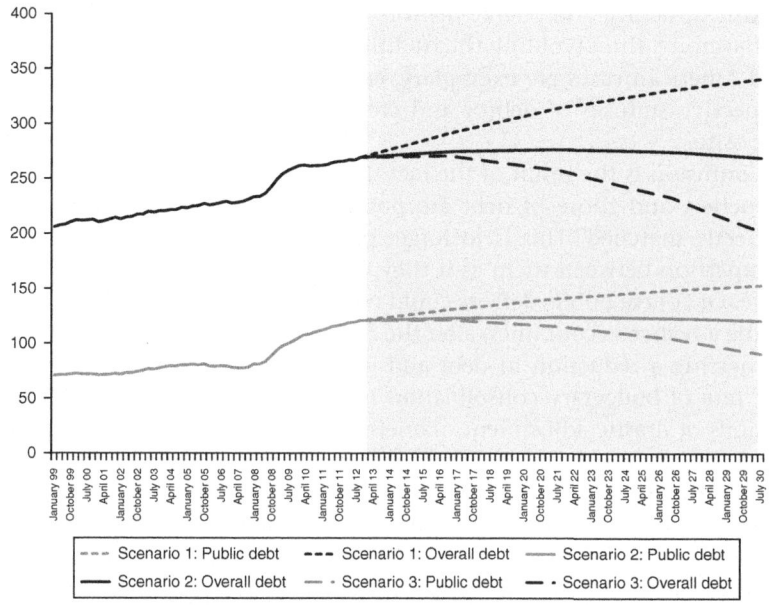

Figure 5.5 Projection for 2015–2030 of private debt from non-financial entities[a] and overall debt[b] as a percentage of GDP

Notes: [a]Weighted average in relations to the GDP of France, Germany, the United Kingdom, Japan and the United States.
[b]Sum of public and private debt owed by non-financial entities.
Sources: IMF, OECD, Eurostat, FED and the authors.

David Graeber's book is enlightening on an aspect that is often underestimated. Debt is the consequence of a social and political balance and the scale of the repayments assumes a very profound transformation of the existing equilibrium. Today, private and public indebtedness is the very mark of the existence of societies that have a middle class, especially those in the developed countries. So much so that it could be claimed that there is continual harping on the subject of debt repayment, despite awareness that no one could reasonably believe that this could be the subject of a sudden and unlikely mechanical solution.

The challenge is to make proposals, other than creating inflation, that would allow governments to claim that the problems could be resolved, thus making it possible to perpetuate the solution to indebtedness by reducing it slightly, something that would favour world growth. Doubtless the politicians would be able to find an equilibrium in this difficulty and enable debtors and creditors to continue to live in harmony, thus avoiding the traditional outcome – war. The Chinese and American cases are exemplary, each avoiding a challenge to their respective statuses of debtor and creditor, while publicly stating the opposite.

Confusion is the result of the fact that the problems of public deficit reduction and those of debt are put simultaneously, as if they were perfectly matched. This is to forget private debt, as well as making a comparison between them as if they were of the same order of magnitude. Of course public deficits could be and should be reduced. In most of the advanced economies, after the record deficits of 2009, we are now witnessing a reduction in debt and it can be stated without risk that the rate of budgetary consolidation is comparable to that of previous periods of drastic adjustment, namely a reduction of 2 to 12 points by late 2013 in comparison with the peak in 2009.[16] Nevertheless, it is clear that this is still insufficient to reduce the debt significantly. At this rate, it would take another thirty years to reduce public debt to 30 or 40% of GDP. In practice, it is a matter of limiting the role of the state in its multiple interventions. In this sense, it is a matter of changing society so as to achieve a public – private rebalancing.

Even if the public deficit could be reduced, the subject of debt remains. It would appear that its reduction is beyond our capabilities. As proof, France took 30 years to reduce its public debt by about 25% between 1950 and 1980 and this was in the very favourable context of strong growth of the Thirty Glorious Years and very high inflation.

According to the forecast released by the OECD,[17] public debt is likely to be very considerable by 2030, at 116% of GDP for the United States, 264% of GDP for Japan, 97% of GDP for the euro zone and 116% of GDP for the OECD as whole. That's way off the mark.

As for private debt, this is an inheritance from the pre-crisis financial expansion. It is thus that numerous advanced economies have accrued an unprecedented amount of private debt through incorrect allocation of their resources. The countries in question, especially those in the euro zone, have also seen their ratio of private debt over GDP increase due to the net slowing of economic activity. If one accepts the words of Mathias Drehmann and Mikael Juselius,[18] who have taken as an indicator the ratio of private debt servicing,[19] the deviation of private debt in relation to its average for the period 1995–2007 can be seen to be a useful tool for predicting the strength of a recession. Why do they make this claim? It is because they have established a correlation between this ratio in the periods preceding a recession or a financial crisis, and the volume of losses in production following these periods. Thus, it is surprising to note that in late 2012 the situation in Sweden was far from the image that this country generally conveys, with a ratio of 6 points above average in the long term. That is also the case for countries on the edge of the euro zone, with an 8 point ratio for Greece and Portugal. On the other hand – and this is another surprise, – it is about 3 points lower for Japan and close to its historic average for the United States, signifying a lower risk of recession. All these assessments could be disputed but they highlight the extent to which the impact of debt, both public and private, is difficult to assess.

Societies always end up finding solutions to impossible equations, which is not the least of their attributes. Debt, from which there seems to be no way out, is just one of them. As always, the solution needs to be original and will more or less resemble perpetual debt. So is it necessary to find out again how to dress it up and imagine the conditions for its implementation? It is this latter point that will take time. We have not yet emerged from lamentations over the debt problem.

Finance versus the real economy

Nothing will stop the growth of liquidity. And basically, no one wants that to happen. What is extraordinary is that the financial industry has its own independent existence, with its own logic, its own growth, and its own life. One could imagine that supervised and controlled financial products would reduce to a trickle, and especially the derivatives. Yet in 2014, exactly the opposite happened. As has been shown, if one takes the development of OTC derivatives between 2008 and 2013, it can be seen that their notional amounts outstanding have continued to increase and have done so on a massive scale. Even the virtuous European Central Bank, which defends the safety of its balance sheet, more than doubled the amount between January 2008 and July 2012. Without such doubling Europe would be experiencing virtual stagnation. Even better, if one restricts oneself to the banks, Dietmar Peetz and Heribert Genreith[20] show to what extent banking assets are increasing much faster than GDP. All this seems to be in the order of the way things develop and nothing is ready for change.

The idea has gradually been imposed that the financial sphere has found its own autonomy, its own valuation and its own capacity to develop. Everything opposes the real economy because its main concern is the short term as opposed to a quest for long-term investments. It is also fond of significant profitability, while the real economy prefers to stabilize rather than increase its results.

Thomas Philippon[21] provides a simple illustration of this phenomenon. The financial industry originally acquired its autonomy on the basis of remuneration. Shown itself to be highly inefficient in information and communication technology, unlike other sectors, that is merely because its priority is deducting the money to finance rewards to the financiers and thus restricting investment in the sector. In fact, thanks to new technology, everything ought to have resulted in a reduction in the cost of transactions. Yet this has not happened.

In addition, whatever happens, investment in finance, within the strict meaning of the term, remains more favourable than the activities of the real economy. Of course, it is very complicated to compare the respective profitability of these investments. We have merely provided elements of response all of which point to the same thing, namely the reinforcement of the incentive to invest in financial products in future years. This is important data since it will affect the very trajectory of the world's future.

Let us begin by investigating the profitability of physical capital in the developed countries in order to get an idea of investment in the real economy.

On average, the profitability of physical capital, i.e. the ratio of company profits after tax but before interest and before dividend distribution, in comparison with net capital is generally stable depending on the region under consideration. In the euro zone, for example, the profitability of physical capital is about 10%; in the United States and the United Kingdom, around 15%. In France, on the other hand, the profitability of physical capital fell to 6.60% in 2013, something that will be no surprise to anyone.

To understand the scale of investment in finance, the investment that makes for the profitability of all of the financial instruments, including derivatives, it is possible to calculate hedge fund performance. In order

Table 5.1 Profitability of physical capital as percentages (after-tax profits, before interest and dividends/net capital in value)

Annual average	Euro zone	United States	United Kingdom	France
1991–2000	9.96	12.60	15.35	9.82
2001–2010	10.73	14.21	14.55	8.91
2012	9.70	15.40	14.45	7.08
2013	9.26	15.40	14.26	6.60

Sources: Datastream, national sources, Natixis and the authors.

The Illusion of Definancialization 121

to do so, certain very specific strategies need to be chosen. These are the global macro strategy, i.e. the strategy linked to anticipation of macroeconomic performance; mergers & acquisitions strategy; event strategy linked to pricing anomalies resulting from corporate bankruptcies; the quantitative directional strategy that uses quantitative techniques and, finally, the emerging market strategy that examines the emerging nations. The historic performances of the various strategies, chosen arbitrarily, reveal them to be very successful.

Why was this specific part of the financial industry chosen? Simply because what is true for the hedge funds is also true for all alternative management. As for more traditional management, it is stimulated because it benefits, in relation to its financing equivalent in the real economy, from very strong liquidity. To illustrate this, let us take the historical performances of certain stock exchange indices such as, for example, the MSCI World Index, the S&P500, DJ Stoxx 600, CAC 40, DAX, Nikkei and the MSCI emerging.

Table 5.2 Annual performance of a few hedge fund strategies as percentages

Annual average	Strategy – HFR Index				
	Global macro	Mergers – acquisitions	Distressed/ Restructuring	Quantitative directional	Emerging markets
1991–2000	21.0	13.5	17.1	24.0	21.4
2001–2010	7.6	6.2	10.2	6.2	13.1
2012	−2.9	1.6	−0.4	−3.0	−8.6
2013	0.5	1.9	9.6	4.5	5.4

Sources: Bloomberg, Hedge Fund Research and the authors.

Table 5.3 Annual performance of certain stock exchange indices as percentages

Annual average	MSCI World Index	S&P 500	DJ Stoxx 600	CAC 40	DAX	Nikkei	MSCI emerging nations
1991–2000	12.1	15.8	16.2	16.1	18.2	−3.7	41.7
2001–2005	1.8	0.4	−0.6	−1.8	1.6	6.0	16.6
2006–2010	2.7	3.0	1.7	−1.0	8.8	−6.1	15.8
2012	13.2	13.4	14.4	15.2	29.1	22.9	13.9
2013	22.9	29.6	17.4	18.0	25.5	56.7	0.9

Sources: Bloomberg and the authors.

Another way of comparing finance with the real economy could consist in creating a parallel between the profitability of retail banking with that of the investment or merchant banks. In fact, the prime objective of a retail bank is to make loans, especially by granting commercial loans. The rate at which these are granted is a good indicator of the profitability of the projects in which these companies are engaged, and thus a good indicator for assessing the real economy. Conversely, the profitability of the activity of the merchant banks is a good indicator of investment in finance.

According to the above table, the profitability of retail bank equity is about 13.5% in France and in the United Kingdom. In Germany, it is half that figure, with profitability at around 6.60%.

Consequently, we can compare this profitability with the profitability of equity in the market trading of the world's major merchant banks in 2010. Depending on the sector, profitability oscillates between 15 and 35%, clearly much greater than for the retail banks. In total, equity profitability from market trading can be estimated at around 20%.

Table 5.4 Estimates of the profitability of retail banking equity in 2010

	Profitability of retail bank equity
France	13.50%
United Kingdom	13.60%
Germany	6.60%

Sources: McKinsey, Day of Reckoning for European Retail Banking (2012) and the authors.

Table 5.5 Profitability of equity from market trading for the world's 13 largest merchant banks in 2010

	Profitability of equity
Currency trading	30%
Rates	19%
Structured rates	15%
Credit	18%
Structured credit	17%
Commodities	20%
Shares	25%
Derivative shares	25%
Trading on own account	35%
Total market trading	20%

Sources: McKinsey, Global Corporate and Investment Banking: An Agenda for Change (2011) and the authors.

In conclusion, this means that there is no significant difference between the overall profitability of the financial sector in comparison with that of the real economy, with the exception of certain financial sectors, and many market trading sectors. It can thus be legitimately considered that market trading will continue to attract massive amounts of capital, whether or not it is regulated, and will reach the heart of the finance industry. What distinguishes the two spheres – finance and the real economy – above all is the huge amount of liquidity available to the former. In fact, the old distinction between investment and speculation, which the economist Nicholas Kaldor[22] described in the 1930s, can be made here. The latter is driven by an expectation of a change in the price of goods purchased or sold for the purpose of their resale or repurchase at a subsequent date rather than from any value added expected from the use thereof.

It should be remembered that Keynes, on the basis of this definition, made the efficiency of the markets dependent on the prices that he considered reflected the value of an asset, through the perspective of investment in the real economy by those involved in the market. In the opposite case, when markets are dominated by speculation, they become their own yardstick and are disconnected from reality. The beauty contest example adopted by Keynes has become famous. To pick the winner of a beauty contest, it is not a matter of choosing from the competitors the faces that those judging the contest consider to be the most handsome but those that they believe will be considered most handsome by the largest number of voters. This is where their shrewdness lies in 'anticipating what average opinion expects the average opinion to be'.[23]

There is one example that could be considered telling, that of agricultural raw materials. For the past six to seven years, there has been surprise concerning the increase in the price of these raw materials which has largely exceeded the growth in demand. There is a suspicion of the imprint of speculation, although this is partly untrue. The main reason lies elsewhere. In the case of these raw materials, contrary to most financial assets, it is the protection instruments that fix the prices.

Agricultural markets are the oldest in the world. Futures contracts have been used in these markets for a very long time in order to protect producers and consumers from all the associated risks. The mechanism for determining the prices on these markets depends on the presence, in smaller or greater numbers, of speculators. These have become dominant, however, their projections no longer being based on the fundamentals of supply and demand, but on the potential attitude of their competitors. The initial mechanism has therefore been distorted. According to Michael W. Masters,[24] the proportion of speculators on the raw materials market increased from 23% in 1998 to 69% in 2008, while the number of agents determined to provide themselves with physical coverage reduced from 77% to 31%. This is yet again another example of disconnection from reality.

The term 'autonomy' best summarizes the position of finance in the world economy. The aim of the financial system in future years will be to develop new financial products, judging to the millisecond where all the gaps lie between the valuations of the same product. To summarize, to be a sector of activity that survives and feeds on its own fuel. No regulation in the world can overcome this implacable logic. All that can be wished is that part of the capacities of this sector might be mobilized to support the real economy in the long term.

The inevitable development of the financial industry for its own benefit can only be controlled in that part of its activities that are totally transparent. The true constraint lies elsewhere, however. Financing the economy assumes that there are abundant savings, long-term investments, an appetite for risk-taking, and financing products dedicated to a productive system. That is a wager that is heavy with consequences since it would involve moving the masses of finance from a world of certainty, one that is profitable since it is largely speculative, and into long-term, risky activities, since they will be connected with real growth and the profitability of which is uncertain. To some extent, this is where politics could once again play a part.

Long-term investment requires renewed financial intermediation that will give priority to long-term investors, whether in the case of sovereign wealth funds, pension funds or insurers. It is these that will now hold the future of the world in their hands. In order to do so, they will have to position themselves as prudent, patient shareholders with a presence in the governance of regulated companies. That is the only way to build a new financial architecture, one that favours long-term investment and can imagine sharing risk between the individual and the collective. This would mean that nothing will happen as it did before. We shall therefore not concentrate exclusively on financial regulation, the limitations of which have been demonstrated. Let us see rather how this finance could be converted into a major player in world growth. All that is required is that no major conflict should break out between the warlords who are the advocates of finance and the rest of the world.

6
Savings, the Ultimate Rare Resource

We have now reached the heart of this book. Having discussed, successively, the serious breakdown of technical progress, the upsets due to ageing, the loss of economic substance in the countries of the OECD, and uncontrolled finance, these themes converge into what creates the balance of the world, the savings accrued by people on every continent and the investments that are the translation of their dreams. Are these savings enough to enable their ambitions to be achieved? We think not, at least not in the way that the balance between investment and savings has materialized in recent decades. Naturally, a new balance will emerge, the expression of the way in which these new constraints will be satisfied. The world will have changed, as will its economic trajectory.

How paradoxical! The world of 2015 seems to be flooded with liquidity, destined to welcome abundant savings and experience extremely low interest rates, rates caused by the monetary policies of the central banks, purveyors of inexhaustible liquidity. Yet we need to show that this situation is unlikely to last. As early as 2009, the issue of insufficient savings on a world scale was raised by Patrick Artus, thus reinforcing our position. A few years later, he went even further by questioning whether savings were being put to the best use. That is indeed what we are arguing.[1]

Not only will investment and savings balance out at different levels to those we know today but the 'key expression' will be *useful savings*, savings available for investment purposes, i.e. for risk-taking. It is in this respect that useful savings risks becoming a rare resource.

The future relationship between savings and investment will be proof of this. Lendable funds need to be provided with a balanced rate of interest on the savings and investment market. Behind the apparent ease there lies a knottier problem, one that is more delicate and more fundamental to the political economy. This balance, that is so impossible for some to find but obvious to others, has resulted in a massive intellectual battle between economists that has raged for two centuries.

The battle rages between the Keynesians and the Neoclassicists. The equality between the two terms Investment vs Savings represents the results of a whole process that assumes that the economic stakeholders will all decide to save and invest. By doing so, they determine new levels of activity in the economy. Yet each agrees to state today that savings and investment are the products of separate developments, linked to its own taxation, the age of those involved and the macroeconomic prospects. The eventual balance depends largely on the overall state of the world economy. The balance represents the strongest constraint with which all economies are confronted and this will continue to be the case in any new configuration.

This means that the coming balance will be a complete break with what happened in previous decades. We shall therefore move from abundant savings to rarer savings, from limited investment to a massive need for investment. The world's macroeconomic trajectory has always been determined by the process that allows these two quantities, the amount of investment and the amount of savings, to come together ex-post, in which the level of balance is decisive for knowing whether or not the world can continue to grow significantly.

Nothing is set in stone. That which determines savings will be radically changed for geostrategic reasons linked to the future forms of globalization and the reasons for changes in the money markets. Here again politics could play a part in encouraging ageing societies not only to save but also to invest. This might be their major role in future years.

The enigma of the balance between savings and investment

Nothing has been discussed at greater length by economists than the balance between savings and investment. This has been the subject *par excellence* of political economics.

A few reminders. For many people savings are synonymous with the virtues of a provident and prudent householder, the bourgeois, whose features have so often been sketched by men of letters. Yet it is but a small step between savings and the accumulation of capital. The bourgeois then becomes a businessman who reinvests his savings in the endless cycle of the accumulation of capital. Investment or, if you prefer, the formation of fixed capital, is made by companies or households in durable goods destined for use in production or domestic activity. The scene is set, the terms defined.

The issue becomes a more sensitive one if one asks questions about what determines savings and investment. The question could then be legitimately asked as to the possibility of an excess or insufficiency of savings and thus of under-consumption or over-consumption. The first theoretical consideration on the subject was provided by Adam Smith. He claimed that all savings released are spent of necessity on job creation, thus stimulating consumption, and on investments, thus on the consumption of consumer durables. Smith brought in his wake the essence of the Classical school. It is a virtuous vision of capitalism *à la* Weber. He basically opened the door to Say's law, in which 'supply creates its own demand'. Saving thus strictly equals investment. There is an identity between the two orders of magnitude, but it is indeed savings that create the initial movement or, to be more precise, it is profits that are entirely reinvested that create the virtuous mechanism. So where are pensioners in this model?

As can be imagined, Smith's model was violently criticized, first and foremost by Marx, who said 'Nothing can be more childish than the dogma, that because every sale is a purchase, and every purchase a sale, therefore the circulation of commodities necessarily implies an equilibrium of sales and purchases'. That would be to forget the over-accumulation of capital that contains within it the seed of future crises. Excess of savings due to a serious inequality between distribution and under-consumption that it presumes is central to the vision of a capitalism that is perfectly unstable and destined to experience repeated crises until its collapse.

In reality, the essential question to be asked is whether savings guide investment or whether the reverse is true. Keynes returns to the notion that savings and investments are identical (a notion that was originally postulated by Jean-Baptiste Say) by operating a conceptual inversion that this was mentioned some time ago. All of this is well known, but deserves to be recalled.

The curves of supply and demand differ profoundly. If this were not the case, insists Keynes, no obstacle would exist to full employment! As far as he is concerned, investment depends heavily on the interest rate, while this is not the case with savings. Currently, we are all Keynesians in one way or another, not through the simplified and thus truncated vision that is often attributed to Keynesian economics, but through his brilliant introduction to the analysis of uncertainty and thus of anticipation. It is a very difficult thought to grasp and one which requires expansion.

As far as we are concerned here, one of the economists who analysed the impact of anticipations is fundamental. Gunnar Myrdal analyses the effect of anticipation in the balance between investment and savings which one calls the 'I-S balance'. He then introduces the *ex-ante* concepts to define the magnitudes projected by agents before they are achieved and *ex-post* for those that have been achieved. It is this Keynesian imbalance, and a natural one, between the *ex-ante* which lies at the origin of economic fluctuations, inflation and unemployment. Obviously, the balance is achieved *ex-post* without this necessarily resulting in full employment.

For the Neoclassicists, the worthy heirs to the Classical school, it is the rate of interest that makes it possible to adjust the two *ex-post* levels of equality between savings and investment. As far as they are concerned savings naturally guide investment. For the Keynesians, the relationship is the opposite, it is investment that determines and generates future savings.

Keynesian thought would impose itself with the success we now know during the French post-war period of great prosperity, characterized by a growth in productivity, in real wages and in investment. Wariness of savings, redistribution of wealth through the welfare state, low rates of interest, public investment, acceptance of inflation – these were the ingredients for success.

From the 1980s, the international financial market as we know it today changed the situation. Henceforth, a disconnection became possible between national savings and national investment. It was the country that led the financial free market, the United States, in which this disconnection was strongest. The U.S. posed the I-S balance in very new terms. It continued to accumulate capital via dynamic investment but – and this was a surprise in view of its scope – it was saving less and less and became indebted to countries with large amounts of available savings, the emerging nations. World savings took refuge in the United States. It is superabundant, confronted with a weaker desire to invest at the very same time that explosive world liquidity fixing long-term interest rates.

Economists expanded their methods and approaches as the free market approach became more widespread. Since then, a consensus has existed to consider that the opening of frontiers has been accompanied with greater disconnection between the flows of savings and investment.

After more than two centuries of questioning, the issue of imbalance between savings and investments remains open for all economists. The veil was partially lifted on the I-S balance by stressing the key role of anticipation, and thus *ex-ante* figures, while the multiplicity of numerous determinants emerged in its full scope.

Ultimately, it can merely be said that if there is an imbalance between savings and investment, it exists *ex-ante* and eventually translates into changes in the interest rates. Consequently, the movements of these rates are series, deep, stable and reveal the fact that savings adjust themselves to investment or the opposite, which we consider to be the key mechanism for adjustment of the world economy. After long decades of an over-abundance of savings, we are entering a new era of world economic history in which savings run after investment that has become the engine.

Three decades of an over-abundance of savings

The figures are surprising. They show a trend in world savings that have remained extremely abundant but that are now confronted for the first time with a rate of investment that appears to have reduced relatively in comparison with what it once was. These changes could only have occurred due to two, mutually reinforcing, movements. On the one hand, consumption in the emerging nations was low. Savings were reinforced by the need to compensate for near non-existent social protection that was incapable of meeting the needs connected with ageing. On the other hand, the developed countries significantly slowed their efforts in improving their production tools. Since the 2000s, the very positive balance in the current account of the emerging nations is observable, as is the negative balance in the developed countries. This translates into low consumption in the emerging countries and high consumption in the developed countries.

This is a very special historic moment, one in which savings are in excess while investment is fairly low. Of course, new factories had to be built in the emerging nations but one does not balance out the other. The most significant part of the graphic is the heavy flow of available savings represented by surplus balances in the current accounts of the emerging nations. Yet, equally, one cannot but be impressed by the impact of uncertainties linked to ageing that translate into quite surprising developments in available savings. In fact, it was from the 1990s onwards that a real divergence could be witnessed between the rates of savings in the developed countries and those of the emerging nations. While the rates were identical in both regions in 1999, with a rate of savings at about 23% of GDP, the situation was very different fifteen years later. In the emerging nations, it culminated at more than 33% of GDP. In the

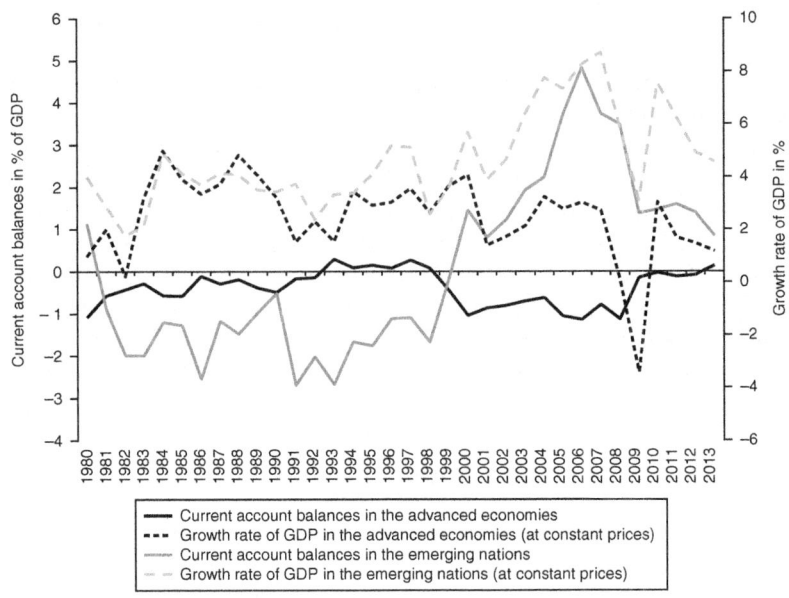

Figure 6.1 Current account balances as a percentage of GDP
Sources: IMF and the authors.

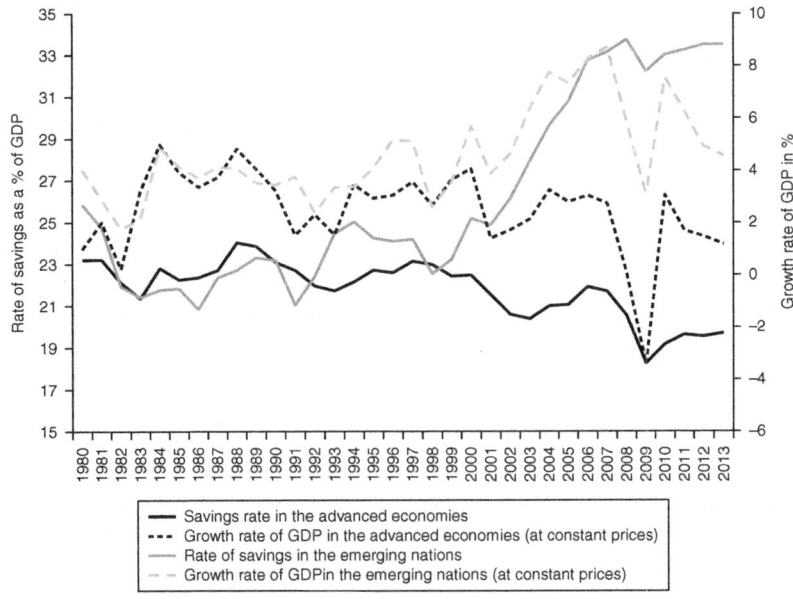

Figure 6.2 Rate of savings as a percentage of GDP
Sources: IMF and the authors.

developed countries, it dropped slightly to 20% of GDP. It pointed to the feeling that people had of being protected or the desire to be protected of the risks linked to old age.

So what has happened to all these available savings? Has a way to invest them been found? It is here that, in practice, the imbalance emerges, investments in emerging nations not having compensated, thus far, for investments in the developed world. In a remarkable report, McKinsey[2] performed the calculation. It assessed the investment deficit at 20,000 billion dollars for the past 30 years. If an analysis is made of the development of the rates of investment during recent years, a similar phenomenon can be observed as that of the rate of savings, but this asymmetry of behaviour between the two groups of countries can only be partially explained by offshoring.

By the late 1990s, the rate of investment was in the order of 23% of GDP in the developed countries as well as in the emerging nations. Since then, there has been a divergence. The rate of investment by the emerging nations reached 33% of GDP in 2015, that of the developed nations 20%.

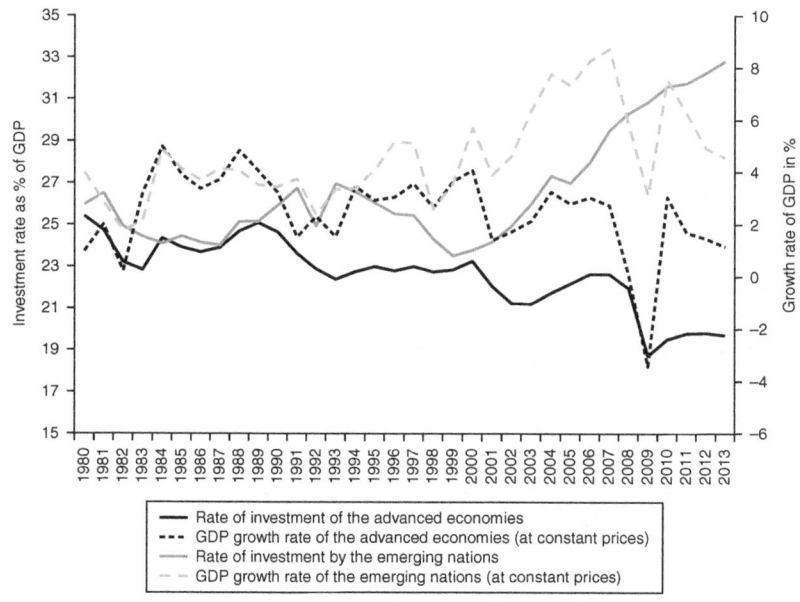

Figure 6.3 Investment levels as a percentage of GDP
Sources: IMF and the authors.

132 A Violent World

These savings clearly exceed investment needs. That which upsets this balance is, clearly, interest rates. One therefore naturally notes a reduction in interest rates after the 1980s. Take the interest rates and 10-year swap rates for France, Germany, the United Kingdom, Japan and the United States since the 1960s. Within these two rates, it is necessary to perceive the financing of the two major issuing categories on the bond market, the various states and their agencies on the one hand and private issuers in various industries on the other. In both cases, it can be seen, despite the various crises, the trend in corporate and sovereign debt is continually downwards in those rates that constitute the basis of finance. While they increased by 6% to more than 16% in the space of only ten years, a continuous decline has been observed since the start of the 1980s. In 2013, they reached very low levels, in the order of 2–3%. Obviously, the rates chosen for our analysis are for the long term, the short-term rates being largely determined by considerations of political economy.

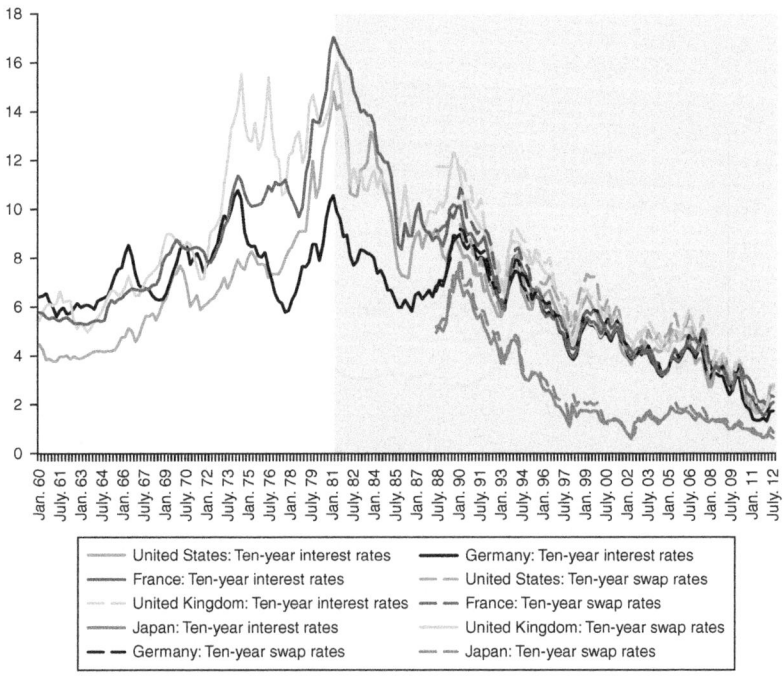

Figure 6.4 Interest rates and ten-year swap rates as percentages
Sources: Bloomberg and the authors.

The numerous interpretations of this phenomenon have been surprising, remote from reality and lacking in credibility. The most traditional of these, proposed by Loukas Karabarbounis and Brent Neiman,[3] claims it is due to the change in the ratio between wages and profits. This is mere tautology, however, in which the underlying theories, especially those concerning the profitability of future investments, are heavy-handed. The 'savings glut' hypothesis, the idea developed by Ben Bernanke[4] is of greater interest. It explains this extraordinary deficit in the U.S. trade balance by basing it on an excess of savings in other countries. The theory is nevertheless disputed by many other economists, including David Laibson and Johanna Mollerstrom.[5] But these interpretations are ancient history. Today, no one is interested in this theory of the United States as victim of the frugality of the rest of the world. What most people are interested in is the future.

The world is changing, savings are decreasing

The reality of coming decades has two themes. The middle classes in the emerging nations, anxious to maintain their way of life, and ageing. These two cumulative phenomena, even if very different in their logic, appear to be likely to result in a weakening of the level of savings and difficulty in financing the necessary investments. As we know, ageing is a synonym for risk aversion.

The BRICS countries – Brazil, Russia, India, China and South Africa – have experienced rapid development in their social welfare systems, though these vary depending on the country. There is nothing exceptional in this development. By the sheer number of individuals that these countries represent, however, the sums committed are very considerable. China managed to increase its health insurance coverage rate from 24% to 94% of the population between 2005 and 2010, representing an addition of nearly 16 million people every month covered for the period.[6] The law of 28 October 2010 organized a complete social security system covering five aspects – sickness, old age, unemployment, maternity and work accidents. South Africa more than doubled its expenditure on social welfare, excluding health, between 2000 and 2005. In Brazil, the Bolsa Familia programme had made a serious dent in the levels of poverty. In response to these social needs, the development of social welfare in the BRICS countries, and in particular in China, has also been a way of rebalancing a growth model that was based mainly on exports.

These systems should make it possible to reduce the precautionary savings that have been created in these countries. According to a recent investigation[7], 'illness and care for ageing parents are among the primary reasons for savings in Chinese households and an improvement in the healthcare and retirement system would increase consumption by between 1.6% and 6.3%'.

Public social expenditure during the course of the last decade represented between 5 and 8% of GDP for India, China, South Korea and South Africa. For Russia and Brazil, expenditure represented around 16% of GDP.[8] The comparable rate of public expenditure on welfare amounted to more than 19% of GDP in the OECD countries. This acceleration in the setting up of social welfare programmes and in the organization of healthcare and retirement systems allows it to be believed that the rate of savings of the emerging nations will gradually reduce and converge towards rates similar to those in the developed countries. It could therefore be suggested that the record level of savings in China, which amounted to 51.2% of GDP in 2012, will gradually follow the pattern of similar countries such as Japan or South Korea.

The calculation could be made on the basis of two theories. One is the introduction of a more significant welfare system in the emerging nations and the other is the demographic phenomenon of ageing. The impact of social welfare first needs to be assessed. Based on the 2.7 billion individuals, mainly living in India and China, who will constitute the middle classes in Asia in 2030[9], it could be assumed that by this time the rates of saving in these countries – China, India, Brazil, Indonesia, South Africa and Russia, – will generally align themselves on the current rate of interest of Japan, which was 21.6% in 2012. In this case, world savings will decrease from 24.6% of GDP in 2012 to 22.4% in 2030, a reduction of about 2.2% of world GDP.[10] In particular, it is the alignment of the rate of savings in China over the Japanese rate that will have the greatest impact on a reduction in savings on a world level because this will contribute to reducing savings by about 1.9%.[11] These figures are obviously debatable as to their accuracy, but they appear to be more or less correct.

An attempt must then be made to measure the impact of demographic ageing. In the case of a country such as France,[12] the impact on retirement will amount to 0.5% of GDP by 2030, and to 1.7% of GDP by 2050. As for its impact on financing needs for the healthcare sector, this will amount to 0.3% of GDP by 2030 and to 1% by 2050. The results obtained in the case of health suggest that an increase in life expectancy will account for nearly half the financing needs in the long term. In total, it is estimated that the impact of ageing on a world level will reduce by 0.1% to 0.2% of the savings rate in relation to GDP. Finally,

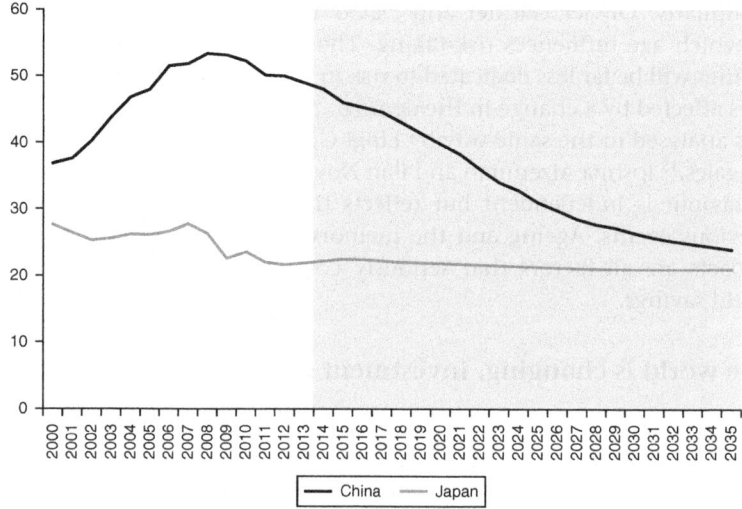

Figure 6.5 Savings rate forecast as a percentage of GDP for China and Japan
Source: The authors.

the world is changing and savings are decreasing. Using our estimates, the world rate of savings will reduce by about 2.3% between now and 2030. This is both limited but very significant. Everything depends on where these savings, which are still pretty significant, are directed.

That is because savings can be hoarded or be used to develop financing, often at little risk. When one considers future needs for financing activities, these investments will be profitable only in the long term. That is the reason why risk aversion and risk-sharing lie at the heart of savings and how they are used.

The use of savings has been upset in reality by the population ageing which is taking place throughout the world – and especially in the developed countries – resulting in the fact that available savings have concentrated in the hands of disarmed populations who are risk-averse. Indeed, André Masson and Luc Arrondel have considered the behaviour of savers in the French case. In Pater (Preferences and property to time and risk) which they published in 2007 and 2009, they state that 'if the Great Recession is likely to last, the phenomenon that will develop as low noise could become louder and generate future savers who have little tolerance for risk and who will be cautious in their investments'.[13]

Similarly, Olivier Garnier and David Thesmar[14] showed the extent to which age influences risk-taking. The inevitable conclusion is that savings will be far less dedicated to risk in the coming years in the countries affected by a change in the demographic structure. The Italian case was analysed in the same way by Luigi Guiso, Paola Sapienza and Luigi Zingales.[15] Joshua Aizenman and Ilan Noy,[16] however, show that savings behaviour is independent but reflects the macroeconomic impact of previous events. Ageing and the memory of previous macroeconomic impacts are all factors that seriously complicate the mobilization of world savings.

The world is changing, investment is increasing

The studies already mentioned presuppose that investment will increase very rapidly.[17] This hypothesis is highly plausible at the very least. World investments could exceed 25% of world GDP in a scenario in which world GDP would grow by 3.2% up to 2030. If this happens, China and India will represent the major part of the general increase with China virtually doubling its share of world investment. On the other hand, the figures are less generous for most western countries. Our investment hypotheses vary with respect to investment in the new industries. In addition to the gigantic effort that the emerging nations will make to adapt their infrastructure to the rise of a huge middle class, the developed countries are under an obligation to reconstruct their production systems which assumes massive investment in the new technology sector.

Like all matters of speculation, the figures for the future are debateable. We have repeated the main forecasts. They are more extensive than those of McKinsey which focus on productive investment over and above infrastructure and housing. As for the figures forecast by the IMF, the OECD and the CEPII, as can be seen, these are extremely conformist. None of them forecast significant changes in savings rates and have not produced any really innovative theories concerning investment for the developed countries. They appear to be believe we are living in an unchanging world. The switch over will occur without impact, without accidents *en route*, without the resurgence of the West's desire to regain the upper hand.

Let us take the theories produced, respectively, by the IMF, the OECD and the CEPII. The short-term analyses of the IMF and the long-term analyses of the OECD and the CEPII are hugely divergent. The IMF shows itself to be relatively confident concerning the will to invest, the

Savings, the Ultimate Rare Resource 137

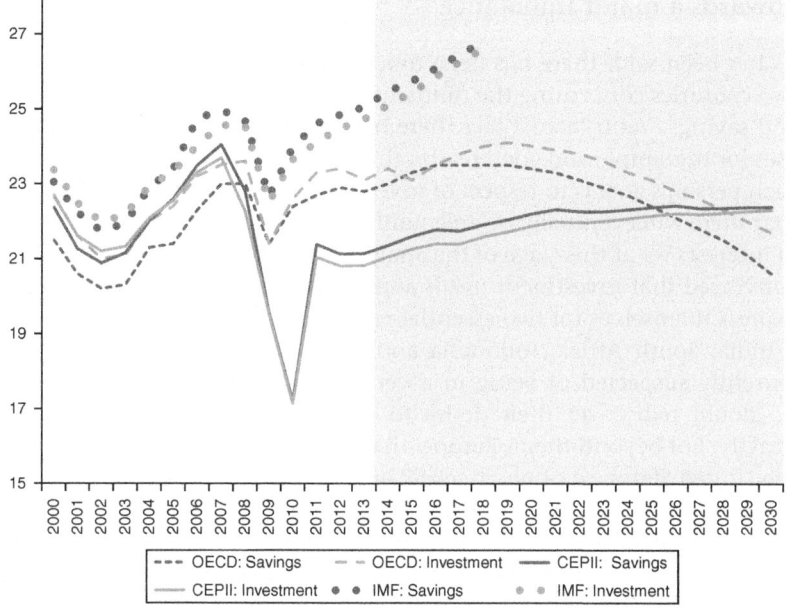

Figure 6.6 Provisions of world savings and investment rates as a percentage of GDP

Sources: (i) OECD, 'Looking to 2060: Long-Term Global Growth Prospects', *OECD Economic Publishing Paper*, no. 3, 2012; (ii) MaGE Model Data and Projections 1980–2050, (iii) CEPII, 2013; IMF, World Economic Outlook Database, October 2013.

OECD predicts the opposite and the CEPII is equidistant from both of them. Where the analyses converge is in the denial of the possibility of major imbalances between savings and investments.

The OECD's estimates project a decreasing rate of savings and investment from 2020. According to that body, the rates will drop from 23% in 2020 to about 13% in 2060. In the long term, there will be an *ex-ante* imbalance, albeit a very slight one, between savings and investment, the main deficit being in savings. As for the CEPII's estimates, these are less pronounced. The rates of savings and investment will remain around the rates observed in 2013, there will be no major change.

We shall thus find ourselves in a world in which years succeed each other in a flat continuum. Under such conditions, the I-S balance will occur in a context that is free of any particular tensions. Consequently the rates of interest will be maintained at a relatively low level.

Towards a major imbalance

As has been said, there has been much theoretical writing for the past two centuries concerning the fundamental balance between investment and savings. Yet in actual fact there have been very few concrete analyses for the simple and good reason that it is very difficult to assess what each person's goal is in respect of investment. It can only be established that there will eventually be an equilibrium obtained by balancing rates of interest. Yet at this stage of the analysis, we believe differently. We are convinced that investment needs and the desire to invest will strongly express themselves for two essential reasons.

India, South Africa, Indonesia and Brazil are all countries that are currently suspected of being in a very parlous situation but they will no doubt rediscover their desire to consume more and invest more heavily. But beyond them, Europe, that has been so greatly decried, and the United States, so often attacked, are also concerned with re-creating the conditions for strong growth. This assumes that both of them, the former tending towards infrastructure, and the latter towards productive investment will massively increase their purchase of machinery of all types in the future and thus their financing needs.

This need for investment, however, for the reasons mentioned above, will find it hard to discover available savings, unless it makes substantial changes to the conditions for their use, for example by changing interest rates but also and above all by a new distribution of risk.

The issue of an insufficiency of savings is a subject already tackled in the past, notably by Patrick Artus beginning of the 1990s'. The macroeconomic conditions were fundamentally different, but the method and the conclusions were remarkable: 'There are sufficient presumptions in favour of a diagnosis of a world insufficiency of savings. It can be admitted that, to a considerable extent, this is the reason for the increase in interest rates even if it is not the only one. Furthermore, savings would appear to be inadequate for sustaining potential growth.'[18] He adds: 'Despite the changes that occurred recently, the international financial system has not always provided solutions to the problems posed in adjusting savings to needs'. This version of events is different from ours, but it rightly emphasizes the major role played by world savings in the economic trajectory that has been followed.

Today, the world has changed fundamentally, having fragmented. Fractures have appeared rendering the world financial system incapable of making the necessary adjustments between local savings and the investments desired by the major economic regions. We have built a scenario for which the figures may be disputed but not the principle. It is a scenario that in its innovative aspects ought to radically change the trajectory of the world economy. If we rely on the calculations we performed earlier, we estimate that world savings will reduce by about 2.3% of GDP by 2030. As a reminder of our theories, the savings rates in the major emerging nations – China, India, Brazil, Indonesia, South Africa and Russia – will gradually align themselves with the current rate of savings in Japan, of the order of 21.6% in 2012, mainly due to the gradual introduction of social welfare systems and demographic ageing on a world scale.

With respect to investment, we estimate that the rate of savings will increase by 2.6% of GDP to reach a world level of about 27.1% of GDP by 2030. In effect, it is possible to imagine a scenario in which all of the OECD countries would return to an investment rate similar to that of the 1970s, namely at around 22% of GDP. With respect to the emerging nations, the rate of investment should remain quite high, with the possible exception of China which might slow it and align itself on a growth rate similar to that of the other emerging nations – India for example.

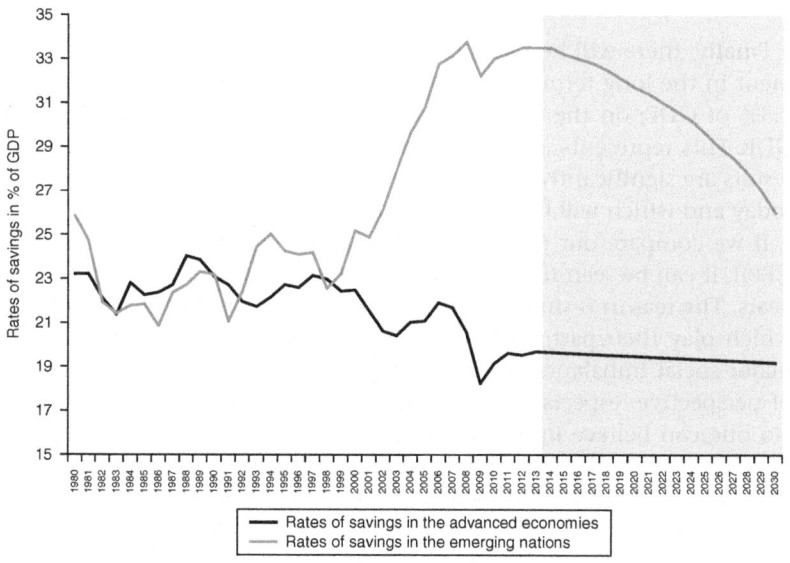

Figure 6.7 Projections of the rates of savings as a percentage of GDP
Source: The authors.

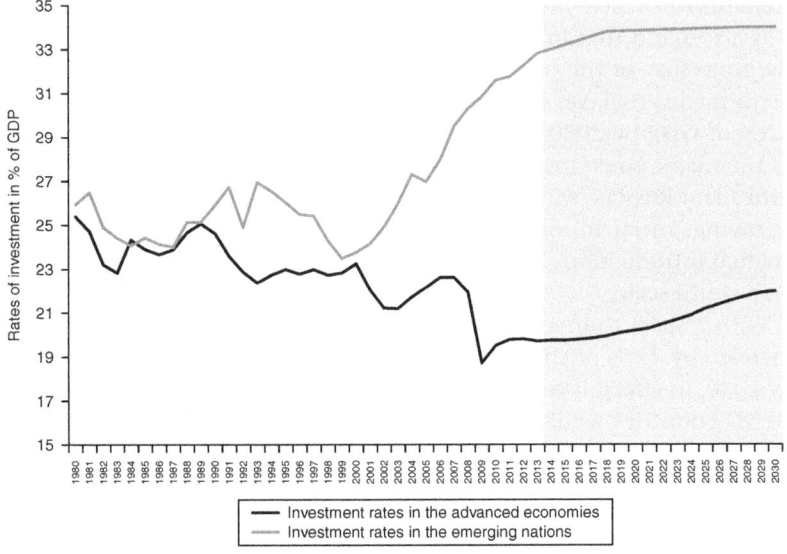

Figure 6.8 Projections of the rates of investment as a percentage of GDP
Source: The authors.

Finally, there will be a major imbalance between savings and investment in the long term. On the one hand, world savings will reduce by 2.3% of GDP; on the other, investment rates will increase by 2.6% of GDP. This represents a need for financing of about 4.8% of GDP. The results are significantly different from those with which we are familiar today and which will be at the source of future conflicts.

If we compare our forecast to those of the OECD, the IMF and the CEPII, it can be seen that there will be significant differentials in future years. The reason is simple. No one can imagine, unlike the institutions which play their part, that the world will follow a route consisting of major social imbalances in the emerging nations, and a world devoid of perspective, especially for young people, in the developed nations. No one can believe in a trajectory devoid of technological disruption which will radically change the organization of production systems and the nature of the items concerned. We currently start out today with three difficulties that will have to be resolved. These are societies that have become unbalanced due to demographic impact, a self-centred financial system and the need for massive investments. Where will there be competition and where will conflict be?

Savings, the Ultimate Rare Resource 141

Table 6.1 'Savings–investment' differential

	2012	2030	Variation
Savings in % of GDP	24.60%	22.30%	−2.30%
Investment in % of GDP	24.50%	27.10%	+2.60%
'Savings – investment' differential	0.10%	−4.80%	

Source: The authors.

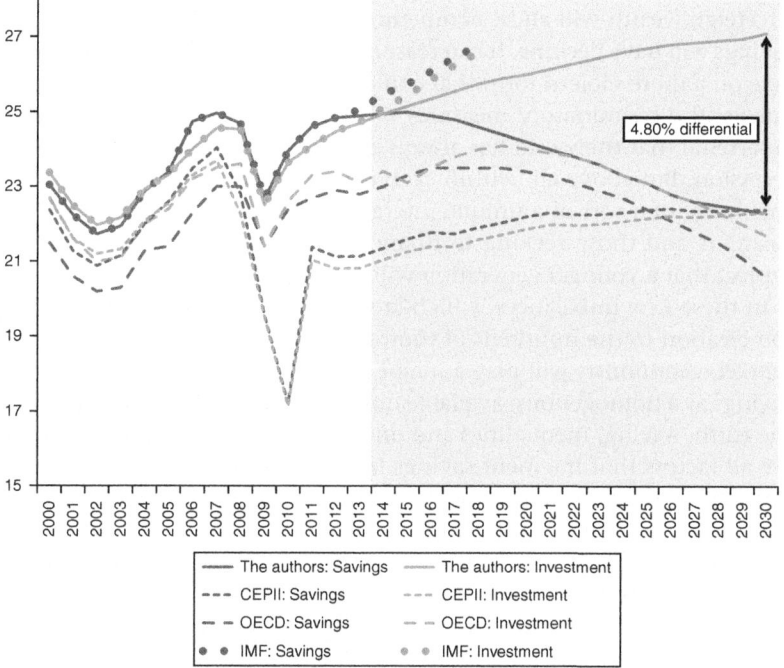

Figure 6.9 Forecasts of the world rate of savings and investment as a percentage of GDP

Sources: OECD, CEPII, IMF and the authors.

One thing is certain: the conflict over savings will take different forms, on a world scale and on the scale of each country. It will first affect each person's ability to attract savings through remuneration and risk-sharing. This is true between countries as well as within each country. The conflict is likely to be about the inability to incentivize or force the savers, who will often be elderly, to invest in risky projects. The divergence between investment and savings may be at the origin of the most serious conflicts with which we shall be confronted.

The increase in interest rates heralded by the IMF, as represented by Andrea Pescatori and David Furceri,[19] the OECD[20] and the OCFE,[21] often deals merely with the problems of short-term economic policy. The increase in rates of interest in the future will in fact be the partial translation of a rebalancing between investment and savings, and this will last for the long term.

Financial centres, investors in every country, pension funds and sovereign wealth will all be competing to recover the rare resource that savings will have become. It can reasonably be assumed that conflict will take on a more violent form that could translate into a war of exchange rates and discriminatory measures pertaining to investment. In short, an arsenal that the world has always employed during periods of major recession. But above all, within each country, the conflict may take on the image of a sort of a unique intergenerational conflict, between the hoarders and those seeking to finance the investment needed for the project that a younger generation will naturally desire to build.

In these new imbalances, which are so significant for growth and for job creation to the hundreds of thousands of new entrants into the job market, economists will play a major role. Why is that? We mentioned savings as a homogenous, available quantity but nothing is further from the truth. Ageing, inequalities and uncertainty about technical progress are all factors that fragment savings into just as many different categories. If these savings are to be made available in such a way that they are invested usefully, one still has to imagine, in the case of the more cautious categories, suitable risk-sharing, for savings for the elderly, for example, or for public generosity. The theory of risk needs to develop into a theory of risk-sharing, translating into the prospect of lots of work for economists.

7
Avoiding the Major Crisis of the Twenty-First Century

Crises, what crises? They will certainly occur, and no mistake. This view is not restricted to the economists. How is it possible not to think of the philosophers, sociologists, anthropologists and novelists who today, as they did yesterday, hold up to us the mirror of a modernity which, today as yesterday, has its share of shadow and evil? A violent modernity that is as destructive for the collective as it is for the individual. It is not by chance that Alain Touraine writes of 'the end of societies'.[1] They will be unable to survive the end of social life and the destruction of their institutions, the result of a financial capitalism that has broken off all its links to the industrial economy, with institutional, political and even cultural control of its resources. Touraine seeks to know how to escape the 'chasm' that is opening up in front of us, in this *'post*-social and *post*-historic' era. While Touraine does not stop there, with this terrible discovery of globalization that is out of control – far from it – he opens the way to a new paradigm, he even leads us into an improbable rapprochement with Arjun Appadurai, someone who does not hesitate to stress the intimate, and even incestuous, relationship between globalization and violence.[2] There are too many authors to list who are warning us against our contemporary deregulation, some speak of folly, such Ulrich Beck,[3] who calls our societies 'risk manufacturers' in which fear predominates or Zygmunt Bauman who constantly lists the destruction of our 'individualistic societies' and many others. Earlier writings expressed forebodings. Claude Lévi-Strauss, studying the Amerindian civilization, in his book *Tristes tropiques*,[4] expresses his anger and consternation when faced with a West whose modernity is predatory, as if by its very nature. If the Old and New World are irreconcilable, it is because the latter, from the pedestal on which 'progress' has been placed, throws its 'ordure in the face of humanity'. Worse still, it 'contributes nothing but war and desolation'. The voice of Lévi-Strauss rediscovers its youth as if it were inviting us to accept different versions of globalization as opposed to the sole western reading of it. One striking phrase by Hannah Arendt expresses the situation as no one else has done: 'One can perfectly conceive that the modern era – which began with an explosion of human activity that was so new so rich in promises – should end in the most inert, sterile passivity that history has ever known'.[5] Will technical progress eventually give birth to the nightmare that could be a society of workless workers? Will people, forgetting the ancient distinction between private life and public life, have nothing in left common but their private interests? From all these readings, one lesson can be learned; that of finding the meaning of the collective, of cooperation as Richard Sennet[6] would have it, a sort of ethos that, as Touraine expresses it, would avoid the chasm.

This long detour has nothing to do with nostalgia or regret. Even less is it the adoption of a reactionary posture in the true sense of the term. No, in reality, this is a matter of rediscovering a sort of frame of reference, one that revives a space-time that has been exceeded, restoring all of its freedom to the former and all of its volume to the latter. Consequently, the problems we have discussed do not belong to a form of practical catalogue containing questions and answers, but rather an attempt to defuse conflicts whose potential results could be disastrous.

Thus, the six constraints identified, difficult to control, restore all meaning to political action at both world and national level. None is insurmountable, but nor are any easy to circumvent. These six constraints reinforce each other in a consistent system, implementing the capacities for action by the authorities, and apparently impose a restraint to growth in the twenty-first century, changing the balances of power between the major regions and transforming society in the way they operate on a daily basis.

Yet it is to this set of constraints that reply should be made in order to hope to avoid a major crisis in the twenty-first century. The five proposals stated at the end of this book are designed to respond to the major constraints described, without suggesting that they are sufficient on their own to resolve all of the problems. Why five and not six? Because any proposal to accelerate technical progress has been deliberately ruled out. As is known, the uncertainty surrounding its progress currently makes it impossible to provide anything but quantitative proposals. The often simplistic manner that countries have of determining the percentage of their GDP to be set aside for R&D shows that they have forgotten the fact that innovation is the product of complex, quantitative systems in which the differential in knowledge plays a predominant role. Similarly, the desire to restrict the role of finance on a world scale constitutes a naïve view and the only goal that one can set for oneself is to create an overall balance between savings and investment.

Thus, any political, world, European or national economy owes it to itself to place at its heart intergenerational consideration, the world management of rare resources, the distribution of income to the detriment of pensioners, the implementation of a regime of currency exchange that will rediscover the ambition of the Bretton Woods agreements and, above all, the sharing of investment risk between the collective and the individual. The world needs to invest in infrastructure, in consumer goods activity, in research and development, in training and in controlling the difficulties connected with the environment. In a word, in the growth model proposed, (the only one that is viable in the long term), the low rate of investment and excessive consumption in the short term should be put on hold in order to enable investment to play its true role in order to revive growth.

Today, it will be difficult and ambitious, but it is nonetheless necessary to express concrete proposals. Yet we have taken this risk by stating them as closely as possible to the analysis taken from each of the chapters. This is how we recommend the progressive disappearance of both frontiers, those separating work from non-work, that fundamentally change the rules for retirement, as well as the conditions for entering the labour market and those dealing with the flood of migrations, thus enabling some of the world's young people to gain access to more developed countries. That is what we have dubbed 'Refocusing the World on its Youth'.

Similarly, we have stressed the extent to which the economist can assist in restricting the squandering of rare resources and subsequently redistributing them optimally, thus rediscovering his/her primary role. Confronted with runaway demographics, it is a matter of building taxation and subsidy mechanisms on a world scale that will make it possible to develop available resources, even though this will require a policy of massive investment, prioritizing the most urgent of them, water, on which everything depends.

Subsequently, we believe it is important to establish that world public debt is a major difficulty to overcome, one for which there is no simple solution. There will be no restructuring drama, no world recession linked to simplistic economic policies in the short term. The daring required for this point should take the form of a rather unorthodox proposal, namely a perpetual world debt whose implementation will enable growth to rediscover the ability to finance itself adequately. Here again, it is a matter of launching a discussion to move away from repetitive, conventional discourse and think about debt reduction.

This theory could not exist without stability in trading and without relative control of the creation of liquidity on a world scale. Rarely was the world more intelligent and creative than at the time the Bretton Woods Agreements were created. It is for this exercise that one must prepare, even if we are living in different times and there are totally different factors at stake.

This is not to forget the demographic impact and its effect on the use of available savings. Ageing is not only sad for individuals, it is also sad for the collective. Fear of risk is what paralyses society. If finance is to rediscover its legitimate role as a basis on which growth can be constructed, it can do so by inventing new formulas for risk-sharing. This is a difficult task because it is based on two unfortunate questions concerning the way society operates, the role of the state and intergenerational transfers.

These proposals should lay down the conditions for renewed world growth. It deserves to be balanced between the major economic regions, financed for the long term despite the major demographic constraint, that of risk aversion linked to ageing. The collective must rediscover its strength in comparison with the individual since the risk for certain investments cannot be borne by it alone. In reality, this is not simplistic Keynesianism that has been reworked for modern tastes, but the idea that investment guides the world and financing it is the main constraint.

Refocusing the world on youth

This proposal is not youthism. For the past half century everything has been done for and by senior citizens, who are protected, the likeable heroes of the post-war period. It does not matter whether a generation was sacrificed. The result is the fact that young people have fewer jobs, fewer prospects, fewer hopes. People are surprised, wrongly, that a part of the qualified European younger generation is leaving their country and this is considered to be the ultimate sign of decline, ridiculous because everyone goes elsewhere to seek what they do not find at home, even though the world as a whole offers no other true vision.

As we have stated several times, the main engine for world development is linked to this rapid demographic growth until the year 2050, at which date it ought to stabilize. Hitherto, the world will be seriously disrupted both by this movement and by the increasing importance of senior citizens in the demographic structure.

Dealing with the intergenerational impact and controlling it is, as far as we are concerned, nothing more than moving this initial frontier between work and lack of work. For a century the world has relied on the now-dated idea that tough working conditions should be compensated for by a sufficiently well financed retirement to make it possible to satisfy the desires of individual well-being. It is also supported by the idea of 'age groups' that has had its day. A division into three ages has been substituted with a more complex division due to the lengthening of life, as well as youth which has so many difficulties that are translated into events. Today, the balance that was so greatly awaited for centuries no longer works. The imbalance between the labour market and financing retirement can only find its solution in the simplistic version of an extension of the length of time spent in work, without the very conditions for the supply of work being adapted to ageing. Our proposal is not only more balanced; it is also more radical. It is to think of the absence of a breach between a working life and rest, pursuing the activities of individuals throughout their life, something that cannot happen without a profound change by putting senior citizens to work.

We lay down the principles of gradual retirement, a proposal that has been widely circulated but which in this case waives the aim of total retirement (except, obviously, in the case of people who are unable to work, as in cases of dependency). This proposal supposes a greater integration between the generations, greater recourse to the know-how of older people, a rebalancing of the financing of retirement and taking over by a collective that is now more homogenous for the most difficult time of life, that of dependency.

A second approach is designed to rebalance the demographic structures. In this sense, one of the actions of world policy to be conducted in the coming decades will be to remove frontiers, those of the population flows. How can the unbearable costs of ageing be covered without relying on the flow of populations that represent a considerable opportunity? This is what can be seen today in Germany, a country in which the active population is reducing without its activity losing dynamism. The population of southern Europe has been responding for several years to the work opportunities offered by Germany. To summarize, we need to be more fluid in the movements of workers within an economic and cultural region, by prioritizing a population capable of adapting to new ways of life. The entire difficulty is based on this contradiction: opening the frontiers, but integrating these populations who have come to mitigate the effects of ageing in the host countries. It is a problem to be resolved not one to be swept aside. Also to be taken into consideration is the natural tendency of the inhabitants of poor countries to move to places that seem to promise them a better way of life. The study performed by Antoine Pécoud and Paul de Guchteneire[7] develops what could be a scenario for migrations without borders. This totally utopian scenario has the merit of throwing light on the fact that population movements are inevitable and should be taken into account as invariable. These movements represent one of the conditions in favour of renewed world growth. Why not imagine the removal of borders, especially for young people, in a manner that is much more significant than the one we know today? Of course, many countries consider that their immigration needs to be selective, and they prefer to welcome in young people who have qualifications. That is not sufficient, however, to solve problems such as those that exist between Mexico and the United States, between Africa and Europe. It is legitimate to consider qualifications as an important criterion but everyone knows that this does not represent tomorrow's true situation. We consider that it is necessary to accept a world in which there is a balanced acceptance of various categories of qualifications.

An inter-generational policy that avoids conflicts between major age groups cannot sacrifice one for the other. The conventional discourse states that the 15–30 year olds will be a sacrificed generation. That may be the case, but the statistics do not show it in such a caricatured way. One merely has the perception that this inequality of access to the labour market seems to be true for all young people throughout the world. What is to be done? There are no miracle solutions to transition from the labour markets that have been so disrupted by the massive transfer of manufacturing during the past 20 years. The return to a balanced trajectory will not occur as rapidly and simply as some people imagine, by reducing levels of pay to young people. One of the few certainties one can have is that it is not possible to imagine a world without frontiers without the younger generations having achieved a satisfactory level of training. The world now devotes less than 5% of its GDP[8] to spending on education, part of which, a very small part, is on initial training. Our suggestion is to accompany this double movement of liberalization of the flows of migration and the constraints represented by retirement by massive investment in early education.

Everyone knows that training will enable individuals to master a variety of languages and will later enable them to integrate into the labour market. Doubling initial expenditure on a world scale, in the context of totally mutualized organization, would appear to be a reasonable goal. Naturally, this would represent a financial transfer from older to young people. It would be difficult to achieve, since the demographic structure of our countries is not ready to allow such reforms to get through easily. Yet it is something that must be done.

Socializing rare resources

It is not a matter of thinking of the whole range of rare resources, as is often done and which seems to be legitimate in considering new growth models. It is always imagined that the main difficulty in the world to come is that of the infernal pair of energy – climate and that in reality, the future of the world depends on a real ability to overcome the changes in both of these. This is very true, and no one could reproach an individual who cares about the survival of humanity for adopting this point of view, but that is not what concerns us. The risk of crisis, of major conflicts, is based on the only resource that is genuinely rare – water. We shall have enormous needs for food in the coming decades, linked to just as impressive a population increase and new nutritional needs. Everyone knows that Earth can satisfy the needs of around 10 billion inhabitants, but the extraordinary difficulty, the greatest of all, is the availability of water. Agriculture consumes about 3,100 billion cubic metres of water annually, 71% of actual world consumption, and if there are not efficiency savings, it will absorb 4,500 billion cubic metres between now and 2030.[9] Naturally, the major centres of demand for agricultural water correspond *de facto* to the regions in which the poorest producers, who practise subsistence farming, live. India will be requiring 1,195 billion cubic metres in 2030, sub-Saharan Africa will need 820 billion and China 420 billion.[10] All this is predictable, as long as the resources are invested, making it a huge financial challenge to be overcome.

Yet what is very problematic today could be considered insurmountable tomorrow. Assuming an average economic growth scenario and if no account is taken of possible gains in water productivity, the annual world needs for water will be 40% in 2030 greater than the currently accessible supply.[11] This global deficit figure actually combines a number of local imbalances, some of which translate into a situation that is even more serious. One third of the world's population, concentrated in the developing nations, will be living in low-lying areas which, if nothing is done, will have a water shortage of 50%. To take full measure of the water challenge, it is indeed the volume of water offered that is accessible, reliable and ecologically sustainable that should be used as the reference point. Yet, as is constantly being said, Africa is the continent that will make it possible to bridge the deficits and solve our problems. Is that realistic? Eighty per cent of people deprived of access to a water source live on that continent and one African in two needs to walk 10 kilometres a day to find a source of drinking water. Yet the continent has major water resources available. What it lacks is the distribution and purification infrastructure that would enable its populations to gain access to drinking water. The African continent contains 660,000 cubic kilometres of water reserves underground.[12] This resource is one hundred times greater than the quantity of water on the surface. Yet 330 million Africans, 40% of the population, do not have access to drinking water, according to the African Development Bank. Africa needs to devote the equivalent of 11.5 billion euros annually merely to create or reinforce the distribution and purification infrastructure. Whilst water exists, some of the water tables are buried at depth, making any drilling project that will be necessary for putting to good use arable land that is currently not in use difficult and costly. It should never be forgotten that 60% of such land in the world is in Africa.

The challenge to produce adequate amount of water is initially a financial one. The problem cannot be contemplated with these solutions except at a world level. The world population will need to be fed, and it is this population that will have to cover the necessary investment. This amounts to considering water, like air, as a public asset, meaning that everyone needs equal access to it, and under the right conditions, without money or any other form of restriction to access being the consequence of a sort of world inefficiency. The vastness of the finance needed has already been mentioned in the Camdessus Report.[13] In fact, no traditional source of finance could bridge the gap between supply and demand for water.

If terrible conflicts over sharing rare resources are to be avoided, it can only be imaged that socialized financing of new water production will be required, based on the taxation of all agricultural assets, simply because the rarity of water will result in a price increase in these assets. In practice, we shall be confronted with a fairly simple transfer of the additional cost linked to an absence of water, destined to finance the farming of the millions of hectares that will be needed to feed the planet. It is thus a matter of releasing the primary constraint, namely lack of water. The question then arises of arable lands since if water, in public ownership, makes it possible to work land that was hitherto unused to the sole benefit of those with natural buying power, Africa will become totally despoiled of its own land.

Such a mechanism is therefore unimaginable. The converted land will need to be sanctified for the production of another publicly owned asset, the food that is necessary for everyone. It would appear that for the first time a world tax could easily be raised since it would be simple in its purpose and implementation.

Taming pensions

When speaking of pensions and debt one enters the world of excess, of smoke and mirrors and of irrationality. How many are those who have evoked the euthanasia of the pensioners or associated debt with collective and individual culpability? Yet a way out must be found for this issue without resorting to a brutal restructuring, led by Greece, since the pensioners are no one but us, represented by the great financial institutions that bear the debt burden.

We have stressed that the world is moving towards a society marked by the weakness of available savings. A substantial part of those who own capital today represent an ageing population, that created its wealth a long time ago and forms an upper globalized layer. Through this, the behaviour and attitudes of a society consisting of pensioners can be found. To be fair, the term 'pension' is more appropriate than 'pensioner'. This is not to insult either the talents or the risk-taking of anyone who was able to create this wealth. Nor can it be ignored that, even today, daring entrepreneurs are at work, creating, devising and developing tomorrow's world. The question of pensions belongs to macroeconomics, the concentration of financial resources, ageing and the financing needs of the world economy.

Yet rent and debt go hand-in-hand to the extent that both of them generate stagnation. The world of today has little fear of inflation, followed by deflation. It needs to finance growth and in order to do so it needs to usefully channel all of the available resources. The new pension and debt proposals have the sole aim of distancing the permanent spectre of debt, the freezing of savings and perceiving the possibility of renewed investment. A reduction in debt, in the traditional sense, can only happen reasonably over the course of several decade and will have the effect of long stagnation since neither the state nor individuals will want to invest. Nor can it be a question of restructuring, which will suddenly deprive creditors of their capital, nor the eternal and hypocritical exit from inflation, which maintains the illusion that the debtor – creditor balance now only depends on uncontrollable phenomena. The world cannot stop growing and that is why we need to invest.

Ever since Sismondi, it has been known that any revival of national or world growth, especially given the demographic changes, will require the conversion of a pensioners' society into a society of investors. The virtuous capitalism of the eighteenth century converted profit into investment. Yet today national and international politics now favour protection of what we have unkindly called the 'pensioners', of the ability to find favourable taxation arrangements so that very often the institutions that claim to represent the pensioner also claim to protect capital as soon as it reaches a high enough level in its eyes. We face a huge stock of debt that needs to be serviced virtually permanently and that prevents any return to growth. Those holding this stock are relatively content with this period of low inflation, and restructuring solutions for debt are conceivable since they will make it possible to lose confidence definitively in any collective destiny. So what is to be done?

Two key words summarize the coming disruptions. They are mutualization and extension of the debt until it becomes perpetual. On the first point, numerous proposals have already been made, basically to deal with future debt. There has been talk of *eurobonds*, the issue of loans at euro zone level in order to mutualize this new debt.

Obviously, Germany has shown itself to have little enthusiasm for this proposal. To attempt to work around this almost Pavlovian rejection, *eurobills*[14] have been suggested. In fact, they work on the same principle as *eurobonds*, except that they only involve short-term loans, those that mature at less than one year. For long-term debt, these countries need to continue to raise funds on their own markets. Another suggestion is the *project bond* which only involves financing major infrastructure projects that are shared within the euro zone. This would mean entering a new stage, since the mutualization of the debt would be linked to the real economy and thus to growth. Hitherto, all of these proposals that will probably come to materialize have had only academic approval, without much interest from politicians. The same fate has befallen those who have attacked the stock of debt, despite their interesting suggestions to separate good from bad debt,[15] and preserve the status of 'senior' debt for the former.

The desire to reduce debt is not, however, new. If one takes the amount of British debt, even when it was becoming the superpower of the nineteenth century, in 20 years it had tripled until it amounted to 250% of its GDP. Numerous resources were introduced in an attempt to reduce it, including 'ideas for amortization, interest reduction, conversion of perpetual debt into lifetime debt of fixed-term annuities and the redemption of certain taxes by making a certain one-time payment'.[16]

Yet it was the extension of this debt over time that was really daring. It was necessary to guarantee a very long term with a guarantee of a fixed rate. If this model is pushed to its extreme, it could be termed 'perpetual debt', which could be imagined to apply totally or partially, with multiple variations. This would be automatically renewed, i.e. reimbursement would at no time be envisaged. Debts would be traded on the secondary market and only the interest would be serviced. There is nothing new in this. Remember that perpetual debt already has a long history. From the second half of the thirteenth century, the Italian governments,[17] which had difficulty in repaying their public debts, decided to change the debt structure and extended them so that they matured in the long term. Nor was France left out, since perpetual debt appears very early in what was known as the *bail à cens*, the exchange of parcels of land against payment of an annual *cens*, a fixed payment due in perpetuity. Many French monarchs put this into practice, including Francis I and Charles X, to honour their commitment to apply the "Law of Milliard des émigrés" and reimburse those whose assets had been confiscated and sold during the Revolution. Throughout the nineteenth century, the French state indebted itself in perpetual pensions at 3% or 5%, but, unlike the land taxes collected under the *Ancien Régime*, these would be reimbursable if the state so wished. The model was lost after 1914. Times had changed and so had the savers, and the state was forced to borrow against commitments to repay quickly.

In fact, the advantages of perpetual debt are without a doubt numerous for countries and that is our main problem today. For what reason? Because they are able to incur the debt without being under the constraint of the due date for redemption. This means they do not need to fear any attacks on the markets, nor the feared credit reference agencies. In France, for example, the average term is about seven years. If reducing the term enabled France to obtain the debt at lower rates this also made it sensitive to the disposition of international markets. This is even more serious since, in the present economic downturn, countries can crystallize the currently very low rates through creating perpetual debt. If growth is on the agenda, they will always be able to buy back their own debts because it is possible, as the British have shown, to move from perpetual debt to debt with a due redemption date.

Above all, this conversion of debt could enable indebted countries, i.e. almost all of them, not to tarnish their image with investors by resorting to sudden restructuring. Remember the trauma in Cyprus in 2013 when the question arose of deducting some of the capital from major bank accounts. The shock is easy to imagine if one of the IMF's proposals, that of imposing a one-off 10% tax on household capital, had been applied to reduce the debt. Perpetual debt would also make it possible to reintroduce less conventional methods, such as purchasing debt securities, into the strategies of the central banks. Eventually, having no more principal to reimburse, perpetual debt would enable countries to be relieved of this burden and be more open to rebuilding daring economic policies.

Obviously, for creditors, institutions and those receiving pensions, the balance sheet is less obvious. The stakeholders, those holding long-term savings, the insurance companies and pension funds, for example, have exchanged their capital against a perpetual pension at a rate fixed in advance. For those who wish it in a period of very low inflation, perpetual bonds could be perceived as being very attractive, if the rate proposed was sufficiently enticing. The real risk, however, is none other than inflation. Even if this perpetual debt could be resold on the secondary market, the person we have called the pensioner risks being the loser. But, with that debt that will mature if there is inflation, he will be so in any case. In fact, it is more a case of convincing savers of the soundness of their own country. Perpetual debt could be compared with a shortage of equity for the state and thus savers would become virtual investors. This notional pensioner needs to be convinced as does the institution representing the savers.

It is not households that are directly concerned but life insurance institutions and other savings vehicles. To incentivize and attract creditors, tax advantages need to be offered, which supposes taking into account all forms of savings, as well as financial balances, especially bank balances, through the management of the assets and liabilities on the balance sheet. It is at the cost of a very creative but rigorous initiative that the freer indebted countries, by means of mutualization of new debts and conversion of the stock of former debts, can invest and find the way to greater growth. Of course, they are taking a risk, but in practice there is little fear of default or even the possibility of puncturing some of the stake. The state will take over the debt and acquire wider flexibility in respect of the markets and the credit ratings agencies, while having virtual equity at its disposal.

Mutualizing new debt and moving from debt to perpetual debt are only some of the proposals among many others and are in no case miracle solutions. There are always attempts to find an acceptable balance between debtors and financiers, with the aim of finding a new capacity for future growth. Technical solutions may not be those mentioned but the world that is overloaded with public and private debt cannot escape a solution of that nature, one that is very innovative. This is simply because it is the only one that will protect us from a decisive conflict between the younger and the older generations.

The incentive to encourage those who own the asset to participate completes the concept of finance placed in the service of the real economy.

A new Bretton Woods?

The current system of trading is one that is dominated by the Western powers. But the world is now happily multicentred and much more balanced. The collapse of the Bretton Woods system corresponded to an intellectual and ideological period in which free trade in all markets appeared to be the only solution for rapid growth. This may have been true in the late 1970s. Since then, clearly, the rate of financial crises has accelerated, the world economy is increasingly difficult to control and a long-lasting solution is becoming impossible to find. The complexity and novelty of the situation leads us to hope to smooth out our currency exchange system and move towards greater stability, perhaps even fixedness, in the relationship between currencies.

Since the 1970s, an initial intellectual and ideological debate has pitted the advocates of a fixed rate of exchange, in the spirit of the Bretton Woods agreements, against those who favoured floating rates of exchange. The latter have won not only on an intellectual level but also in practice. Yet, after 40 years of a flexible exchange rate system, it seems clear that this option has contributed significantly to the imbalances of the international system.

The second discussion is of a geostrategic nature. Numerous voices have been raised in favour of a rebalancing of the international monetary system. It would appear that transition towards a more 'multipolar' system, using in all its calculation processes and developments a basket of currencies such as the dollar, the euro and the yuan is inevitable. One of the expected effects is the attenuation of the asymmetric nature of the adjustments and consequent reinforcement of equity in the world monetary system. On the other hand, the stability of the system would not be automatically achieved from the outset. At first, short term volatility in exchange rates is likely to be worsened by greater mobility of capital. Nevertheless, moving from a hegemonic to a multicentre system looks promising. There have been numerous discussions and proposals, especially concerning the possibility of assigning a more important role to the Special Drawing Rights (XDR or SDR). That is the opinion of Agnès Bénassy-Quéré and Jean Pisani-Ferry.[18] Jacques Mistral is also favourable to a return to XDRs because they are a stabilizing factor through the automatic diversification of reserves. Everything will depend 'on how the basket of currencies will behave, nothing more or less'.[19] This multi-currency system is in fact in the image of the multi-centre world that we have entered, which makes it possible, faced with recurrent instability, to be more efficient in linking the interests of the various stakeholders.

Other opinions have been expressed insisting on the need for liquidity in the world economy. For Emmanuel Farhi, Pierre-Olivier Gourinchas and Hélène Rey,[20] XDRs are not a suitable instrument for these needs since it is too complex to issue them.

As can be seen, everyone is trying to revert to a more stable model, one that is more respectful of the new realities, more susceptible to removing the spectre of an exchange rate war. Our discussion is neither intellectual nor geostrategic. It is rather a matter of adopting a philosophical position concerning the future of the world. That is the reason why one cannot be satisfied with minimum of reform. If an enterprise as ambitious as the Bretton Woods agreements saw the light of day in the aftermath of the most tragic war in human history, it is not by chance. Let us remember that the desire of the nations was to impose the conditions of an order guaranteeing stability, appeasement, pacification and healing. Today, it is exactly through this prism, these values, that the international monetary system needs to be rethought. A return to a new Bretton Woods would indeed mitigate this inevitable slide of nations into a war which today may be about currencies but tomorrow could adopt more violent forms.

Risk-sharing

At the start of the twenty-first century, the aim of the vast majority is to flee from risk or, more specifically, the perception that one has of it. The consequences of this attitude that has been so rare for two and a half centuries have names that signify serious difficulties in the long run, such as the principle of precaution, stagnation, protectionism, closing borders, reindustrialization and a currency war. To emerge from this difficulty, without otherworldliness and without cynicism, it is a matter of sharing and thus mutualizing risk at all levels of human activity. In reality, the problem arises in the relationship between the collective and the individual, who is often elderly and thus risk-averse. Subsequently, there was a sharing of activities between the major economic regions and those that everyone agreed to preserve for transferring value chains for the production of goods and services destined for a globalized market. On this last subject, two solutions currently offer themselves, that of a sudden reconquest of activities by countries that consider themselves to have been badly affected by too significant and too swift a transfer of business activity. The second is to imagine the creation of zones destined to trade with each other without, however, exercising a monopoly on the production of goods and services and without building territories that are increasingly autonomous. The second solution appears to be the more satisfactory. It is based essentially on producing higher quality goods in the emerging nations and the development of new activities in the developed countries. A world is unthinkable in which the industrial geography and services in these countries will remain unchanged. Some people speak of the green economy, the sustainable economy; others mention the development of technologies.

Regardless of the scenario, the distribution of business activity will be profoundly changed. The developed nations can choose to once again direct major financing into investment for developing activity in their territory, which will produce a satisfactory evening out of trade balances. However, the question remains of how this can encourage economies and their savers to invest their available resources in their own countries, knowing that they are likely to be less profitable. This is indeed the unresolved question of the allocation of financial resources, manpower and production on a world scale. There is a temptation, in the countries whose population is ageing, to abandon any production activity on their territory, even if it means converting them into economic deserts ripe for international tensions and conflict. Very innovative solutions will have to be invented if risk-sharing is to be rendered acceptable. In this respect, the respective roles of the collective, in this case, and more usually the state, and the individual need to be changed in two ways, namely, taxation of savings and risk-sharing, since the amount of investment needed to recreate the industrial manufacturing network cannot occur without protection for the saver involved.

Once again the respective roles of the state and the individual lie at the heart of national development. It is decades since certain people wanted to reduce the state to its simplest expression, when others were breathing life back into it. Our position is clear. In a world dominated by uncertainty, the state main role is to accept its share of risk. For example, as Mariana Mazzucato[21] claims, it is through close collaboration between the state and the public services that innovation will emerge. Companies cannot develop if the government does not invest in fundamental research at the outset, since they will not have the financial and strategic capacities to do so. Far from being the victims of exclusion, they would benefit from the first of these qualitative leaps to transform the scale of their production.

There are thus numerous situations in which the public sector and the market have a shared interest in the implementation of certain projects, be they small or large. Yet these projects cannot get off the ground – not because they are not profitable but because they are more especially affected by low-frequency risk, i.e. risks that are rare but extremely expensive. This is the case in particular with the construction of infrastructure whose costs are difficult to estimate at the outset. This same infrastructure is presumed to pay for itself in the long term if, once again, public intervention makes this possible. Protection against risk means accumulating capital well in advance. In order to cover this type of risk, the frontier between what relates to the market and what relates to that which is not on the market is more uncertain than for high-frequency risk in which market competence is indisputable. Consequently, true state intervention is required to design optimal risk-sharing. Yet the type of sharing offered in current legislation and practice is hardly feasible. A very typical obstacle, one that is suited to the past, concerns European regulations with respect to state aid. The result is a ridiculous situation in which it is relatively easy for the government to finance a project, such as building infrastructure or public equipment, by making the private sector shoulder the long-term risk. On the other hand, it is much harder to achieve the opposite risk-sharing situation in which long-term risk is borne by the government rather than the private sector.

We therefore believe that risk-sharing is based on the specific role of a government entity which would be responsible for covering extreme and long-term risks, while the private investor would cover more current, short- and medium-term risk. That is the only solution for mitigating the consequences of the current shortage of long-term investment. This means relaunching products that the market and the state are both interested in implementing, for reasons which may be very different, but which they will not be able to achieve, due to lack of management skills and sufficient financial resources from the public sector and a lack of desire for risk-taking on the part of private stakeholders. Dealing with this type of problem means reassigning a very special role to the state which will become the indispensable risk-taker. Why the state? Because its size gives a much greater capacity to spread the risk over a large number of projects, even if this capacity is more restricted than might be thought due to the strong correlation between long-term investments and macro-economic developments. A second argument would give the state a comparative advantage. The state can finance itself through debt under optimum conditions that the private sector is unable to, due to the lesser risk of default thanks to its ability to finance deficit through taxation. Of course, the economic cost linked to the distortions introduced by taxation will attenuate this advantage and could even reverse it when the state's profits from tax are reduced or become non-existent. Nevertheless, it has the ability to share and dilute the risk linked to these investments between all tax-payers as soon as they agree to recoup the cost through a broad-based taxation device. Beyond the legalistic and economic arguments, the ability to imagine and implement new risk-sharing mechanisms, i.e. a new organization of the relationship between the state and the individual, is a condition *sine qua non* for a return to growth on a world scale. Finance today has nothing in common with what it once was, the financing of tomorrow needs to be just as inventive. The state will find, well beyond what has just been mentioned, a new risk-sharing mechanism. That is quite simply because, as is the case today, no one wants to invest in the future.

* * *

The conviction of the authors of this book is simple. The trajectory of the world economy needs to be thought of in a completely different way to the one with which we are currently familiar. The difficulty with which we are all confronted is the result of a profound unfamiliarity with the networks of constraints with which the world economy will have to contend. No one ever imagined credible and acceptable solutions without trying to predict the future. The silliest, most simplistic solutions have been proposed by various people with reference to a past that has largely been superseded. We have tried to provide the outlines of this world economy as it will develop in the next 15 years. This diagnosis and the solutions contain many inaccuracies and lots of imperfections. Nevertheless, the world will not be able to avoid a really serious crisis and its dramatic consequences unless it clearly understands the main elements of which the future macroeconomic context will consist. The recommended solutions are based on paths that are still largely inadequate but which relegate to their rightful place the hesitant macroeconomic policies with which we are familiar today.

Notes

Introduction

1. Francis Fukuyama, *The End of History and the Last Man*, New York: Free Press, 1992.
2. National Intelligence Council, Global Trends 2030: Alternative worlds, 2013.
3. White paper entitled 'Défense et sécurité nationale', French Ministry of Defence, 2013.
4. Scenario whereby the inequalities between countries will explode, creating victors and vanquished, and within countries in which social tensions are rapidly increasing.
5. Kishore Mahbubani, *The Great Convergence: Asia, the West and the Logic of One World*, Public Affairs, USA, 2013.
6. Samuel Huntington, *The Clash of Civilizations and the Remaking of World Order*, New York: Simon & Schuster, 1996.
7. Michael Walzer, *Just and Unjust Wars: A Moral Argument with Historical Illustrations*, New York: Basic Books, 1977.

1 The Major Breakdown in Technical Progress

1. Adolphe Blanqui, *History of Political Economy from Antiquity to Our Days*, London: Routledge, 2000. Originally published in French in 1837.
2. Clayton M. Christensen, *The Innovator's Dilemma: When New Technologies Cause Great Firms to Fail*, Boston, MA: Harvard Business School Press, 1997.
3. Jacques Brasseul, *Petite Histoire des faits économiques et sociaux* [*Little History of Economic and Societal Events*], Paris: Armand Colin, 2010 (2001).
4. Robert L. Heilbroner, *The Making of Economic Society*, New Jersey: Prentice-Hall, 8th edition, 1989 (1962).
5. Nathan Rosenberg and Luther E. Birdzell, *How the West Grew Rich, The Economic Transformation of the Industrial World*, New York, NY: Basic Books, 1986.
6. Niall Ferguson, *Civilization: The West and the Rest*, London: Penguin Books, 2011.
7. Albert E. Musson, 'Continental Influence on the Industrial Revolution in Great Britain', in Barrie M. Ratcliffe (ed.), *Great Britain and Her World, 1750–1914. Essays in Honour of W.O. Henderson*, Manchester: Manchester University Press, 1975, pp. 71–85.
8. Patrick Verley, *L'échelle du monde. Essai sur l'industrialisation de l'Occident* [*The World Scale. An Essay Concerning the Industrialization of the West*], Paris: Gallimard, 1997.
9. Paul Bairoch, *Victoires et déboires. Volume 1: Histoire économique et sociale du monde du 16e siècle à nos jours* [*Victories and Defeats. Volume I: The Economic and Social History of the World from the Sixteenth Century to Today*], Paris: Gallimard, 1997.

10. Paul Valéry, *La crise de l'esprit* [*The Crisis of the Mind*], 1919.
11. Marcel Mauss, *Les civilisations. Éléments and formes* [*Civilizations: Elements and Forms*], Paris: Les Éditions de Minuit, 1929.
12. David S. Landes, 'Why Europe and the West? Why Not China', *Journal of Economic Perspectives*, Spring 2006, pp. 3–22.
13. Marc Bloch, *L'évolution de l'Humanité* [*The Evolution of Humanity*], Routledge, London: Feudal Society, 1989.
14. Angus Maddison, *Development Centre Studies: The World Economy: A Millennial Perspective*, OECD: Paris 2002.
15. Robert J. Gordon, 'Is U.S. Economic Growth Over? Faltering Innovation Confronts the Six Headwinds', NBER, Working Paper No. 18315, August, 2012.
16. Lecture given during a Seminar organized by CEPREMAP and DARES, Paris, 6 December 2014.
17. Tyler Cowen, *The Great Stagnation: How America Ate All the Low-Hanging Fruit of Modern History, Got Sick, and Will (Eventually) Feel Better*. New York, NY: Dutton Adult, 2011.
18. Kenneth Rogoff, 'Innovation Crisis or Financial Crisis?', *Business Standard*, 8 December 2012.
19. Patrick Artus and Marie-Paule Virard, *Croissance zéro* [*Zero Growth*], Paris: Fayard, 2015.
20. Edmund Phelps, *Mass Flourishing: How Grassroots Innovation Created Jobs, Challenge, and Change*, Princeton, NJ: Princeton University Press, 2013.
21. Erik Brynjolfsson and Andrew McAfee, *The Second Machine Age: Work, Progress, and Prosperity in a Time of Brilliant Technologies*, New York, NY: W.W. Norton & Company, 2014.
22. Carl Benedikt Frey and Michael A. Osborne, 'The Future of Employment: How Susceptible Are Jobs to Computerization?', WHO Working Paper, 17 September 2013.
23. Jeffrey D. Sachs and Laurence J. Kotlikoff, 'Smart Machines and Long-Term Misery', NBE Working Paper No. 18629, December 2012.
24. Jeremy Rifkin, *The Third Industrial Revolution: How Lateral Power is Transforming Energy, the Economy, and the World*, London: Palgrave MacMillan, 2013.
25. Philippe Chalmin (ed.), *Cyclope: les marchés mondiaux* [*Cyclope: World Commodities Markets*], Economica, 2005.
26. Source: Bloomberg. West Texas Intermediate oil spot price, raw materials futures index.
27. Food and Agriculture Organization of the United Nations.
28. Philippe Chalmin, '2009, an II de la crise alimentaire' [2009, year II of the food crisis], *Le Monde économie*, no. 19896, 13 January, 2009.
29. This is the case with respect to agricultural produce and oil; the metals market, however, is generally decreasing slightly in price.
30. The World Bank, The Sustainable Energy for All Global Tracking Framework Report, 2013*.
31. UN, consultable at: www.un.org/fr/events/worldwateryear/factsfigures.html
32. FAOSTAT, Food and Agriculture Organization of the United Nations.
33. Ye Jianping, Zhang Zhengfeng, Wu Zhenghong, *Current use of arable land in China, problems and perspectives*, Land Management Department, Peoples University of China, 2007.

34. Philippe Aghion, Philippe Askenazy, Renaud Bourlès, Gilbert Cette, Nicolas Dromel, 'Distance à la frontière technologique, rigidités de marché, éducation and croissance' [Distance to the Technological Frontier, Market Inflexibility, Education and Growth], *Économie and Statistique*, no. 419–420, August 2009.
35. Richard L. Florida, *The Rise of the Creative Class: And How It's Transforming Work, Leisure, Community, and Everyday Life*, New York, NY: Basic Books, 2002.
36. David S. Landes, *The Wealth and Poverty of Nations*, New York, NY: W.W. Norton, 1998.
37. Gregory Clark, *A Farewell to Alms. A Brief Economic History of the World*, Princeton N.J: Princeton University Press, 2009.
38. *Disruptive Technologies: Advances That Will Transform Life, Business, and The Global Economy*, McKinsey Global Institute, May 2013.
39. Ministère du Redressement productif, *La nouvelle France industrielle* [*The New Industrial France*], annual report, 2013.
40. Report of the 'Innovation 2030' Commission, chaired by Anne Lauvergeon, 2013.
41. Dipesh Chakrabarty, *Provincializing Europe*, Princeton, N.J.: Princeton University Press, 2000.

2 The Curse of Ageing

1. Extract from a lecture at Queen's University, Canada, 16 August 2011.
2. Arata Tendō, *Itamu Hito* [*The Mourner*], Tokyo: Bungeishunju, 2008.
3. This passage draws heavily on the introduction to Jean-Hervé Lorenzi and Pierre Dockès' book, *Le choc des populations: guerre or paix* [*The Population Impact: War or Peace*], Paris: Fayard, 2010.
4. Fernand Braudel, *Civilisation matérielle, économie and capitalisme, 15e–18e siècles* [*Material Civilization, the Economy and Capitalism, 15th–18th centuries*], Paris: Armand Colin, 1979.
5. Philippe Trainar, 'Le vieillissement, un phénomène mondial' [Ageing, a world phenomenon], in Pierre Dockès and Jean-Hervé Lorenzi (eds), *Le choc des populations, Guerre or paix*, Fayard, 2010, pp. 157–171.
6. Jean-Hervé Lorenzi, op. cit.
7. United Nations, *World Population Ageing*, Report of the Department of Economic and Social Affairs, 2013.
8. Ibid.
9. Ibid.
10. Andrew Mason and Ronald Lee (eds), *Population Aging and the Generational Economy. A Global Perspective*, Cheltenham, UK: Edward Elgar Publishing Limited, 2011.
11. David E. Bloom, David Cunning and Günther Fink, 'Implications of Population Aging for Economic Growth', NBER, Working Paper No. 16705, 2011.
12. Donghyun Park, Sang-Hyop Lee and Andrew Mason (eds), *Aging, Economic Growth, and Old-Age Security in Asia*, Cheltenham, UK: Edward Elgar Publishing Limited, 2012.

13. Ronald Lee and Andrew Mason, 'Population Aging, Intergenerational Transfers, and Economic Growth: Asia in a Global Context', in James P. Smith and Malay Majmundar (eds), *Aging in Asia: Findings from New and Emerging Data Initiatives*, Panel on Policy Research and Data Needs to Meet the Challenge of Aging in Asia, Washington, DC: The National Academies Press, 2012, pp. 77–95.
14. Jean-Hervé Lorenzi, *Le fabuleux destin d'une puissance intermédiaire* [*The Fabulous Destiny of an Intermediate Power*], Paris: Grasset, 2011.
15. Brigitte Dormont, 'Les dépenses de santé: une augmentation salutaire?' [Healthcare Expenditure: a Salutory Increase] (2009), in Philippe Askenazy and Daniel Cohen (eds), *16 nouvelles questions d'économie contemporaine*, Paris: Albin Michel, 2010.
16. Jean-Michel Charpin, *Perspectives démographiques and financières de la dépendance* [*Demographic and financial prospects for dependency*], final report, 2011.
17. Michel Duée and Cyril Rebillard, *La dépendance des personnes âgées: une projection à long terme* [*Dependency in the Aged: a long-term projection*], INSEE Working Group, INSEE, April 2004.
18. Consultable at: www.france-blog.info/pdf/Les%20retraites%20en%20France.pdf.
19. *The Ageing Population*, www.parliament.uk.
20. COR, *Retraites: perspectives actualisées à moyen et long terme en vue du rendez-vous de 2010* [*Retirement: prospects actualized in the medium and long term for the 2010 appointment*] eighth report of the Conseil d'orientation des retraites, 2010.
21. Lionel Ragot, in Jean-Hervé Lorenzi and Hélène Xuan (eds), *La France face au vieillissement. Le grand défi* [*France facing ageing: the great challenge*], Paris: Descartes et Cie, 2013.
22. National Institute of Population and Social Security Research, *Population Projections for Japan: 2011 to 2060*, 2012.
23. André Masson, *Vieillissement et croissance* [*Ageing and growth*], Seminar organized by the Caisse des dépôts et consignations, 2011.
24. This passage largely repeats the article by Alain Villemeur, to whom we offer our thanks, and the article by Jacques Pelletan, entitled 'Productivité dans une économie vieillissante: quels enseignements tirer de la littérature?' [Productivity in an ageing economy: what lessons can be learned from the literature?], working document for the Chair in Demographic Changes and Economic Changes, 2011.
25. Benjamin F. Jones (ed.), *Age and Great Invention. The Review of Economics and Statistics*, 92(1), February 2010.
26. Robert M. Solow, 'Technical Change and the Aggregate Production Function', *The Review of Economics and Statistics*, (39)3, August 1957, pp. 312–320.
27. Gary S. Becker and H. Gregg Lewis, 'On the Interaction between the Quantity and Quality of Children', in *Journal of Political Economy*, (81)2, March–April 1973, University of Chicago Press, pp. 279–288.
28. Simon Kuznets, 'Population and Economic Growth', *Proceedings of the American Philosophical Society*, (111)3, 1967, Published by: American Philosophical Society, pp. 170–193. Julian L. Simon, *The Ultimate Resource*, Princeton University Press, 1981.

29. Paul M. Romer, 'Endogenous Technical Change', *Journal of Political Economy*, 98(5), 1990, pp. 71–102.
30. David M. Cutler, James M. Poterba, Louise M. Sheiner and Lawrence H. Summers, 'An Aging Society: Opportunity or Challenge', *Brookings Papers on Economic Activity*, 1990.
31. Jaypee Sevilla, 'Age Structure and Productivity Growth', *Institute for Future Studies*, Working Paper, August 2007.
32. James Feyrer, 'Demographics and Productivity', *Review of Economics and Statistics*, 89(1), February 2007, pp. 100–109.
33. Paul Beaudry and David A. Green, 'Population Growth, Technological Adoption and Economic Outcomes in the Information Era', in *Review of Economic Dynamics*, (5)4, 2002, pp. 749–774.
34. Christian Pfeifer and Joachim Wagner, 'Is Innovative Firm Behavior Correlated with Age and Gender Composition of the Workforce? Evidence From a New Type of Data for German Enterprises', CESIS Electronic, Working Paper No. 291, 2012.
35. This pessimistic vision was expressed as long ago as 1946 by Alfred Sauvy and Robert Debré in a cry of alarm in the face of the 'invasion of the elderly' (*Des Français pour la France* [The French for France] Gallimard, 1946). More recently, see Stefanie Wahl (in *Regard sur l'économie allemande* [A Look at the German Economy] in Problèmes économiques, 2007, illustrating such a vision for Germany, or the report by the World Bank (*From Red to Grey, The Third Transition of Aging Population in Eastern Europe and the Former Soviet Union*, 2007) concerning the countries of Eastern Europe and the Former Soviet Union.
36. Models for the general balance of the overlapping generations (see for example, Miles D., 'Modelling the Impact of Demographic Changes upon the Economy', The Economic Journal, 109, 1999, pp. 1–36; Auerbach A., R. Hagemann, L. Kotlikoff and G. Nicoletti, 'The Economics of Aging Populations: The Case of Four OECD Economies', OECD Staff Papers, 12, 1989, pp. 111–147.).
37. Joaquim Oliveira Martins, Frédéric Gonand, Pablo Antolin, C. de la Maisonneuve and K.Y. Yoo, 'The Impact Of Ageing On Demand, Factor Markets And Growth', OECD, Working Paper,(7), 2005.
38. 1.8%.
39. Alain Villemeur and Jacques Pelletan, 'Productivité dans une économie vieillissante: quels enseignements tirer de la littérature?' [Productivity in an ageing economy: what lessons can be drawn from the literature?], *Working Document of La Chaire, Demographic Transitions – Economic Transitions*, 2011.
40. The 'poorest' and 'richest' are taken to mean the 10% poorest and the 10% richest respectively.
41. Centre for Strategic Analysis, 'Vivre ensemble plus longtemps: enjeux et opportunités pour l'action publique du vieillissement de la population française' [Living together longer: challenges and opportunities for public initiatives concerning the ageing of the French population], Reports and Documents No. 28, 2010.
42. Centre d'analyse stratégique, 'Les technologies pour l'autonomie: de nouvelles opportunités pour gérer la dépendance?' [Technologies for self-sufficiency: new opportunities to manage dependence], Monitoring Report No. 158, December 2009.

43. Jacques Pelletan, op. cit.
44. Vivre ensemble plus longtemps [Living together for longer], op. cit.
45. Robert E. Hall and Charles I. Jones, 'The Value of Life and the Rise in Health Spending', *The Quarterly Journal of Economics*, (122)1, February 2007, pp. 39–72.
46. *Leviticus*, XIX: 32.
47. Moses I. Finley, *The Elderly in Classical Antiquity*, lecture given at the University of Nottingham, 5 March 1981.
48. George Steiner, *Lessons of the Masters*, Cambridge, MA: Harvard University Press, 2005, p. 184.
49. George Steiner, in *Esprit*, June 2004.
50. Ibid.
51. Andrew Mason and Ronald Lee, *op. cit.*
52. Bruno Palier, 'The Emerging Intergenerational Conflict', *Policy Network*, February 2014.
53. Jeroen Spijker and John MacInnes, 'Population Ageing: The Timebomb that Isn't?', *Project Syndicate*, December 2013.
54. Hyppolyte d'Albis, 'La realité des transferts intergenerationnels (État, marche and famille)' [The reality of intergenerational transfers (State, market and family)], seminar by La Chaire Transitions démographiques, transitions économiques, May 2013.
55. Laurence J. Kotlikoff and Scott Burns, *The Clash of Generations*, MIT Press, USA, 2012.
56. Source: OECD. The unemployment rate among young Spaniards aged 15–24 years in the fourth quarter of 2013 was 55.6%.
57. Study linked to the 'Generation what?' operation conducted by France Televisions, in partnership with *Le Monde* and Europe 1, in 2013 among 210,000 French people aged between 18 and 34 and based on 21 million replies.
58. Chloé Woitier, 'Méprisés, les 18–25 ans songent à la révolte' [The despised 18–25 year-olds are thinking of rebelling], *Le Figaro*, 26 February 2014.
59. Ibid.

3 The Irresistible Explosion of Inequalities

1. David Ricardo, *The Principles of Political Economy and Taxation*, Dover edition, 2004. Originally published: London, New York: J. M Dent & Sons, 1911.
2. Richard H. Tawney, *Equality*, London: Allen and Unwin Books, 1964 (1931).
3. John Stuart Mill, *Principles of Political Economy*, vol. 1, London: John W. Parker, 1848, p. 123.
4. John Locke, *Two Treatises of Government – Chapter V: Of Property – 30*, Merchant Books, April 2011.
5. Adam Smith, *An Inquiry into the Nature and Causes of the Wealth of Nations*, Jefferson Publication, USA, 1776.
6. Aristotle, *Politics*, Second Edition, *Carnes Lord*, The University of Chicago Press, Chicago and London, Printed in the United States of America, 2013.
7. Friedrich A. Hayek, *The Road to Serfdom*, Chicago, IL: University of Chicago Press, 1994.
8. John Kenneth Galbraith, *The Affluent Society*, New York, NY: Houghton Mifflin, 1961, p. 32.

9. Thomas Robert Malthus, *Principles of Political Economy*, London: John Murray, 1820.
10. Frédéric Bastiat, *Harmonies économiques* [Economic Harmony], Paris: Guillaumin, 1864 (1850).
11. Paul Leroy-Beaulieu, *Essai sur la répartition des richesses* [Essay on the Distribution of Wealth], Paris: Guillaumin, 1997 (1881).
12. Nikolai Bukharin, *The Economic Theory of the Leisure Class*, Monthly Review Press, January 2011 (first published January 1st 1970).
13. François Bourguignon, *La mondialisation de l'inequality* [The Globalization of Inequality], Paris: Seuil, 2012.
14. Classification performed by *L'Expansion*, 26 June 2012.
15. *The Wall Street Journal*, 30 January 2014.
16. John Rawls, *A Theory of Justice*, Cambridge, MA: Harvard University Press, 1971.
17. Amartya Sen, *Inequality Re-examined*, Oxford: Clarendon Press, 1992.
18. 1% of the highest incomes.
19. In 2012, the wealthiest centile of the U.S. population captured 19.34% of total income, the same level as during the periods that preceded World War I and the crash of 1929. In 1980, it captured 8.18% of total income. Sources: Facundo Alvaredo, Anthony Barnes B. Atkinson, Thomas Piketty and Emmanuel Saez, *The World Top Incomes Database*, 2013, consultable at: http://topincomes.g-mond.parisschoolofeconomics.eu.
20. Mario Pezzini, 'An Emerging Middle Class', *OECD Development Centre*, 2012 report, pp. 3–28.
21. Ibid.
22. Abhijit V. Banerjee and Esther Duflo, 'What Is Middle Class about the Middle Classes around The World?', *The Journal of Economic Perspectives*, vol. 22, no. 2, 2008.
23. Ernst Engel, 'Die Lebenskosten Belgischer Arbeiter-Familien früher und jetzt' [The Cost of Living in Belgian Working-class Families, then and now], *International Statistical Institute Bulletin*, vol. 9, 1895, pp. 1–74.
24. Zhou Xiaohong, *Survey of the Chinese Middle Class*, Beijing: Social Sciences Academic Press, 2005.
25. Nan Chen, 'China: le mythe de la classe moyenne' [China's missing middle class], in *Problèmes économiques*, no. 3052, 2012, pp. 38–42.
26. Calestous Juma, 'Le nouveau moteur de l'Afrique' [The New Engine of Africa], *Problèmes économiques*, no. 3052, October 2012, p. 24.
27. Ibid.
28. McKinsey Global Institute, Lions on the Move: The Progress and Potential of African Economies, June 2010.
29. Leslie T. Chang, *Factory Girls: From Village to City in a Changing China*, Spiegel & Grau, New York, USA, 2008.
30. Chrystia Freeland, *Plutocrats: The Rise of the New Global Super-Rich and the Fall of Everyone Else*, London: Penguin Books, October, 2012.
31. Moses N. Kiggundu, 'La lutte contre la pauvreté and le changement social progressif au Brésil: enseignements destinés aux autres' [Anti-poverty and progressive social change in Brazil: lessons for other emerging economies], *Revue internationale des sciences administratives*, vol. 78, 2012, pp. 785–808.
32. Oxfam, *Even it up: Time to End Extreme Inequality*, report, January 2014.

33. In other words, trading income.
34. OECD, 'The economic crisis reduces income and has repercussions on inequality and poverty', results from the OECD wealth distribution database, May 2013.
35. Thomas Piketty, *Capital in the 21st century*, English edition, Trans. Arthur Goldhammer, Cambridge, MA: Harvard University Press, 2014.
36. Trans. Note: 'The Glorious Thirty' were France's thirty post-war years (1945–1975).
37. Simon Kuznets, *Shares of Upper Income Groups in Income and Saving*, NBER, working paper, 1953.
38. Simon Kuznets, 'Economic Growth and Income Inequality', in American Economic Review, vol. 45, no. 1, March 1955, p. 171–218.
39. Hélène Chaput, Kim-Hoa Luu Kim, Laurianne Salembier and Julie Solard, 'Les inégalities de patrimoine s'accroissent entre 2004 and 2010' [Inequalities in assets increased between 2004 and 2010], *Insee Première*, no. 1380, November 2011, pp. 1–4.
40. From a study published in the Sunday Times, Saturday 10 May 2014.
41. Richard Fry and Paul Taylor, 'An Uneven Recovery, 2009–2010. A Rise in Wealth for the Wealthy; Declines for the Lower 93%', Pew Research Center, April 2013.
42. François Ewald, *L'État-providence* [The Welfare State], Paris: Grasset, 1986.
43. OECD, 'The economic crisis reduces incomes and impacts on inequality and poverty', results from the OECD income distribution database, May 2013.
44. Gosta Esping-Andersen, *Trois leçons sur l'Etat-providence* [Three Lessons concerning the Welfare State], Paris: Seuil, 2008.
45. André Masson, 'Trois paradigmes pour penser les rapports entre les générations' [Three paradigms for considering the relationship between the generations] in Jean-Hervé Lorenzi and Hélène Xuan (Eds), *La France face au vieillissement: le grand défi* [France facing Ageing: the Great Challenge], Paris: Descartes & Cie, 2013.
46. Chrystia Freeland, *Plutocrats: The Rise of the New Global Super-Rich*, London: Penguin Books, 2012.
47. Daron Acemoglu, Suresh Naidu, Pascual Restrepo and James Robinson, 'Democracy, Redistribution and Inequality', NBER, Working Paper, no. 19746, December 2013.
48. Tyler Cowen, *Average is over Powering America Beyond the Age of the Great Stagnation*, Dutton Adult, New York, USA, 2013.
49. Hannah Arendt, *The Human Condition*, Chicago, IL: University of Chicago Press, 1958.
50. Michel Aglietta, *Régulation and crises du capitalisme* [Regulation and Crises of Capitalism], Paris: Calmann-Lévy, 1976.
51. Adolf Berle and Gardiner Means, *The Modern Corporation and Private Property*, Transaction Publishers, USA, 1932.
52. Max Weber, *Die Protestantische Ethik und der 'Geist' des Kapitalismus* [The Protestant Ethick and the 'Spectre' of Capitalism], Archiv für Sozialwissenschaft und Sozialpolitik, 1905.
53. David Boyle, *Broke: How to Survive The Middle-Class Crisis*, Fourth Estate, 2014.
54. Joseph Stiglitz, *The Price of Inequality: How Today's Divided Society Endangers Our Future*, W.W. Norton & Company, USA, 2013.

55. Gabriel Zucman, *La richesse cachée des nations. Enquête sur les paradis fiscaux* [The Missing Wealth of Nations. An investigation of tax havens], Paris: Le Seuil, 2013.
56. Michael Kumhof and Romain Rancière, 'Inequality, Leverage and Crises', IMF Working Paper, November 2010.
57. Raghuram Rajan, *Fault Lines: How Hidden Fractures Still Threaten the World Economy*, Princeton, NJ: Princeton University Press, 2010.
58. Michael Kumhof and Romain Rancière, *op. cit.*
59. Ibid.
60. Collected by Philippe Coste and published in December 2013. Consultable at: www.lexpress.fr/actualite/monde/amerique-nord/robert-reich-les-americains-doivent-partager-la-richesse_1303125.html.
61. Paul Collier, *The Bottom Billion: Why the Poorest Countries are Failing and What Can Be Done About It*, Oxford: Oxford University Press, 2007.

4 The Impact of Deindustrialization

1. Source: U.S. Bureau of Labor Statistics. In 2002, the cost of industrial labour was US$27.36 per hour in the United States, US$23.53 per hour in Europe and US$0.60 per hour in China.
2. On 11 December 2001, China became the 143 member of the WTO.
3. Mathias Thoenig and Thierry Verdier, 'Innovation défensive and concurrence internationale' [Defensive Innovation and International Competition], *Économie et Statistique*, no. 363–365, 2003, pp. 19–28.
4. Lilas Demmou, 'Le recul de l'emploi industriel en France entre 1980 and 2007. Ampleur and principaux déterminants: un état des lieux' [The decline in industrial employment in France between 2008 and 2007. Extent and main determining factors: an inventory], *Économie et statistique*, no. 438–400, 2010, pp. 273–296.
5. Avraham Ebenstein, Ann Harrison, Margaret McMillan and Shannon Phillips, 'Why are American Workers Getting Poorer? Estimating the Impact of Trade and Offshoring Using the CPS', Cambridge, MA: National Bureau of Economic Research, June 2009.
6. Patrick Artus, 'Y a-t-il des raisons profondes, non conjoncturelles, pour les-quelles le monde se désindustrialiserait?' [Are there deep-seated reasons, not connected with the recession, as to why the world is deindustrializing], *Éco Hebdo, Recherche économique*, no. 1, Natixis, 3 January 2014, pp. 1–6.
7. This passage was inspired by the report from the Economic Analysis Council by Lionel Fontagné and Jean-Hervé Lorenzi (eds), *Désindustrialisation, délocalisations* [Deindustrialization, Offshoring] *La Documentation française*, 2005.
8. Patrick Verley, *La révolution industrielle* [The Industrial Revolution], Paris: Gallimard, 1997.
9. Paul Bairoch, *Mythes and paradoxes de l'histoire économique* [Economics and World History: Myths and Paradoxes], Paris: La Découverte, 1999.
10. Alain Redslob, *La cité de London* [The City of London], Paris: Économica, 1983.
11. 'Natural Experiments in Financial Reform in the Nineteenth Century: The Davis and Gallman Analysis', in Jeremy Atack and Larry Neal (Eds),

The Origins and Development of Financial Markets and Institutions. From the Seventeenth Century to the Present, New York, NY: Cambridge University Press, 2009, pp. 241–261.
12. Lance E. Davis and Robert E. Gallman, *Evolving Capital Markets and International Capital Flows: Britain, the Americas, and Australia, 1865–1914*, New York: Cambridge University Press, 2001.
13. Source: U.S. Bureau of Economic Analysis.
14. Source: U.S. Bureau Labor of Statistics.
15. Maxime Amiot, 'Automobile: le grand retour des exportations américaines' [Automobiles: the big comeback of U.S. exports], *Les Échos*, 13 January 2014.
16. Sylvie Cornot-Gandolphe, 'Impact du développement du gaz de schiste aux États-Unis sur la pétrochimie européenne' [The Impact of Shale Gas development in the United States on European Petrochemicals], IFRI note, October 2013.
17. There were 16.8 million units in 2014.
18. 1 to 1.5 metric tonnes per year of capacity.
19. IHS, *America's New Energy Future: The Unconventional Oil and Gas Revolution and the US Economy*, vol. 3, *A Manufacturing Renaissance*, report, September 2013.
20. American Chemistry Council (ACC), *Shale Gas, Competitiveness and New US Chemical Industry Investment: An Analysis Based on Announced Projects*, report, May 2013.
21. Boston Consulting Group, *Made in America, Again. Why Manufacturing Will Return to the U.S*, report, August 2011. Boston Consulting Group, *Made in America, Again. U.S. Manufacturing Nears the Tipping Point*, March 2012. Boston Consulting Group, *Made in America, Again. The U.S. as One of the Developed World's Lowest-Cost Manufacturers*, August 2013. Euler Hermes Economic Research, 'The Reindustrialization of the United States', *Economic Outlook*, no. 1187, December, 2012. Euler Hermes Economic Research, 'La réindustrialisation des États-unis se confirme' [Confirmed Reindustrialization of the United States], April 2014.
22. Boston Consulting Group, *Made in America, Again. The U.S. as One of the Developed World's Lowest-Cost Manufacturers*, August 2013.
23. Fraser Institute, *Survey of Mining Companies*, report, 2013.
24. Source: U.S. Energy Information Administration.
25. Suzanne Berger, *Making in America: From Innovation to Market*, Cambridge, MA: MIT Press, 2013.
26. OECD Statistical Sources Database. Consultable at: https://stats.oecd.org/Index.aspx?DataSetCode=MSTI_PUB.
27. '2014 Global R&D Funding Forecast', *R&D Magazine*, Battelle, December, 2013.
28. National Science Board, 'Science and Engineering Indicators 2012'.
29. Ibid.
30. Federal Reserve, FRED Economic Research Data. Consultable at: http://research.stlouisfed.org/fred2/series/LFEAINTTUSA647S.
31. Suzanne Berger, *Notre Première Mondialisation. Leçons d'un échec oublié* [Our First Globalization. Lessons from a Forgotten Failure], Paris: Le Seuil, 2003.
32. Dani Rodrik, *The Globalization Paradox, Democracy and the Future of the World Economy*, New York, NY: W. W. Norton & Company, Inc., 2012.

33. Norman Angell, *The Great Illusion*, 1909 (quoted by Suzanne Berger).
34. Dani Rodrik, *op.cit.*
35. Philippe Martin, Thierry Mayer, Mathias Thoenig, *La mondialisation est-elle un facteur de paix?* [Is Globlalization a Factor for Peace] Paris: Cepremap, Éditions ENS rue d'Ulm, 2006.
36. Montesquieu, *The Spirit of the Laws*, 1748 (First English translation by Thomas Nugent 1750), New York, NY: Cosimo Classics.
37. Pankaj Ghemawat, *World 3.0: Global Prosperity and How to Achieve It*, Boston, MA: Harvard Business School Publishing, 2011.
38. World Trade Organization (WTO), *World Trade Report 2013*, 2013.
39. Speech by the Director-General of the WTO, Pascal Lamy, on 30 May 2012 to the Thai Chamber of Commerce.
40. According to *Global Trade Alert*, www.globaltradealert.org.
41. WTO, *World Trade Report*, 2013.
42. United Nations Conference on Trade and Development (UNCTAD).
43. Nicolas Baverez, 'Guerre et paix entre les monnaies' [War and Peace between Currencies] *L'Histoire*, no. 382, December 2012, p. 8.
44. Nicolas Baverez, *op. cit.*
45. Ted Truman, *Message for the G20: SDR Are Your Best Answer*, Opinions VoxEU, 6 March 2009.
46. Jacques Mistral, *Guerre and paix entre les monnaies* [*War and Peace between Currencies*], Paris, Fayard, 2014.

5 The Illusion of Definancialization

1. Bank for International Settlement, *OTC Derivatives Statistics At End-June 2013*, Monetary and Economic Department, Statistical Release, November 2013.
2. Esther Jeffers and Dominique Plihon, '*Le shadow banking system et la crise financière*' [*The Shadow Banking System and the Financial Crisis*], *Cahiers français*, no. 375, June 2013, pp. 50–57.
3. Estimate performed by the Financial Stability Board (FSB) in *Global Shadow Banking Monitoring Report 2013*, based on total financial assets held by '*other financial intermediaries*, (OFIs)', 14 November 2013.
4. Source: National Flow of Funds Data.
5. With the entry into force on 1 November 2007, of the European Directive concerning the financial instruments markets (FIM).
6. 'Investing not betting', Finance Watch, position paper, 2012.
7. Barry Eichengreen, '*10 questions à propos de la crise des prêts subprimes*' [*Ten Questions about the Crisis in Subprime lending*], *Revue de la stabilité financière*, no. 11, Banque de France, February 2008, pp. 19–29.
8. Extract from the final communiqué of the G20 dated 2 April 2009.
9. These measures are extracted from the 83 annual report of the BIS, 23 June 2013.
10. Commitments by Los Cabos, calculations of the Organization for Economic Cooperation and Development (OECD) – taken from the *AGEFI Hebdo*, of 12–18 December, 2013.
11. Finance Watch, *Basel 3 in 5 Questions*, May, 2012.

12. André Oliveira Santos and Douglas Elliott, *Estimating the Costs of Financial Regulation*, IMF, 11 September 2012.
13. The Institute of International Finance, *The Cumulative Impact on the Global Economy of Changes in the Financial Regulatory Framework*, September 2011.
14. David Graeber, *Dette: 5000 ans d'histoire* [*Debt : The First 5,000 Years*], Paris: Éditions Les Liens qui Libèrent, 2013.
15. Bank for International Settlements, *83rd Annual Report*, June 2013.
16. Bank for International Settlements, *op. cit.*
17. 'Medium- and long-term scenarios for growth and world imbalance', *OECD Economic Outlook*, 2012.
18. Mathias Drehmann and Mikael Juselius, 'Do Debt Service Costs Affect Macroeconomic and Financial Stability', *BES Quarterly Review*, Bank for International Settlements (BIS), September 2012, pp. 21–35.
19. Sum of interest payments and reimbursements of the principal divided by GDP.
20. Dietmar Peetz and Heribert Genreith, 'The Financial Sector and the Real Economy', *Real World Economic Review*, no. 57, 2011, pp. 41–47.
21. Thomas Philippon and Ariel Reshef, 'Wages and Human Capital in the U.S. Financial Industry: 1909–2006', NBER, working paper, no. 14644, January 2009.
22. Nicholas Kaldor, 'Speculation and Economic Activity', *Review of Economic Studies*, October 1939, pp. 1–27.
23. John Maynard Keynes, *The General Theory of Employment, Interest and Money*, Chapter 12, 1936.
24. Michael W. Masters, Testimony before the Commodities Futures Trading Commission, UK: Palgrave Macmillan, August 2010.

6 Savings, the Ultimate Rare Resource

1. Patrick Artus, Va-t-il y avoir insuffisance de l'épargne mondiale? [Will there be insufficient world savings?], *Flash Economie*, no. 130, 20 March 2009; Patrick Artus, Flash Economie, L'épargne mondiale est abondante, mais mal utilisée [World savings are abundant but incorrectly used], *Flash Economie*, no. 626, 25 August 2014.
2. McKinsey Global Institute, *Farewell to Cheap Capital? The Implications of Long-Term Shifts in Global Investment and Savings*, 2010.
3. Loukas Karabarbounis and Brent Neiman, 'Declining Labor Shares and the Global Rise of Corporate Savings', *NBER Working Paper* No. 18154, June 2012.
4. Ben S.Bernanke, 'The Global Savings Glut and the U.S. Current Account Deficit', *speech given to the Virginia Association of Economists*, 10 March 2005.
5. David Laibson and Johanna Mollerstrom, 'Capital Flows, Consumption Booms and Asset Bubbles: A Behavioural Alternative to the Savings Glut Hypothesis', *NBER Working Paper* No. 15759, February 2010.
6. International Social Security Association, *Social Security Coverage Extension in the BRICS Countries: A Comparative Study on the Extension of Coverage in Brazil, The Russian Federation, India, China and South Africa*, 2013.

7. McKinsey Global Institute, *If You've Got it, Spend it: Unleashing the Chinese Consumer*, 2009.
8. OECD, *Employment Prospects in the OECD*, 2011. The data refers to 2005 for Brazil, 2006–2007 for South Africa and India and 2008 for China.
9. The OECD forecast is that the middle classes will increase in number from 1.8 billion people in 2009 to 4.9 billion in 2030. The Asian continent alone will account for 66% of the world's middle classes in 2030 as against 28% in 2009. Source: Mario Pezzini, *An Emerging Middle Class*, OECD Observer, 2012.
10. Calculations based on available savings rates on the IMF database and taken from GDP projections of the CEPII MaGE model.
11. Ibid.
12. Lionel Ragot, 'Les conséquences macroéconomiques du vieillissement' [The Macroeconomic Consequences of Ageing], in Jean-Hervé Lorenzi and Hélène Xuan (dir.), *La France face au vieillissement. Le grand défi [France facing up to ageing, the great challenge]*, Paris, Descartes & Cie, 2013.
13. André Masson and Luc Arrondel, *L'épargnant dans un monde en crise. Ce qui a changé [The Saver in a World in Crisis. What has Changed]*, CEPREMAP, Éditions rue d'Ulm, 2011.
14. Olivier Garnier and David Thesmar, *Épargner à long terme et maîtriser les risques financiers [Long-term savings and controlling financial risk]*, report by the Conseil d'analyse économique, 2009.
15. Luigi Guiso, Paola Sapienza, Luigi Zingales 'Time Varying Risk Aversion', *NBER Working Paper* No. 19284, 2013.
16. Joshua Aizenman and Ilan Noy, 'Public and Private Saving and the Long Shadow of Macroeconomic Shocks', *NBER Working Paper* No. 19067, 2013.
17. McKinsey Global Institute, *Farewell to Cheap Capital? The Implications of Long-Term Shifts in Global Investment and Savings*, 2010.
18. Patrick Artus, *Épargner,investir and croître [Saving, Investing and Growing]*, report by the 'Allocation internationale de l'épargne' Group, Commissariat général du plan, June 1991.
19. IMF, *World Economic Outlook*, 2014.
20. OECD, 'Évaluation générale de la situation macroéconomique' [General Assessment of the Macroeconomic Situation], *OECD's Ecnomic Perspectives*, 2013.
21. OFCE, 'La hausse des taux long est-elle inévitable?' [Is an increase in long rates inevitable?], *OFCE review*, October 2010.

7 Avoiding the Major Crisis of the Twenty-first Century

1. Alain Touraine, *La fin des sociétés* [The End of Society], Paris: Seuil, 2013.
2. Arjun Appadurai, *Condition de l'homme global* [The Future as Cultural Fact: Essays on the Global Condition], Payot 2013.
3. Ulrich Beck, *Risikogesellschaft*, 1986. Translated into English as 'Risk Society: Towards a New Modernity', New Delhi: Sage, 1992.
4. Claude Lévi-Strauss, *Tristes Tropiques*, published by the Penguin Group, in Penguin Classics, England, 2011. (First published by Plon 1955, trans. John Weightman and Doreen Weightman, 1973) – also translated as *A World on the Wane*.

5. Hannah Arendt, *The Human Condition*, Chicago, IL: University of Chicago Press 1958, p. 363.
6. Richard Sennett, *Together: The Rituals, Pleasures, and Politics of Cooperation*, USA: Yale University Press, 2012.
7. Antoine Pécoud and Paul de Guchteneire (eds.) *Migration without Borders. Essays on the Free Movement of People*, Oxford: Berghahn Books in Association with UNESCO, 2007.
8. According to the World Bank, public spending on education throughout the world amounted to only 4.94% of GDP in 2010.
9. Water Resources Group, *Charting our Water Future*, 2009.
10. Ibid.
11. Ibid.
12. A. M. MacDonald, H. C. Bonsor, B. E. O. Dochartaigh and R. G. Taylor, 'Quantitative Maps of Groundwater Resources in Africa', *Environmental Research Letters*, 2012.
13. James Winpenny, *Financing Water for All*, report by the World Panel, chaired by Michel Camdessus, World Water Council, March 2003.
14. Thomas Philippon and Christian Hellwig, 'Eurobills, not Eurobonds', Vox EU, 2 December 2011.
15. Jacques Delpla and Jakob von Weizsäcker, 'The Blue Bond Proposal', *Bruegel Policy Brief*, May 2010.
16. Raphaël-Georges Lévy, *Revue des Deux Mondes*, vol. 149, 1898, pp. 277–306.
17. Luciano Pezzolo, 'Government Debts and Credit Markets in Renaissance Italy', Department of Economics, University of Venice, Working Paper, 2007.
18. Agnès Bénassy-Quéré and Jean Pisani-Ferry, 'Quel système international pour une économie mondiale en mutation rapide?' [What should the international system be for a world economy in the process of rapid change?], *Réformer le système monétaire international*, Conseil d'analyse économique, 2011.
19. Jacques Mistral, *Guerre et paix entre les monnaies* [*War and Peace between Currencies*], Paris: Fayard, 2014.
20. Emmanuel Farhi, Pierre-Olivier Gourinchas, Hélène Rey, 'Quelle réforme pour le système monétaire international?' [What reform should there be for the international monetary system?], *Réformer le système monétaire international*, Conseil d'analyse économique, 2011.
21. Mariana Mazzucato, *The Entrepreneurial State: Debunking Public vs. Private Sector Myths*, Anthem Press, USA 2013.

Index

Abe, Shinzō, 99, 101
Acemoglu, Daron, 67
Africa, 23, 31, 36, 59
　mobile phones, 60–1
　water, 24, 148–50
ageing, 35, 37, 47, 134, 146
　employment, 39, 42–4, 46
　impacts of, 36–40
　innovation in, 39–40, 43–4
　intergenerational conflict, 44–9
　Japan, 30–1, 37–8, 41, 44
　life span, 31, 35, 37–8, 42
　productivity, 40–4
Aghion, Philippe, 26
Aglietta, Michel, 68, 70
agricultural water, 149–50
Aizenman, Joshua, 136
Al-Mansur, Abu Yusuf Yaqoub, 15
Alvaredo, Facundo, 166n19
Angell, Norman, 93
Appadurai, Arjun, 143
Arendt, Hannah, 68, 144
Aristotle, 53
Arrondel, Luc, 135
Artus, Patrick, 82, 125, 138
Atkinson, Anthony Barnes B., 166n19
Australia, 77, 78
Averroës, 15

Bairoch, Paul, 11, 84–5
Banerjee, Abhijit, 59
Basle 3, 113, 114
Bauman, Zygmunt, 143
Baverez, Nicolas, 98
Beaudry, Paul, 40
Beck, Ulrich, 143
Bénassy-Quéré, Agnès, 155
Berger, Suzanne, 91, 93, 95
Berle, Adolf, 68
Blankfein, Lloyd, 56
Blanqui, Adolphe, 6
Bloch, Marc, 15

Bourguignon, François, 56
Boyle, David, 69
Brasseul, Jacques, 9
Braudel, Fernand, 14, 28, 31, 33
Brazil, 25, 59, 62, 78
　savings and investment, 138–9
　social welfare changes, 133–4
Bretton Woods system, 96, 99, 145–6, 155–6
Brynjolfsson, Erik, 20
Bukharin, Nikolai, 55
Burns, Scott, 48
Byzantine Empire, 9

Canada, 77, 78, 96
capitalism, 9, 11, 63, 143, 152
　corporatism, 20
　crisis of, 98
　feudal form of, 67
　property-owning, 68
　vision of, 127
CEPII (French public research centre), 136–7, 140–1
Chakrabarty, Dipesh, 29
Chang, Leslie T., 61
chemical industry, 88–90
Chile, 48, 59
China, 25–6, 60, 61
　economic growth, 15–16
　exchange rates with U.S., 100–101
　industry's share of added value on world scale, 78
　power and offshoring, 80–1
　protectionist policies, 97
　R&D (research and development) expenditure, 91–2
　savings and investment, 138–9
　savings rate forecast, 135
　social welfare changes, 133–5
　water, 24, 149
Christensen, Clayton M., 8
Clark, Gregory, 28

Clinton, Bill, 7
Collier, Paul, 73
conflict, 3, 24
  inequality at heart of, 71–3
  sharing rare resources, 150
Cowen, Tyler, 18, 67–8
crash of 1929, 1, 71, 98, 166n19
crisis, 1
  constraints, 143–6
  financial, 74–5, 107–12
  rare resources, 21–6
  risk-sharing, 156–9
culpability, 115, 151

d'Albis, Hyppolite, 48
dark trading, 107, 110
Davis, Lance, 87
Debré, Robert, 164n35
debt, 115–24
  country, as percentage of GDP, 116–18
  pensions, 151–5
  perpetual, 152–5
definancialization, 102–3
  debt, 115–24
  dismemberment of financial system, 107–12
  finance *vs.* real economy, 119–24
  liquidity, 103–12
  utopia of regulation, 112–15
deindustrialization
  1995–2005, 76–87
  American hope, 87–101
  finance, 102–3
  financial crisis, 74–5
  London temptation, 83–7
  offshoring, 74, 76–7, 79, 81, 89, 131
  outsourcing, 18, 42, 76, 92, 96
democracy, 52–3, 61, 63, 67, 93–5
demographics
  life span, 31, 35, 37–8, 42
  links with economy, 32–6
Dormont, Brigitte, 37
Drehmann, Mathias, 118
Duflo, Esther, 59

economic growth
  inequality and, 51–8
  linking demographics and, 32–6

natural resources, 21–6
  slowdown, 16–21
  technical progress in promoting, 12–16
education, 20
  ageing, 35, 37, 40–1, 46
  declining, 17–18
  growth theory, 27
  inequalities, 57, 59, 70
  spending on, 148, 173n8
Eichengreen, Barry, 110
Ellison, Larry, 56
energy, natural resources, 22–3
Engel, Ernst, 59
equity, 91, 108, 111, 113–14
  intergenerational, 66
  private, 68
  profitability of, 122
  reinforcement of, 155
Esping-Andersen, Gosta, 65
ethanol, conversion of grain to, 25
euro-bonds, 152
Europe, 16, 85, 104
euro zone, 88–9, 97, 99, 106, 116–20, 152
Ewald, François, 64
exchange rates, 100–101

Farhi, Emmanuel, 156
FDI (foreign direct investment), offshoring, 79–80
Ferguson, Niall, 10
fertility rate, 30–1, 33–5
feudal system, collapse, 9–10
financial crisis
  deindustrialization, 74–5
  dismemberment of financial system, 107–12
  financialization, British economy, 86–7
financial system
  debt, 115–24
  finance *vs.* real economy, 119–24
  regulation, 112–15
Finley, Moses I., 45
Florida, Richard, 27
food chain, resources, 21–2
food security, 25–6
Fordism, 12, 51, 60, 62, 65

France, 2, 16, 65, 70, 78
  ageing and productivity, 41–2, 44, 46
  debt, 116–18
  GDP (gross domestic product) growth, 12, 13, 17
  health and welfare, 37–8, 48–9
  interest rates and ten-year swap rates, 132
  jobs in industry, 81–2
  productivity, 18–19, 90
  profitability, 120, 122
  Thirty Glorious Years, 63, 69, 118
Freeland, Chrystia, 61, 66–7
Frey, Carl, 20–1
Fukuyama, Francis, 2
Furceri, David, 142

Galbraith, John Kenneth, 54
Gallman, Robert, 87
Garnier, Olivier, 136
GATT (General Agreement on Tariffs and Trade), 96
GDP (gross domestic product), 76
  banking, 109–10
  current account balances as percentage, 130
  forecasts of world rate of savings and investment, 141
  growth per hour worked, 12, 13
  investment levels as percentage of, 131
  projections of rates of investment, 140
  projections of rates of savings, 139
  rate and potential growth rate, 17
  rate of savings as percentage, 130
Genreith, Heribert, 119
Germany, 2, 27, 65, 70, 78, 147
  ageing, 41, 46
  debt, 116–18
  GDP (gross domestic product) growth, 12, 13, 17
  interest rates and ten-year swap rates, 132
  jobs in industry, 81–2
  productivity, 18–19, 41, 90
  profitability, 122
Ghemawat, Pankaj, 96

globalization, 3, 11, 18, 44, 126
  deindustrialization, 75–7, 79, 81
  finance, 102, 111
  inequality and economy, 51, 56, 58, 60, 70, 72
  political trilemma, 93–5
  uncertainty over, 93–101
  violence and, 143–4
Glorious Thirty, 63, 69, 118
Gordon, Robert, 7, 17–18, 21
Gourinchas, Pierre-Olivier, 156
Graeber, David, 115, 117
Great Britain
  deindustrialization, 75
  London temptation, 83–7
  number of technological inventions, 85
  see also UK (United Kingdom)
Great Depression, 58, 71, 72, 85, 98
great stagnation, 18, 56
Greece, 46, 62, 119, 151
Green, David, 40
Guchteneire, Paul de, 148
Guiso, Luigi, 136

Hayek, Friedrich August von, 54
health and welfare, expenditure, 31, 36–7, 39–43, 116
healthcare, 6, 39, 47, 134
  expenditure, 37, 42–3
  social welfare programmes for, 134
Heilbroner, Robert, 9
Hobbes, Thomas, 16, 66
Huntington, Samuel, 4
hyperglobalization, 94–5

IMF (International Monetary Fund), 16, 71, 94, 96, 114, 136, 140, 142, 153
imitators, 26
India, 25, 59, 97
  savings and investment, 138–9
  social welfare changes, 133–4
Indonesia, 59, 77, 78, 134, 138–9
Industrial Revolution, 6–14, 17, 20, 27–8, 83–5
inequality, 3
  assets and income, 50–1
  end of egalitarian myth, 58–66

inequality – *continued*
  growth and, 51–8
  theories of, 55–6
innovation
  ageing and demographics, 39–40
  caring for elderly, 43–4
  phenomenon, 7–12
innovators, 26, 40
Institute of International Finance, 114
intelligence, technological war, 26–9
International Labour Office, 13, 80, 81
investment
  balance between savings and, 125–9
  changing world increasing, 136–7
  forecasts of world rate of, 141
  as percentages of GDP, 131, 137
  projections of rates, 140
  savings-investment differential, 141
  toward major imbalance with savings, 138–42
  see also savings
Ireland, 46, 62
Israel, 24, 27
Italy, 20, 48, 70, 77, 78, 90

Japan, 27, 65, 76, 78, 104, 106
  ageing, 30–1, 37–8, 41, 44, 46
  debt, 116–18
  GDP (gross domestic product) growth, 13, 17
  interest rates and ten-year swap rates, 132
  jobs in industry, 81–2
  productivity, 18–19, 90
  savings rate forecast, 135
  social welfare changes, 134–5
Jeffers, Esther, 108
jobs, 21
  ageing, 30–1, 42, 46–9, 146
  deindustrialization, 75–82
  inequality, 50, 52, 60, 65–6, 71
  manufacturing, 87–90
  savings, 127, 142
  women in market, 65–6
Jobs, Steve, 56
Johnson, Ronald B., 56

Juma, Calestous, 61
Juselius, Mikael, 118

Kagan, Robert, 73
Kaldor, Nicholas, 123
Karabarbounis, Loukas, 133
Keynesian/Keynesianism, 76, 123, 126–8, 146
Kotlikoff, Laurence, 20–1, 48
Krugman, Paul, 80
Kumhof, Michael, 71, 72
Kuznets, Simon, 55, 58, 61–3
Kuznets curve, 58, 63

Laibson, David, 133
Landais, Camille, 56
Landes, David, 14, 27
Latin America, 28, 36, 97
Lee, Ronald, 36, 37, 45
Lee, Sang Hyop, 36
Lehman Brothers, 106
Leroy-Beaulieu, Paul, 55
Lévi-Strauss, Claude, 143–4
life span, 31, 35, 37–8, 42
Liikanen, Erkki, 113
Locke, John, 52, 66
London temptation, 83–7
Lula da Silva, Luis Inácio, 62

McAfee, Andrew, 20
Machiavelli, Niccolò, 33
MacInnes, John, 47
McKinley Tariff (United States), 85
McKinsey Global Institute, 28, 131, 136
macroeconomic liquidity, 103–5
Maddison, Angus, 13, 15, 17
Maimonides, Moses, 15
Malthus, Thomas, 33–4, 53–5
Mantega, Guido, 99
manufacturing jobs, United States, 87–92
Marx, Karl, 33, 46, 63, 127
Mason, Andrew, 36, 37, 45, 47
Masson, André, 38, 66, 135
Masters, Michael W., 124
Mauss, Marcel, 14
Mazzucato, Mariana, 157

Means, Gardiner, 68
Méline Law (France), 85
Mexico, 59, 77, 78, 89, 148
middle class, 11, 18, 25, 59
  Brazil, 25, 62
  in emerging nations, 25, 133–6
  erosion of, 67–8
  Fordism as triumph of, 51
  inequality and conflict, 71–3
  patrimonial society against, 66–71
  private and public indebtedness, 117
  role of, 58–62
Mill, John Stuart, 52, 53
Mistral, Jacques, 101, 155
Mollerstrom, Johanna, 133
Montesquieu, 33, 95
Moore's Law, 18
mortality rate, 33, 35, 47
Myrdal, Gunnar, 128

Naidu, Suresh, 67
nation-states, 10, 93–5
natural order, 50, 52–3
natural resources
  crisis of rare, 21–6
  socializing rare, 149–55
Neiman, Brent, 133
Newcomen, Thomas, 13
Noy, Ilan, 136

Occupy Wall Street, 67
OECD countries, 2, 22
  deindustrialization, 75, 77, 90, 102
  expenditures, 134, 139
  inequality, 59, 62
  unemployment by age group, 46
offshoring, 74, 78
  capital transfer in foreign direct investments (FDI), 79–80
  deindustrialization, 76–87
oil and gas, resources, 23
Osborne, Michael, 20–1
OTC (over-the-counter) derivatives, 105–6, 108, 110, 113, 119

Palier, Bruno, 47
Park, Donghyun, 36
Pécoud, Antoine, 148

Peel, Sir Robert, 86
Peetz, Dietmar, 119
pensions, debt and, 151–5
Pescatori, Andrea, 142
petrochemical industry, 88–9
Petty, William, 16, 39
Pfeifer, Christian, 40
Phelps, Edmund, 19–20
Philippon, Thomas, 120
Piketty, Thomas, 56, 62–3, 69, 166n19
Pisani-Ferry, Jean, 155
Plato, 53
Plihon, Dominique, 108
political economy, 50–1, 56, 126, 132
political trilemma, 93–5
Portugal, 15, 46, 119
principle of precaution, 14, 156
productivity
  ageing populations, 40–4
  growth rate by country, 19
  reindustrialization, 90–1
profitability, 69, 104, 119–20, 122–4, 133, 135
protectionism, 84–5, 97, 156

Quesnay, François, 52

R&D (research and development), 27, 29, 40, 91–2, 144–5
Ragot, Lionel, 38
Rajan, Raghuram, 71
Rancière, Romain, 71, 72
Rawls, John, 57
Reagan, Ronald, 58
regulation, financial systems, 112–15
Reich, Robert, 72
reindustrialization, 75, 83, 88, 90–3, 98, 101, 156
resources, *see* natural resources
Restrepo, Pascual, 67
Rey, Hélène, 156
Ricardo, David, 51–4
risk-sharing, 156–9
Robinson, James, 67
Rodrik, Dani, 93–5
Rousseau, Jean-Jacques, 57, 66

180 Index

Russia, 14, 24, 61, 97
   savings and investment, 138–9
   social welfare changes, 133–4

Sachs, Jeffrey, 20–1
Saez, Emmanuel, 56, 166n19
Sapienza, Paola, 136
Sauvy, Alfred, 21, 164n35
savings
   balance between investment and, 125–9, 138–42
   changing world decreasing, 133–6
   forecasts of world rate of, 141
   interest rates and ten-year swap rates, 132
   over-abundance of, 129–33
   as percentages of GDP, 130, 137
   projections of rates, 139
   rate forecast for China and Japan, 135
   savings-investment differential, 141
   see also investment
Say, Jean-Baptiste, 127
Say's Law, 127
Schmitt, Carl, 5
securitization, financing, 108, 111–12
Sen, Amartya, 57
Sennet, Richard, 144
shadow banking, 107–9
Shuttleworth, Mark, 19
Singapore, 24, 27
slowdown
   globalization, 75
   potential growth, 16–21, 22
   technical progress, 2, 7–8, 12, 82
Smith, Adam, 53, 54, 127
Smoot-Hawley Tariff Act, 98
social security, 40, 44, 48, 65, 133
Solow, Robert, 12, 39
Solvency 2, 113
South Africa, 59, 133–4, 138–9
South Korea, 26, 77, 78, 134
Spain, 15, 20, 46, 62
Special Drawing Rights (XRD or SRD), 155–6
Spencer, Herbert, 54
Spijker, Jeroen, 47

Steiner, George, 45
Stiglitz, Joseph, 70
Sweden, 27, 41, 46, 119
Switzerland, 27, 70

Takahashi, Shigesato, 30
Tawney, Richard H., 52
tax evasion, 67, 70
technical progress, slowdown, 2, 7–8, 12, 82
technology, war of intelligence, 26–9
Tendō, Arata, 30
Thesmar, David, 136
Thirty Glorious Years, 63, 69, 118
Touraine, Alain, 143, 144
Toynbee, Arnold Joseph, 14
training, 26, 32, 65, 145, 148
Truman, Ted, 99
Turkey, 24, 64

UK (United Kingdom), 78, 104, 132
   ageing, 38, 46
   debt, 116–18
   GDP (gross domestic product), 12, 13, 17
   inequality, 63, 65, 69
   jobs in industry, 81–2
   London temptation, 83–7
   productivity, 18–19, 90
   profitability, 120, 122
United States, 27, 64, 85, 104, 132
   bank credit, 106
   debt, 116–18
   exchange rates, 100–101
   GDP (gross domestic product), 13, 17, 42, 87, 91
   jobs in industry, 81–2
   manufacturing jobs, 87–92
   offshoring, 76, 78
   productivity growth, 16, 18–19, 90
   profitability, 120
   R&D (research and development) expenditure, 91–2
   wealthiest centile, 58, 166n19

Valery, Paul, 14
Verley, Patrick, 11

Vickers, John, 113
Volcker, Paul, 113

Wagner, Joachim, 40
Walzer, Michael, 5
war of the generations, 47
water, 24–5
  resources, 22, 23–5
  sharing, 149–50
Weber, Max, 69, 127

WTO (World Trade Organization), 79, 94, 96–7, 168n2

youth/younger generation, refocusing world on, 146–9

Zhou Xiaohong, 60
Zingales, Luigi, 136
Zollverein Agreements (Germany), 85
Zucman, Gabriel, 70

The manufacturer's authorised representative in the EU is Springer Nature Customer Service Centre GmbH, Europaplatz 3, 69115 Heidelberg, Germany. If you have any concerns regarding our products, please contact ProductSafety@springernature.com

Printed and bound by CPI Group (UK) Ltd, Croydon, CR0 4YY

23/03/2026

02076663-0015